What People Are Saying . . .

"Get this book! It will tell you all you need to know about long-term care and includes information about state-specific issues." – Irwin C. Cohen, Affiliated Financial Specialists, Inc., Chicago, IL, featured speaker at the Million Dollar Round Table (MDRT) Conference, Las Vegas, NV, June 25, 2003

"Our entire stock of your long-term care books sold out in fifteen minutes. It was like a tornado went through here!" – Ileo N. Lott, Marketing Manager, Million Dollar Round Table (MDRT) Power Center, Las Vegas, NV, June 26, 2003

"I would like to thank you . . . Our chapter members were impressed and informed by your presentations. Several . . . remarked . . . it was the best meeting we had presented in the past twenty years." – Michael Holman, President, NAIFA – South Puget Sound, WA

In regard to "Long-Term Care . . . Alternatives and Solutions," Bill Upson's first book:
"Mr. Upson has obviously done his homework before writing this book. I would say it is one of the most thorough books on this subject . . . I would certainly recommend keeping a copy of this book in your library if you want to learn more about long-term care. As a reference book, this one is excellent." – The Financial Planning Association of the East Bay

"Your assistance in the areas of financial planning and meeting long-term insurance needs has proven beneficial for me personally and for the corporation. You have effectively reduced my personal taxes and provided the diversification my pension plan needed to assure long-term growth on a conservative basis." – Edward D. Grieve, V.P. Marketing, United Van Lines

"I want to thank you . . . The attendees spoke highly of your presentation on long-term care . . . Your extensive background and experience was quite evident in the wealth of knowledge that you shared." – Marshall L. Schield, Schield Management Company

"Over the years, I found that I needed someone I could trust to responsibly handle my personal, business, insurance and estate planning needs. Bill has far exceeded my expectations." – Jack King, investor and client

"I recently became a widow and found myself feeling very vulnerable. My husband had always been quite protective of me and, consequently, I wasn't very knowledgeable about financial matters. Bill and his staff guided me through everything: investments, a trust, long-term care insurance . . . Now I feel self-confident and much more secure. Most of all, however, I feel grateful. Thank you, Bill!" – Martha Callinicos, client

"Thank you for participating in our conference. Fine speakers like you are the reason we have achieved . . . our excellent reputation for high-caliber education." – Kay Phelan, Conference Director, California CPA Education Foundation

ISBN # 0-9678982-3-4=0A=

Printed in U.S.A.

Published by:
St. Bernie's Press
P.O. Box 5558
Walnut Creek, CA 94596
1 (800) 765-0561

To order additional books, call (800) 765-0561, or visit our website:
www.longtermcarebooks.com

Prologue

ACKNOWLEDGEMENTS

> *"The child you were is the child you will become!"*
>
> *William Upson*

Without the help of many individuals and organizations this publication would not have been possible. I would like to thank them for their special efforts on behalf of all who read this publication.

They are, in alphabetical order, as follows:

Nanette Conkel, Jennifer and Mark Denno, Beverly DeVeny, Linda Dorn, Linda Fodrini-Johnson, Roxanne Foster, Sheron Irons, Steve Klamm, Esq., Janice Kraft, Celia Mason, Elly Rabben, Alan Silver, Dan Sullivan, Elaine Swyt, Bryan Upson, and Peter Upson. This publication would not have come to a final draft without the significant efforts of the talented staff of Galaxy Press, especially Bob and Tom Meyer.

Inspiration for this publication came from individuals whose courage about their personal circumstances, or those of their countrymen, has led to the charitable organizations of their choice receiving equal shares of the profits from this publication as sales are realized. These include the Alzheimer's Foundation (President Ronald Reagan), the Diabetes Foundation, the Eagle Scholarship Endowment Trust, Habitat for Humanity (President Jimmy Carter), the Paralysis Foundation (Christopher Reeve), and the Parkinson's Foundation (Michael J. Fox).

> *"Two roads diverged in a wood and I – I took the one less traveled by, and that has made all the difference."*
>
> **"The Road Not Taken"** *by Robert Frost*

Habitat for Humanity® International

Building houses in partnership with God's people in need

June 8, 2000

William Upson
St. Bernie's Press
P. O. Box 5558
Walnut Creek, CA 94596

Dear Bill,

It was so good to be with you and to visit with you at the building site in Concord, California on Monday, June 5.

Thanks for giving me the autographed copy of your new book, <u>Long Term Care</u>, and thanks also for giving the check to John Shanley representing a portion of the profits made from sales of this book over the past few weeks. I believe John will be forwarding that check to Americus and, when he does, a receipt will be issued to you.

Please know that we are honored and grateful to you for designating Habitat for Humanity as one of the organizations to benefit from the sale of your book. We will be faithful and diligent to be good stewards in using the money.

I have read over your book, and I find it extremely well written and incredibly timely.
You can see that I am copying Linda Fox who is the person on our staff responsible for benefits. I am going to pass your book along to her because I am sure she will find it both interesting and helpful.

Thanks again for the book and for designating Habitat for Humanity to be a beneficiary of profits from the sale of this publication.

Again, Bill, it was great to be with you in Concord earlier this week. I send my very best regards to you.

In joyous Christian partnership, and with gratitude,

Milliard Fuller
President

Dear Reader,

This book is designed to educate you about what to do *before* you become ill, or when you become seriously ill or disabled, what you *should* do. We urge you to consider how you will meet long-term care needs for yourself and your family. We have tried to provide you with as many options as possible on how to prepare for this potential crisis.

As a financial asset manager and insurance advisor, I felt compelled to write this book as a result of numerous experiences I have had with clients, family, and friends who have needed long-term care. Those who planned well maintained their ability to choose the type of care they wanted and also preserved their estates. Others have lost their chance to choose their own care, having been financially, and in many cases, emotionally and physically devastated in the process.

Our goal is to see people preserve their assets while maintaining their freedom to choose the type of care that best meets their needs. This book explains what long-term care is and who may need it. It provides checklists to determine your individual needs. It provides guidelines on choosing a professional who can help you design a plan that will preserve the physical, emotional, and financial well being of you and your family.

All of the stories you will read in this book are true. Some are heart wrenching, while others, thankfully, have positive outcomes. The names have been changed out of respect for the individuals and families involved.

Please take the time to educate yourself and your family about long-term care. It may affect you when you least expect it. It could mean the difference between financial and emotional security or winding up in a government-mandated facility far from home and family. Scary? Yes! Only you can decide to plan for a secure future, *but do it now.*

Throughout the humbling process of writing and compiling this book, I have come to believe that I can do no greater good than to follow the philosophy and guiding principles of the following:

"You are not here merely to make a living. You are here in order to enable the world to live more amply with greater vision with the finest spirit of hope and achievement."
— *President Woodrow Wilson*

"Live out of your imagination, not your history."
— *Stephen R. Covey*

Sincerely,

Bill Upson
Chartered Financial Consultant (ChFC)
Chartered Life Underwriter (CLU)

Table of Contents

Introduction

Martha

Martha was 78 years old, very active and in good health when her son Steve began talking to her about purchasing long-term care insurance. She refused to consider the coverage.

The insurance was expensive, she thought, and besides, *if she bought a policy, maybe there would be some chance she would have to use it and end up in a nursing home.* "I'd rather die than go to a nursing home," she told her son. Steve offered to pay the premiums for her, insisting that it would protect her assets. (Several years before, she had inherited $495,000 from a relative, and she planned to donate it all to her favorite charities upon her death.) Again, she refused.

A year later Martha began having a series of strokes and she did need skilled nursing care. Medicare paid for the first seven days and then stopped paying because her condition was not improving (Medicare requires that you are getting better to continue payment). She continued to need nursing home and home health care for 12 years. When she came home she continued paying for her home health care. In total, she spent the whole $495,000 on home care and nursing facilities.

Martha eventually ended up on Medicaid with no assets. Had Steve been successful in securing long-term care insurance for his mother before she became ill, the premium would have cost her a maximum of $4,000 for one year's coverage (before she started having strokes). Most likely she would have been able to help her charities with more than $500,000 of assets at her death. Medicaid spent more than $100,000 on her care before she died and liens against her residence paid off the expenses Medicaid incurred.

Becky and Tom

Becky and Tom, a married couple, were in their late 30s when they realized that Becky was having trouble controlling her physical movements. After numerous medical tests, doctors determined that she was suffering from Huntington's chorea, a progressive disorder involving degeneration of nerve cells in the brain, a condition from which Becky's mother had died. This disorder, over a period of between three and twenty years, would render her totally incapable of caring for herself. Unfortunately, since Becky and Tom discovered this problem before talking to an insurance advisor, they were not able to find insurance to cover the costs of long-term care that Becky would need.

Sadly, these stories are not uncommon. We meet with people every day who want to purchase long-term care insurance or make other arrangements to protect their assets **after** they find out a loved one has a serious health problem. As with any other insurance, once a problem has been discovered, it is usually too late to buy coverage. It is far wiser to plan ahead for long-term care needs while you're still young and healthy, and when you can purchase it at a preferred rate. Rates are not affected by advancing age once you have purchased coverage.

Costs for long-term care escalated to $183 billion in 2003 in the U.S., according to the U.S. Government Accountability Office (GAO), and they estimate the cost will be $379 billion by 2050. Only about 2% of this expense is covered by Medicare. Medicaid (Medi-Cal in California) pays for approximately half of the remainder, but it requires that people exhaust nearly all of their resources before they are eligible for assistance. The other half of the cost is paid for by individuals and their families.

With an average cost in the U.S. of $203 per day ($74,095 per year) for a private room in a nursing home this can quickly become an impossible burden to pay. Annual expenditures range from $41,975 ($115 daily) in Louisiana to $193,815 in Alaska ($531 daily). Considering the average stay in a nursing home is two-and-a-half years, the cost for such a stay would average $177,828, depending on the type of facility and region of the country.[1] If you need home health care, costs can be approximately twice as much. These expenses can wipe out assets that a couple has spent a lifetime accumulating. In fact, the Congressional Subcommittee on Aging has determined that 70% to 80% of nursing home residents deplete their assets within 12 months of entering a facility.

Our population is aging – 36.3 million Americans, 12% of the population, are now over 65.[2] By the year 2020 people 65 and over will account for about one in six Americans, or 17% of the population.[3] The numbers will continue to grow as the "baby boomer" generation (Americans born between 1946 and 1964) continues to age. The number of people over 65 will be close to 66 million, as reported by *Time* magazine. The percentage of people who live to "old, old" age is also increasing. Estimates by the Administration on Aging indicate that the percentage of people 85 and older will climb by as much as 250% by 2040, from 4.3 million today to 10.75 million.[4] That age bracket is the fastest-growing segment of the American population today.

In 1998, 1.5 million people over age 65 lived full-time in some type of residential care facility. About 40% of the Americans currently age 65 and over will spend some time in a nursing home at some point in their lives. Of those who enter a nursing home, 50% will stay an average of 2.5 years, and 10% will stay there five years or longer.[5]

We would never think of driving our cars uninsured, or not having fire insurance on our homes. Approximately 1.9 million people have already purchased private long-term care insurance, yet that number comprises only about 5.9% of Americans over age 65.[6] Why wouldn't we want to protect ourselves from the most draining cost we could face over our lifetime, especially one with such a high probability of occurring?

Planning in advance for your long-term care needs, whether through a long-term care insurance policy or other methods such as reverse mortgages, special savings programs, life insurance policies with long-term care riders, or family and community support, must be undertaken by you. This book discusses the most important steps you can take to ensure your financial and emotional future.

The following chapters will explain

- Why long-term care involves the whole family
- What government programs (such as Medicare) cover
- What kinds of care are available
- What your options are for paying for long-term care
- How to select a plan.

Chapter 12 also discusses estate planning and its relationship to planning for long-term care.

1 What Is Long-Term Care and Who May Need It?

Dave and Judy

Dave and Judy decided they needed a financial review when they both turned 80 years old in 1991. Up to that point they felt they had taken good care of their financial and insurance needs. They had not relied upon their children to oversee their personal affairs. One of their children lived nearby, while the other lived more than a thousand miles away.

In meeting with them we quickly discovered that they had significant exposure to long-term medical and nursing costs that were far above what their insurance policies covered at the time. The long-term care insurance policies they had purchased were written prior to major changes made to insurance regulations in 1990. Their policies covered only extremely serious illnesses and allowed coverage only after a mandatory three-day hospital stay followed by immediate transfer to a skilled nursing facility. Less than one percent of claims filed on such policies are ever paid since qualification for benefits is nearly impossible.

Our first recommendation was to immediately replace these policies with comprehensive policies that provided significantly better benefits, which they agreed to do. The new policies provided for skilled, intermediate and custodial long-term nursing care, and home health care services. The benefit "triggers" (access to policy payout benefits) were far easier to meet even though the policies were more expensive. After all, access to benefits that pay expenses incurred is the reason we all buy insurance.

Several years later they needed to access that coverage. Judy developed senile dementia and lived in a nursing home of her choosing for more than seven years. Dave received around-the-clock care at home for four years for similar problems. Care for the two of them cost more than $180,000 per year. Their new long-term care policies covered $80,000 per year of this cost.

Fortunately, they had also agreed to change their Medicare supplement policy to a higher-quality plan in 1991, which paid up to 100% of most medical expenses. They now have both died. These policies saved their estate more than $350,000 over the course of four years. Even with the policies, additional expenses amounted to nearly $500,000. While this is still taking a significant toll on their estate, by careful planning they both received the type of care that allowed them to live independently and with dignity during their later years.

What is Long-Term Care?

Long-term care is assistance with those activities of daily living that an individual cannot accomplish alone. These services are typically provided following an injury or illness, or when advanced age and frailty render individuals unable to care for themselves. Long-term care encompasses a wide array of services; from part-time help for a person at home, to permanent residence in an assisted-living or nursing facility, or even around-the-clock skilled care in a special facility. *Figure 1-1* shows that the risk of needing such care is far greater than most individuals realize. *Figure 1-2* shows that youth does not protect us from this need.

1

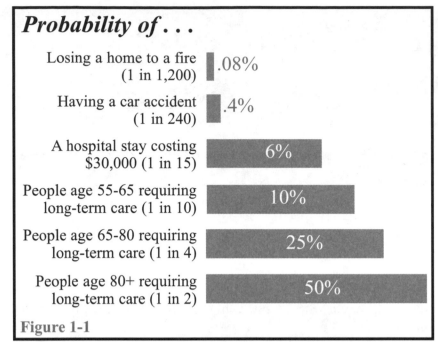

Probability of . . .

Losing a home to a fire (1 in 1,200) .08%

Having a car accident (1 in 240) .4%

A hospital stay costing $30,000 (1 in 15) 6%

People age 55-65 requiring long-term care (1 in 10) 10%

People age 65-80 requiring long-term care (1 in 4) 25%

People age 80+ requiring long-term care (1 in 2) 50%

Figure 1-1

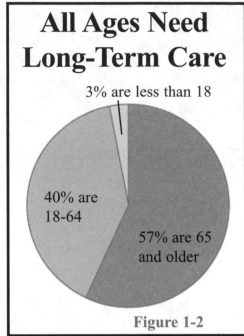

All Ages Need Long-Term Care

3% are less than 18

40% are 18-64

57% are 65 and older

Figure 1-2

Long-Term Care may include:

- <u>Personal care</u> (also called custodial care): help with bathing, grooming, transferring from a chair to a bed, taking medications, and other activities of daily living. Services at this level are provided either at home or in a residential facility;

- <u>Home health care</u>: medically-oriented services provided to a person at home by a nurse or other medical personnel, usually on a part-time basis;

- <u>Intermediate care</u>: care provided by skilled personnel, such as a speech, physical or occupational therapist – on an intermittent basis rather than daily. Services at this level are provided at home or in a residential facility;

- <u>Adult day care</u>: a program of therapeutic, social and health activities with services offered on a per-day basis. These services are provided at specialized centers that are either free-standing or part of a larger medical facility;

- <u>Assisted-living facility</u> (also called residential care facility): a facility that provides personal care and some medical care for people who live in the facility (usually called "residents"). These facilities may also provide recreational activities and/or educational and support programs for residents and/or family members, as well as a full or modified meal program;

- <u>Skilled nursing</u>: care provided by licensed personnel, such as nurses, for people who are under a physician's order 24 hours a day. This care is provided in a hospital, nursing home, assisted-living facility, or at home. A Skilled Nursing Facility (SNF) is an independent facility or specialized unit of a larger medical facility that provides this level of care;

- <u>Respite care</u>: part-time, occasional care for a person while his or her at-home caregiver, such as a spouse or adult child, takes time away from 24-hour-a-day care;

- <u>Hospice care</u>: care for individuals and their families in the last days and weeks of the individual's life.

WARNING! In any situation where the caregiver is unskilled or uncertified (and especially if the provider is working in the individual's home), the provider should be required to provide complete details about his/her background (e.g., DUI, felonies, drug tests, etc.).

Many people who are now in their seventies and eighties assumed that their children would take care of them as they aged. That has frequently turned out not to be the case. There are several reasons for this in planned family support structures.

First, people are now living longer. Parents and grandparents may need care for the last 20 to 35 years of their lives. The adult child caregiver is typically in the middle of raising a family at the same time. In fact, the typical caregiver is a woman in her mid-40s who has children under 18 living at home. People in this "sandwich generation" find themselves overburdened financially, physically and emotionally, trying to take care of two, sometimes three generations at the same time.

A recent national study conducted by the American Association of Retired Persons (AARP) indicates the following impact on the working caregiver's job performance.

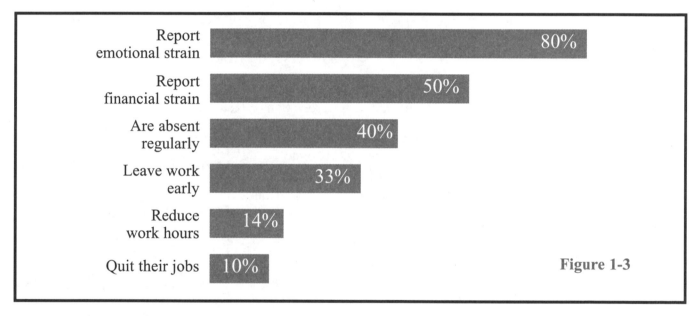

Report emotional strain — 80%
Report financial strain — 50%
Are absent regularly — 40%
Leave work early — 33%
Reduce work hours — 14%
Quit their jobs — 10%

Figure 1-3

Second, hospitals are releasing patients earlier than in the past. A parent who returns home from the hospital is more likely to be ill or frail, more so than he or she would have been in the past, requiring a higher level of care than the child may be able to provide.

Third, in many families, economics dictate that both spouses work. This leaves less time and energy to care for an aging or ill parent. Both spouses and their children may be away from the home for 12 or more hours, leaving the ill person alone for long periods of time.

Older people also have common attitudes, such as:

● The government will take care of them in their old age;

● They have adequate resources to take care of their own long-term care needs;

● "Whatever is going to happen will happen, and we'll deal with it then."

We will see in the course of this book that waiting to deal with the situation is, in fact, the absolute worst way to plan for the latter days of our lives. The costs of nursing home care are rising by approximately 7-9% per year. With continued decreases in government support, the best, and sometimes the only way to ensure that you get the type of care you want when you most need it is by planning ahead.

For those who do have substantial resources, the benefits of planning ahead include:

- Preserving your estate;

- Benefitting from sound financial advice;

- Good tax planning;

- Maximizing the estate transfer at the lowest tax;

- Providing the full range of choices available to you.

Elder Care's Cost to Firms Pegged at $29 Billion Yearly

Workers caring for elderly relatives cost their employers as much as $29 billion a year in lost productivity. This expense is likely to grow as the population ages.

The 14.4 million Americans who juggle jobs and care for the elderly often are late arriving to work, leave work early, or take long lunches to carry out their responsibilities. According to a study based on the first national survey of caregivers, as many as ten percent of these Americans ultimately quit their jobs.

The study by Metropolitan Life Insurance[1] was based on a national survey of caregivers carried out by the National Alliance for Caregiving and the American Association of Retired Persons.

"We found that two out of three caregivers are employed and half said caregiving has an impact on their work," said Joyce Ruddock, a gerontologist and vice president of the MetLife Mature Market Group. "All this means is lost productivity for our nation's businesses."

She noted that the costs associated with caregiving will rise dramatically as the population continues to age. The nation's 76 million baby boomers will begin turning 65 in 2011, according to the Census Bureau. "Businesses who turn their backs on family caregivers will pay a tremendous price," said Ruddock, who helped present the research to the U.S. Senate's Special Committee on Aging.

Some companies are beginning to wake up to the need. Thirty percent of major U.S. employers now offer eldercare programs, up from 13 percent in 1991, according to a survey of 1,050 companies by Hewitt Associates.

WORKING AND GIVING

- 52 percent of those caring for an elderly relative or friend are employed full time.
- 54 percent of working caregivers have made changes at work to accommodate their caregiving responsibilities.
- 81 percent of working caregivers say their employer is understanding of their caregiver responsibilities.
- The average age of caregivers is 46; 73 percent are women.
- The average age of a care recipient is 77.

Source: National Alliance for Caregiving

The National Alliance for Caregiving survey — the first of its kind in a decade — found that more than 23 percent of U.S. households have caregivers and 14.4 million caregivers work full or part time.

The average caregiver is a 46-year-old woman who spends 18 hours a week caring for her 77-year-old mother, according to the survey of 1,509 people.

Surprisingly, more than 20 percent of caregivers are ages 18 to 35.

"Eldercare is something that everyone will very likely experience in their lifetime," said Dorothy Howe of the AARP. In its study of the survey results, MetLife focused on caregivers who work full time and spend nine hours or more a week caring for an elderly relative.[2]

As medical advances allow people to live longer and the first baby boomers hit age 60 this year, protecting yourself against a long-term care risk is more important than ever. With average nursing home costs nationally at about $57,700 per year and as high as $70,000 in some areas[3] and the average length of stay being 2.5 years (892 days), you can see how this could be a serious drain on your assets.[4]

Long-Term Care is Not Just For the Elderly

It is important to realize that long-term care is not just for the aging, as was seen in *Figure 1-2*. Remember, forty percent of people in nursing facilities today are under age 65.

The average hospital stay is now two days. People recovering from a serious accident or illness will find themselves quickly released from a hospital to a separate facility for continued rehabilitation or skilled nursing care. Most medical policies require a three-day hospital stay and immediate transfer to a rehabilitation or skilled nursing facility for this benefit to be paid by the insurance company. Therefore, most individuals will not be covered by that insurance if forced to leave the hospital in less than three days.

What You Can Do at This Point

1. Plan a family meeting that lets everyone know what is in place, what your wishes are and where you need help now *and* in the future.

2. Review your options and needs with a trusted advisor.

3. Determine your current assets and liabilities.

4. Determine costs in your area for various levels of nursing and intermediate custodial care so that you can properly evaluate your resources and your capabilities.

2 Long-Term Care is a Family Issue

Long-Term Care Assistance At Home

When one person in a family needs long-term care, it affects the entire family:

- The lifestyle of the spouse changes dramatically;

- An adult child may have to spend more time helping an older parent; or

- Parents must focus on helping their temporarily or permanently disabled child.

In most situations, the family's financial picture changes, sometimes drastically. The emotional stressors on the family are tremendous and the health of the caregiver often begins to suffer.

Most people who need long-term care assistance receive care at home for some period of time. It is important to be realistic about what kind of family support will be available to you or other members of your family when the need for long-term care arises.

Figure 2-1: The Need for Assistance in the Home Rises as People Age

Age	% of adults who need in-home assistance
Under 65	15%
65-79	17%
75-84	28%
85+	49%

Source: *Taking Care of Tomorrow, A Consumer's Guide to Long-Term Care,* California Department of Aging, 1998.

Virginia

Virginia, who is 84 and blind, lives alone. If it weren't for Norma, her in-home care provider, Virginia says, "I couldn't do anything but sit here on my couch." Norma spends 33 hours a month with Virginia, taking her shopping, cleaning house and paying her bills. Norma spends six hours of her own time taking Virginia to the doctor because she isn't paid for that time by the county, state, or federal programs that support in-home care.

Norma receives the minimum wage and no benefits. Everyone agrees that in-home care workers provide a valuable service by taking care of elderly and disabled people in their homes and keeping them out of expensive institutions. Federal, state and county governments do share the cost, yet none are willing to pick up the extra expense of higher wages or benefits to fully care for the individual.[1]

Here are some of the critical issues to think about:

- Do you have family?

- Do your children live nearby, or must they travel great distances to plan for your care, or to help you daily? Are there adequate public services available to help with your needs?

- Are your children willing and able (both financially and emotionally) to assist in meeting your needs?

- Are your anticipated needs also the needs that you want your children to provide for you, such as bathing you, helping you eat, or helping you go to the bathroom?

- How much time and energy, given their other commitments, will they realistically have?

Community Resources

Most cities and communities have developed resources to help keep older people independent in their homes. These resources can be of great assistance to family members as they develop a long-term care plan for a parent, or for a temporarily or permanently disabled family member.

Community and private services in the community may include:

- Home health care: temporary or occasional care by a nurse or other medical personnel;

- Personal care: help with bathing, grooming, and transferring from a chair to a bed;

- Homemaker services: housekeeping, bill paying, cooking, and grocery shopping;

- Hospice care: support for people with terminal illnesses;

- Respite care: short-term care that provides temporary relief to caregivers;

- Adult day health care: provides some medical care, plus physical, occupational and speech therapy, usually as a specialized service requiring transportation to and from the facility;

- Adult day support centers: day care that provides recreation and social stimulation for the person needing care (such as church groups, social groups);

- Special day care services for people with special needs unable to take part in group activities, such as those with ALS (Lou Gehrig's disease).

When people start seeking care for these situations they often do not know where to start. There are usually local, volunteer, or government agencies that can provide them with basic information, but frequently what is needed is help in coordinating and assessing the situation.

The following services are provided by one agency located in my hometown of Walnut Creek, CA:

- In-home assessment and long-term planning session;
- Consultation;
- Financial services;
- Mental health assistant;
- Personal assistant;
- Alzheimer's disease expertise;
- 24-hour crisis intervention.

- Placement service;
- Counseling;
- Care management;
- Socialization;
- Live-in attendant;
- Transition care management;

Geriatric Care Managers

A Geriatric Care Manager is a health and human services professional such as a gerontologist, social worker, counselor, or nurse, with a specialized body of knowledge and experience related to aging and eldercare issues. A Professional Geriatric Care Manager (PGCM) is a geriatric care manager who is a member of the National Association of Professional Geriatric Care Managers (GCM) and has committed to adhering to the GCM Pledge of Ethics and Standards of Practice. The PGCM assists older adults and persons with disabilities in attaining their maximum function. The PGCM strives to respect the autonomy of the individual and delivers care coordination and support services with sensitivity to preserve the dignity and respect of each individual. In addition, the PGCM is an experienced guide and resource for families of older adults and others with chronic needs.

Questions to Ask When Looking for a Geriatric Care Manager

People calling themselves "care managers" have many different backgrounds. Very few states have licensing for these professionals; however, many are licensed in their state in other fields. The GCM recognizes the following certifications as being "Certified Care Managers": CMC, CMM, C-ASWCM, and C-SWCM. It is important for the wise consumer to ask questions which include:

- Are you a member of the National Association of Professional Geriatric Care Managers?
- Are you certified as a care manager? Do you hold other professional licenses or certifications?
- How long have you been providing care management services?
- Are you available for emergencies?
- Does your company also provide home care services?
- How will you communicate information to me?
- Can you provide me with references?

Care managers do not specialize in all areas. Care managers who primarily work with older adults generally bring more to their practice than an expertise in geriatrics. They bring knowledge of aging issues that allows them and their staff to overcome the myths relating to aging and to focus on the problems at hand. At the same time they bring an experience of working with resources in your community. They are more aware of real life problems, health and otherwise, that emerge as persons age and what tools are available to address them. You will want to hire someone who regularly handles clients in the area of your concern.

Once You Have Found a Care Manager

When you have found an appropriate care manager, he or she will most likely do an on-site assessment. During the assessment, you will be asked to give an overview of the reason you are seeking help and introduce all of the parties involved. After you have explained your situation, ask:

- What resources will it take to resolve this situation?
- Are there any alternative courses of action?
- What are the advantages and disadvantages of each alternative?
- Who will be working with you?
- How many professionals may be involved? What about off-hours and back-up?
- How are fees computed?
- How are travel time and mileage handled?
- How are services terminated?

Ask Questions First

Ask lots of questions before choosing your care manager, such as:

- What are the primary services provided by this agency/business?
- What other services does this agency/business provide?
- How many care managers are there in this agency/business?
- Is there a fee for the initial consultation and, if so, how much is it?
- Given the nature of your problem, what information should you bring with you to the initial consultation?
- Should other family members/friends/caregivers come to the initial consultation?
- What will the initial consultation include?
- Do they have knowledge about long-term care policy claim procedures and the tax consequences of the services they are providing?

Discussing Fees

There are many different ways of charging fees and each care manager will choose to work differently. You will also want to know how often he/she bills. Some care managers bill weekly, some bill monthly, some bill upon completion of work. Ask about these matters at the initial conference and ask to have them in writing, so there will be no surprises. If you don't understand, ask again. If you need clarification, say so. It is very important that you feel comfortable in this area.

In addition to fees, most care managers will charge for out-of-pocket expenses. Out-of-pocket expenses may include charges for mileage, caregiving supplies, long distance telephone calls, and other such costs. Find out if there will be any other incidental costs. Be sure to discuss and make sure you have all questions answered before proceeding with an agreement for services. You should expect a written agreement including fees before the commencement of services.

Get It in Writing

Once you decide to hire the care manager, ask that your arrangement be put in writing. The writing can be a letter or a formal contract. It should spell out what services the care manager will perform for you and what the fee and expense arrangements will be. REMEMBER – even if your agreement remains oral and is not put into writing, you have made a contract and are responsible for all charges for work done by the care manager and his/her staff.

Do I Really Need a Geriatric Care Manager?

Before making the effort, step back a moment and try to determine whether you actually have a problem in which a professional geriatric care manager needs to be involved. There are many places to find a care manager in your city or state. The Web site *www.caremanager.org* includes a searchable directory of professional geriatric care managers who belong to GCM. The GCM headquarters are located at 1604 N. Country Club Road, Tucson, AZ 85716-3119, and their phone number is 520-881-8008. You may also want to check with local agencies or hospitals to obtain a list of local referrals. Health professionals and elder-law attorneys are other excellent referral sources.[2]

Information for the section on Geriatric Care Managers provided by Linda Fodrini-Johnson, MA, CMC, MFT, Executive Director of Eldercare Services, 1808 Tice Valley Boulevard, Walnut Creek, CA 94595; telephone 925-937-2018. Their website is: www.eldercareanswers.com

Other Resources

The cost and availability of services varies from community to community. You can find out about these resources from agencies that provide services for older people and those with disabilities. In California a key resource is the Area Agency on Aging (there are 33 such agencies throughout the state). Every state has similar programs. These agencies also typically have information on the location of senior centers, senior nutrition sites, Meals on Wheels, Alzheimer's resource centers and other community programs and services.

Local churches, religious groups, state-funded counseling services, associations for people with a specific illness (such as Alzheimer's disease), and community outreach programs may also offer specialized programs or may be able to refer you to additional community resources. Volunteer programs are also beginning to be implemented around the country to assist families caring for a loved one at home. (*See the section in Chapter 16, Volunteer Support, on the "Caring Hands" program in Walnut Creek, CA, a nationwide program in selected areas.*)

If you are looking for resources for someone out of state, the Eldercare Locator, a nationwide toll-free information and referral service, can give you telephone numbers of programs in all areas of the United States. The toll-free telephone number is 1-800-677-1116.

Talking to Your Parents About Long-Term Care Needs

The subject of aging and losing the ability to care for one's own day-to-day activities is difficult for many people to face, much less discuss. Children need to be respectful of their parents' wishes, while at the same time being realistic about their parents' capabilities and needs. The transition from living an independent life to needing assistance with basic activities is not an easy one.

As the financial and investing world has become more complex, many older people have trouble understanding the complicated investments and insurance policies they purchased when they were younger. Frequently, as time passes, the products and policies have changed what is provided or covered. The tax consequences may also have changed through the years, sometimes dramatically. You must educate yourself about these issues, enabling you to help your parents understand the specifics of their situation.

The following guidelines can help you talk about these issues with your parents:

- Realize that at some point your parents will need some assistance, if just for grocery shopping, house cleaning, etc.;

- Be alert to changes in your parents' physical, mental and emotional situation;

- When you sense that your parents are ready and prepared to talk about the subject, be willing to listen and have an open, honest dialogue about their short-term or long-term care needs;

- Call on professional advisors to help you understand the ramifications of decisions about long-term care for the whole family, and to learn about various alternatives.

Professionals you may want to speak with include: an attorney, an accountant, a financial/investment advisor, and an insurance broker or agent. Make sure these people are well versed in long-term care issues.

In California and most other states, insurance agents and financial consultants selling long-term care insurance must be licensed by the state Department of Insurance. They must have special training and have completed a number of continuing education courses before they can renew their licenses. You can obtain this information by calling the California Department of Insurance at 1-800-927-HELP (4357) (calling from within California) or 213-897-8921 (outside California).

Make certain you select advisors you respect and trust, then tell them all the facts. They can only help you to the extent you give them full and reliable information. If you do not give them your parents' full health and financial status, they may make the wrong recommendations. That could cause an insurance company to decline coverage, or to provide coverage at a higher cost. Federal or state programs could possibly provide coverage at no cost, but qualifying can be difficult (*see Chapter 4 regarding Medicaid and Medi-Cal*).

Safeguard Vital Financial and Legal Documents

In order for family members to make decisions regarding health care, serious illnesses or insurance coverage(s), it is important to have financial and legal information at hand. It is also essential to identify and catalogue all assets of the estate to prevent enormous shrinkage of assets (loss of value) due to income, capital gains and estate taxes, or due to the cost of health care needs that could have been covered by insurance.

You will need to collect all personal and financial information in one master file. Store originals of valuable or negotiable documents such as deeds, automobile titles, stock certificates, birth and death certificates, adoption and citizenship papers, contracts and IOU's (indentured certificates) in a safe or a safety deposit box. Items that must be quickly available upon a family member's death or disability should be kept with the family attorney or in another safe but easily accessible place.

(An excellent nationwide service available for this purpose is provided by a California firm headquartered in Walnut Creek called Video Inventory Services. They can provide video documentation of your vital records and store them on CD or videotape so you can store them, access them, and review them whenever necessary and at your leisure. The company will also keep a separate copy in a secure location in backup storage if you desire. You can contact this company toll-free at 1-866-791-3144 for more information or to place an order.)

Importance of Tax Information

Although it may seem unnecessary when you are planning for long-term care needs, the gathering of information on income taxes, estate taxes and ongoing income flow is critical to making the "right" decisions at this time. Professional advisors and/or family members must be aware of the income sources of the person requiring medical and/or long-term care attention. As a professional financial advisor, the author has encountered many such situations where a client requiring services, through simple inattention, was unclear on current income sources, was unclear whether taxes were paid or delinquent, and was unclear if other liabilities were being missed.

The reason this is so important is that the wrong financial decisions could be made by a person stepping in as a caregiver, unaware of the ramifications of different investment, insurance coverages, or other planning previously established. There are choices in the general discussion of estate planning techniques and income tax considerations that apply to these situations and this is provided later in the book.

Taking Care of the Caregiver

As the caregiver of a person with long-term care needs, you may be tempted to try to provide everything yourself. It is crucial to realize that there is a limit to what you can provide and it is best for everyone involved not to take on too much of the effort. It becomes difficult to give good advice to your loved one, or to make sound decisions, when you are overwhelmed with his or her day-to-day needs. We have seen too many people in our practice whose lives and those of their children began to suffer as they tried to do it all alone. In addition to making the caregiver less capable of providing quality care, it can also lead to animosity among family members, depression, or even life-threatening illnesses.

There are programs available in most communities that can help at-home caregivers, including adult day care programs and respite care. The programs allow the caregivers a break, to rest and restore themselves, or take care of matters in their own lives. Local churches, hospitals, senior citizens' groups, or centers may have references to help you find resources in your area.

Sometimes the caregiver suffers the most . . .

Bill and Margaret

Bill and Margaret retired at 65 in New Hampshire. Their children were living in various parts of the U.S. and overseas. At age 73, Bill suffered a stroke that permanently blinded him and created other health problems. Due to the severity of his illness, he spent some time hospitalized and then recovered at home with Margaret's help. As family members came to provide care and assistance it was immediately recognized that he could no longer handle his income taxes, other financial documents, or investments, something he always loved to manage. At this point, the children took over that responsibility.

Margaret did her best to provide for his needs at home, but over time Bill's health declined appreciably. The stress of caring for him took its toll on her. She began to experience health problems that led to her death shortly thereafter.

Bill was now completely on his own in a farmhouse in the middle of New Hampshire and needed to move close to, or in with, one of his children. Arrangements were made to bring him to the home of one of the sons. It was quickly determined that the three-story residence was inadequate. With no one home during the day to care for the frail 75-year-old man with multiple needs, it became necessary to find a retirement center for Bill.

He was eventually placed in an assisted-living facility located close to family for visits. At a cost of $3,000 a month, this facility provided room and board and included many stimulating activities. Not only did he feel more comfortable and relaxed, but his health actually improved over a three-year period, until he died at age 79.

This true story emphasizes the fact that family members, whether a spouse, siblings, children, or other close relatives, may find it close to impossible to meet many of the needs that are required for a person in declining health. Bill's stay at the assisted-living facility included monitoring of his medications, help with his clothing and food preparation, and assistance in showering and toileting. These became, over time, activities of daily living, which further increased the cost of his care, but made it possible for him to stay at that facility rather than moving to a skilled or custodial nursing facility. His family was then free to provide loving support and companionship without the added stress of trying to care for him when they could not adequately provide for his daily needs.

Family and Medical Leave

In early 1993, President Bill Clinton signed the Family and Medical Leave Act (FMLA), ending a nearly decade-long struggle to enact legislation that would allow people to take time off from work to care for their families or themselves. Before this law was enacted many American employees were unable to take time off from work in family emergencies for fear of losing their jobs.

In fact, according to the official U.S. Bureau of Labor Statistics, only 37% of all working women in firms with 100 or more employees were eligible for unpaid maternity leave upon the birth of a child. In the decades before this law, untold thousands of employees were forced to choose between caring for their families and keeping their jobs.

The FMLA was developed to address this dilemma. It guarantees employees of companies with more than 50 employees up to 12 weeks of unpaid leave per year, to care for a newborn or newly adopted child, to care for certain seriously ill family members, and/or to recover from their own serious health conditions. Although this law is relatively straightforward, some employees and employers may be unsure about how it actually works. The series of responses that follow are designed to answer frequently asked questions about the FMLA. They are generally based on the regulations explaining the FMLA issued by the U.S. Department of Labor, which enforces the law.

1. When can I take family or medical leave?

- If you are having a baby or adopting a child;
- If your child, spouse or parent has a serious health condition;
- If you have a serious health condition, including pregnancy.

The FMLA gives you the right to take time off ("leave") without losing your job.

"Family Leave" means time off to care for another person in your family: a newborn or newly adopted child, a child, a spouse, or a parent with a serious health condition. "Medical leave" means time off to seek medical treatment for, or to recover from, your own serious health condition.

2. How much leave can I get?

The FMLA allows you to take either family leave or medical leave, or both, for up to a total of 12 weeks per year. This means that if you are on family or medical leave and not out for more than 12 weeks in a year, your job is protected.

3. How do I know if I can take family or medical leave?

Not everyone is covered. There are generally three conditions:

- First, your employer must have 50 or more employees on the payroll for 20 workweeks during the current or preceding calendar year. To determine whether the law applies to your employer, find out how many employees are on the payroll, including those on leave and working part-time. For you to be covered 50 employees must work within 75 miles of your work site.

- Second, you can count employees at different work sites within 75 miles to reach the 50-employee threshold. For example, if your employer has 25 employees at your work site, and 25 working at another site 10 miles away, the employer must comply with the FMLA. But if the two work sites are 100 miles apart, then the employer would not be eligible.

- Third, you must have worked for your employer for at least 12 months *and* for at least 1,250 hours during the last year. If you worked 25 or more hours for 50 weeks in a year you would have worked the required total of 1,250 hours. (Specific rules apply to teachers and some highly paid "key" employees.)

4. Does the law guarantee paid time off?

No. The FMLA only requires unpaid leave. However, the law permits an employee to elect, or the employer to require the employee, to use accrued paid leave, such as vacation or sick leave, for some or all of the FMLA leave period. When paid leave is substituted for unpaid FMLA leave, it may be counted against the 12-week FMLA leave entitlement if the employee is properly notified of the designation when the leave begins.

The Americans with Disabilities Act (ADA) requires certain employers to make reasonable accommodation to allow employees with disabilities to do their jobs. If your disability requires that you be out of work for more than 12 weeks, or requires that you return to work on a flexible schedule, or at a less strenuous job, you may be able to argue that these are reasonable accommodations under the ADA.

3 Medicare

Medicare is Spending Less for Home Care Services

Home health care has become big business in the U.S., and with a growing senior population there is the potential for greater growth in this industry. In 1999, more than 20,000 home care providers delivered services to nearly 8 million individuals who required medical care in their homes. According to the National Association for Home Care, the annual expenditure for these services was $36 billion. Two years earlier home care service expenditures were a record $41 billion. You might ask, how can home care service expenditures decrease as the demand for home care and the cost of other medical services continue to rise sharply?

Medicare pays about 40% of the cost for home care services. However, the Centers for Medicare and Medicaid Services presently projects that Medicare's share of payments for home care services will continue to decline through 2008. From 1998 to 1999 Medicare's spending for home care services fell from $14 billion to $9.5 billion. This is a decrease of nearly one-third. Medicaid and private insurance combined provide about 25% of the reimbursements for home care services. This leaves more than one-third of the costs of home services to come out-of-pocket or from other sources — and this percentage will grow.

It is also interesting to note that the National Center for Health Statistics reports that 63% of those receiving home care services are over age 65 and that 65% of those receiving home services are women. Home care services are a cost-effective alternative to costly Skilled Nursing Facilities and hospitals. Home health services are provided to all ages, with 37% of care being received by those under 65.

Robert and Lynn

Robert was a retired surgeon with Medicare insurance when he required heart surgery. One week after the surgery he was transferred to a skilled nursing facility (SNF) for physical therapy and other rehabilitation services. His Medicare caseworker kept close tabs on his recovery. As soon as the caseworker was informed that he was not responding to the physical therapy, she informed Robert's wife, Lynn, that Medicare would no longer pay the costs of the skilled nursing home. Medicare rules require that patients be improving in order to continue receiving benefits.

Since Robert had always handled all of the family's financial matters, Lynn had no idea what to do. She sat staring at the bills on her table day after day. She felt confused and helpless. Seventy-four days after he entered the SNF, Robert died.

By then, the medical and nursing home bills owed (for Robert's care, but required to be paid by Lynn) totaled $77,000. Lynn eventually paid all the bills, but it consumed a third of her assets. Upon Robert's death she also lost some pension benefits and Social Security income. With her reduced resources, Lynn was forced to move to another less expensive part of the country, change her lifestyle, and seriously limit her spending.

Good Medicare supplementary insurance and long-term care nursing home coverage would have paid most of Robert's long-term care expenses. It would have given Lynn more to live on and less to worry about as she faced the last days of Robert's life and her future alone.

Most of us assume that our medical insurance will cover all of our health needs, but most plans do not cover most levels of nursing or home care. Many cover home care in a limited way, but will not cover a home health aide. Most HMOs contract with groups of physicians called IPAs (Independent Physician Associations). The IPA contracts for skilled nursing and home health care. Depending upon the organization to which your doctor belongs you may have excellent benefits, or you may have none at all. Some IPAs have patient liaison personnel called case managers who make sure that their patients get the level of care they need. They know that, in the end, this will actually save money by avoiding unnecessary readmission to the hospital. Other organizations are less accommodating. These policies are especially important for the Medicare HMOs many seniors are now joining.

Check your health insurance policy to see if the most basic home health care services and skilled nursing services are covered. None of these policies, including Medicare and Medigap plans, cover either custodial or protracted home and skilled nursing care (if so, for very limited periods).

MEDICARE FACTS

- Medicare now pays based on a prospective payment system through the use of diagnosis related groups, or "DRGs." Each DRG is only one of 503 possible classifications of diagnoses in which patients with similar lengths of stay and resource use are grouped together for billing purposes. The patient's actual diagnosis is converted into a DRG that is used to calculate the hospital's reimbursement. In 1983, DRGs were implemented in all acute care, non-specialty hospitals throughout the United States. They were implemented to contain the costs for the Medicare Program. Instead of hospital reimbursement being based on retrospective charges (after the delivery of care), the reimbursement system changed to a DRG fixed payment or "prospective payment" system, meaning hospitals are compensated for a patient's care based on the qualifying DRG.[1]

- Hospitalization for hip fractures decreased from 22 days to 13 days.

- The percentage of patients who could walk at all when discharged from the hospital dropped from 56% to 40%.

- The percentage discharged directly to nursing homes rose from 35% to 60%.

- Since the start of the new program, a new study found that the percentage of hip fracture patients remaining in a nursing home one year after their hospitalization rose from 9% to 33%.

Jack

Jack was 63 years old. He was a big man and lived with his frail wife in their own home. His wife, Elizabeth, had medical problems of her own and he had been her caretaker for years. They had no children living in the area. When Jack suffered a stroke their roles reversed. Because Jack was less than 65 years old he did not have Medicare. He did have comprehensive health insurance.

Jack spent three days in the hospital (acute care) and was discharged to a nursing home that specialized in rehabilitation, as he needed physical, occupational, and speech therapies. His insurance covered eight weeks in the nursing home, but when he failed to improve for over one week, his coverage ended.

Jack needed either 24-hour home care or long-term care in a custodial facility. Elizabeth and Jack did not have the necessary extra bedroom for the full time live-in caregiver that Jack needed, and Elizabeth was not able to take care of Jack's needs herself.

Jack was transferred to an area nursing home. Jack and Elizabeth had to pay for Jack's on-going custodial care out of their savings. The cost for this care in California, in the fall of 2002, was $140 to $175 per day, plus substantial additional costs for personal items as needed. Before Medicaid coverage began, Elizabeth and Jack had spent over $100,000.

When one's spouse has need of custodial care and receives Medicaid benefits the spouse is allowed to keep approximately $101,640 (2007) in savings. The community spouse (the spouse staying at home) keeps his or her monthly income, regardless of amount. If the amount is less than $2,541 per month (in 2007) the community spouse may be able to keep more of the institutionalized spouse's spend-down assets.[2] For many people this clearly would destroy their retirement savings as well as severely affect the stay-at-home spouse's lifestyle. In addition, Medicaid may put a lien on the family home to collect the costs that government care provided.

What are Medicare, Medicaid and Medi-Cal?

Many people are confused about the distinctions among Medicare, Medicaid and Medi-Cal.

- Medicare is a national health insurance program for people 65 or older, younger people with certain disabilities, and people with permanent kidney failure who need dialysis (called End-Stage Renal Disease, or ESRD), or a transplant. Medicare is run by the Centers for Medicare and Medicaid Services (CMS). The Social Security Administration assists CMS by enrolling people in Medicare and by collecting Medicare premiums. Medicare is the federal medical insurance program for Americans who are 65 and older. This insurance is available to all citizens and legal residents at age 65. The same benefits are available to everyone who qualifies, no matter what their level of income or assets. Mcdicare is extremely limited in its long-term care coverage.

- Medicaid is a joint federal and state program for the poor which pays some medical and assisted living expenses. It does pay for certain types of long-term care, but primarily only in skilled nursing facilities and only for people with very few assets.

- Medi-Cal is California's version of Medicaid. It covers the basic medical and assisted living costs of the poor. Medi-Cal, like Medicaid, requires that people have very few assets to qualify. In California, the limit for a single person is $2,000 in non-exempt assets and $35 per month of income for personal needs if institutionalized. (Other states have other programs.)

More detailed information regarding Medicare follows. (*For information regarding Medicaid and Medi-Cal, please see Chapter 4.*)

What Medicare Covers

Part A – Hospital Insurance helps pay for necessary in-patient medical care in a hospital, skilled nursing facility, or psychiatric hospital, and for hospice and home health care.

Medicare Part A is financed through the Social Security payroll withholding tax paid by workers and their employers and the Self-Employment Tax paid by self-employed people. You do not have to pay a monthly premium for Part A if you or your spouse worked in Medicare-covered employment for at least 10 years, if you are at least 65 years old, and if you are a citizen or permanent resident of the

United States. Certain younger disabled people and those with ESRD also qualify for premium-free Part A. If you do not qualify for premium-free part A, you may buy it if you are at least 65 and meet certain other requirements.

Part B – Medical Insurance helps pay for necessary physician services, outpatient hospital care, and other medical services and supplies not covered by Part A. Both Parts A and B have deductibles and co-payments and Part A has benefit limitations as well.

Everyone who enrolls in Medicare Part B must pay a premium which was pegged at $93.50 per month in 2007.[3] Most enrollees have it deducted from their monthly Social Security check. You are automatically enrolled in Part B when you become eligible for premium-free Part A, unless you state that you do not want it. Even if you do not qualify for premium-free Part A you can usually buy Part B if you are 65 or older.

Part C – Medicare Advantage (formerly known as Medicare+Choice) is available if you are entitled to Medicare Part A, enrolled in Part B, and provided you reside in the plan's service area. There are two options under Part C. With the Coordinated Care Plans, you can be enrolled in a Health Maintenance Organization (HMO), Point of Service (POS), Regionally Expanded Preferred Provider Organization (PPO), or a Provider-Sponsored Organization (PSO). The second option is to set up a Health Savings Account (*see Chapter 7*) in conjunction with private fee-for-service plans offering at least the same benefit coverage levels as Medicare Parts A and B, or high deductible coverage. Call 1-800-MEDICARE or visit *www.medicare.gov* to determine what plan choices are available in your area.[4]

Part D – Prescription Drug became available in January 2006. Beneficiaries have several choices for getting their drug coverage, including:

- People who are in or want to be in the original, fee-for-service Medicare program can enroll in a Part D prescription drug plan (PDP) that contracts with Medicare;

- People who are in or want to enroll in a Medicare Advantage managed care plan (HMO, e.g.) can enroll in that plan's Part D Medicare Advantage-Prescription Drug plan (MA-PD); or

- People who are in or want to join a Medicare Advantage Private Fee For Service (PFFS) plan can get their Part D prescription drug coverage through the PFFS plan if it is offered, or through a PDP if it isn't included as a benefit of the PFFS.

Although enrollment in Part D is voluntary, people with Medicare who choose not to enroll when they are first eligible may have to pay a higher premium if they later decide to enroll in a Part D plan.

Figure 3-1		(View Online at www.longtermcarebooks.com)	
Standard Part D Drug Benefit in 2007			
Coverage	**Drug Costs**	**Part D Plan Pays**	**Beneficiary Pays**
Annual Deductible	$0 - $265	$0	$265
Initial Coverage Limit	$266 - $2,400	75% (up to $1,650)	25% ($499)
No Coverage (Doughnut Hole)	$2,401 - $3,850	$0	100% ($3,850)
Out-of-Pocket Limit	Over $3,850	95% of remaining costs	Up to 5% of remaining costs

Source: Medicare & You 2007, *U.S. Department of Health & Human Services, Centers for Medicare & Medicaid Services, www.medicare.gov, CMS Pub. No. 10050, September 2006, page 45.*

They will also need to wait until the annual enrollment period at the end of each year to sign up. Benefits will begin on the first day of the following year. If someone already has drug coverage that is at least as good as the Part D, they can keep their existing drug coverage without facing a premium penalty later. The chart on the previous page outlines what the "standard" Part D drug coverage looks like in 2007. The premiums, deductibles, and coverage limit amounts will increase annually. Coverage limits include a gap in coverage ("doughnut hole") during which a beneficiary must pay all his or her drug costs before the Part D plan begins paying again.[5]

Medicare and Long-Term Care

Medicare pays less than 2 percent of all nursing home costs. Medicare pays only for stays in skilled nursing facilities (facilities that provide 24-hour nursing care) that are Medicare-approved, and only if admission directly follows a hospital stay of at least three days. (*Note: Only 7 percent of skilled nursing facilities in the country in 2007 are Medicare-only certified*). Coverage is limited to 100 days per episode of illness. This means that after 100 days of nursing home care, benefits may not be available if the person returns to a nursing home later with the same illness.[6]

In order to qualify for Medicare payment for skilled nursing care in a skilled nursing facility an individual must:

- Have received inpatient hospital care for at least three days;
- Enter an SNF for the same reason that required the hospital stay; and
- Enter that SNF within 30 days of the hospital stay.

The longest skilled nursing home stay that Medicare will pay for completely is 20 days. After the first 20 days, if you still require *skilled care*, Medicare will pay only a part of the nursing home bill. You will have to pay a co-payment for each of the next 80 days. It must also be determined that you are getting better and that you still need *skilled nursing care* seven days a week and/or rehabilitative services at least five days a week for Medicare to continue to pay for nursing home care.

Medicare will not pay for any nursing home stays where you only need help with the activities of daily living, such as eating, getting dressed, or going to the bathroom. These are considered to be custodial functions and you must pay for these services.

Figure 3-2   (View Online at www.longtermcarebooks.com)

Number of Days in a Skilled Nursing Facility Covered by Medicare

Days	Medicare Pays	You Pay
1 - 20*	100% of approved amount	$0
21 - 100	All approved, less $124 deductible	$124 per day
101+	$0	100%

*Medicare will pay 100% for ONLY the first 20 days

Source: "Medicare Premiums and Deductibles for 2007. Copyright 2006 Center for Medicare Advocacy, Inc. www.medicareadvocacy.org.

Figure 3-3 (View Online at www.longtermcarebooks.com)

2007 MEDICARE AND SOCIAL SECURITY RATES

MEDICARE

Part B monthly premium*	$93.50
Part B deductible	$124.00
Part A deductible – hospital stay per benefit period	$992.00

MONTHLY SOCIAL SECURITY BENEFITS

2006 cost-of-living adjustment (COLA) (As of January, 2007)	3.3%
Average, all retired workers (after COLA)	$1,044.00
Average, couple both receiving benefits (after COLA)	$1,713.00
Maximum benefit (age 65 and 10 months)	$2,116.00

ANNUAL RETIREMENT EARNINGS TEST FOR EARLY RETIREES

(The Retirement Earnings Test determines whether Social Security benefits are payable. A person's earnings for a taxable year are the sum of pay for services as an employee plus all net earnings from self-employment [minus any net loss from self-employment] for that year. If you are under Full Retirement Age [FRA] when you start getting your Social Security payments, $1 in benefits will be deducted for each $2 you earn above the annual limit. In the calendar year you attain FRA, $1 in benefits will be deducted for each $3 you earn above a higher annual limit up to the month of FRA attainment.)

Exempt amount under FRA (2007)	$12,960.00($1,080/month)
Exempt amount at FRA (2007)	$34,440.00 ($2,870/month)

MAXIMUM TAXABLE PAYROLL EARNINGS

Social Security	$97,500.00
Medicare	no limit

TAX RATES (2007)

Employee	7.65%
Social Security portion	6.20%
Medicare portion	1.45%
For self-employed	15.30%

* Due to the Medicare Modernization Act, beginning in 2007, single beneficiaries with annual incomes over $80,000 and married couples with incomes over $160,000 will pay a higher percentage of the cost of Medicare Part B coverage, reducing Medicare's share. These higher-income beneficiaries will pay a monthly premium equal to 35, 50, 65, or 80 percent of the total cost, depending on their income level.

Sources: "Social Security and Medicare Changes for 2007." Copyright © 2007 New York Life Insurance Company. Website: http://www.newyorklife.com/cda/0,3254,10994,00.html; and "2007 Social Security Changes." Copyright © 2007 United States Social Security Administration. SSA Press Office, 440 Altmeyer Bldg., 6401 Security Blvd., Baltimore, MD 21235. Website: http://www.socialsecurity.gov/pressoffice/factsheets/colafacts2007.htm.

Figure 3-4

(View Online at www.longtermcarebooks.com)

MEDICARE PAYMENTS IN 2007*

Part A - Hospital Insurance	You Pay	Medicare Pays
Hospitalization First 60 days	$992 for first 60 days	All but $992
Days 61-90	$248 per day	All but $248 per day
Days 91-150	$496 per day	All but $496 per day
Days 151+	**All**	**Nothing**
Skilled Nursing Facility First 20 days	Nothing	All
Days 21-100	Up to $124 per day	All but $124 per day
Days 101+	**All**	**Nothing**
Hospice Care All days	Limited costs for drugs and inpatient respite care	All other costs
Home Health Care All days	Nothing for services; 20% of approved amount for durable medical equipment**	100% of approved amount; 80% of approved amount for durable medical equipment**
Blood	For first 3 pints unless the blood is donated	100% after first 3 pints

Part B - Medical Insurance	You Pay	Medicare Pays
Medical Expenses	$131 deductible,*** plus 20% of approved amount and limited charges above approved amount	80% of approved amount after $131 deductible. Reduced to 50% for most outpatient mental health services
Outpatient Hospital Services (co-insurance or co-payment varies depending on service)	$131 deductible,*** plus 20% of billed amount for physical, occupational and speech-language therapy	80% of approved amount after $131 deductible based on hospital cost
Outpatient Mental Health Care	50%	50%
Home Health Care	Nothing for services; 20% of approved amount for durable medical equipment*	100% of approved amount for services; 80% of approved amount for durable medical equipment*
Blood	For first 3 pints unless the blood is donated, then 20% for additional pints	80% after first 3 pints

*Effective January 1, 2007

**Coverage includes only part-time intermittent care

***There is *one* $131 deductible for Outpatient Hospital Services and/or Medical Expenses

Home Care

There were significant changes in the Home Care benefit under 1997 legislation, the Balanced Budget Act of 1997 (PL 105-33). These changes created a home care benefit under both Part A and Part B of Medicare. Home Health Care benefits under Part A are defined as benefits instituted after a hospital stay of at least 3 days and which is initiated within 14 days of discharge, or home care benefits provided to recipients who were in a skilled level nursing facility for at least 14 days after discharge from a hospital. This Part A benefit is limited to 100 visits per spell of illness. A visit is defined as one visit by a nurse; or a visit by a physical, occupational or speech therapist; or a four hour visit by a home health aide. A Spell of Illness is defined as beginning on the first day on which a beneficiary receives post-institutional home care services and which occurs in a month in which the beneficiary was entitled to Part A benefits. A Spell of Illness ends with the close of the first 60 consecutive days thereafter in which the beneficiary is not an inpatient of a hospital, skilled level nursing home, or receiving home health services. All other Home Health Care not within this definition are classified as Part B home care.[7]

In order to qualify for Medicare at-home care, an individual must meet the following requirements:

- The beneficiary must require and receive intermittent skilled nursing, or physical, occupational or speech therapy;
- The beneficiary must be homebound (essentially this means the person cannot leave home without assistance);
- The services must be ordered under a physician's plan of care; and
- The services must be provided through an agency approved by Medicare.

Each year Medicare may change the amount of the deductibles it will allow for a hospital visit, the frequency of hospital visits, the availability of skilled nursing facilities, and the amount of home health care provided.

Joan and Larry

Joan contracted a rare disease called ataxia. An estimated 150,000 people in the United States are affected by the hereditary and sporadic ataxias; a group of neurological disorders characterized by a lack of coordination as a common symptom. Hereditary ataxia affects the cerebellum and spinal cord and is passed from one generation to the next through a defective gene. The two most prevalent types of hereditary ataxia are Friedreich's (recessive) ataxia and Marie's (dominant) ataxia. Also common are the sporadic ataxias which occur spontaneously in individuals with no known family history of ataxia. The symptoms can include muscle weakness and loss of coordination in the arms and legs, visual impairment, slurred speech, and aggressive scoliosis (curvature of the spine). The strain that Joan contracted attacked her nervous system and resulted in chronic pain and itching throughout her illness.

During the last seven months of her life, Joan required hospital and nursing home care, as well as hospice services. She and her husband, Larry, incurred $2 million in costs for her care. Fortunately, all of their costs were covered by their insurance coverages, including nursing home policies provided by their employer. *This one instance, out of thousands occurring annually, underscores just how important and crucial it is that you take the time and the effort to review and monitor your insurance coverage while you are still in good health.*

For more information on ataxia, please refer to the National Ataxia Foundation on the Web at *http://www.ataxia.org*. Their phone number is: 1-763-553-0020 (Minneapolis, MN).

Medigap Insurance

Medigap insurance is designed to supplement Medicare's benefits. These policies are sold by private insurance companies and are regulated by federal and state law. The medical plan must be clearly identified as Medicare supplemental insurance and it must provide specific benefits that help fill the gaps in your Medicare coverage. Other kinds of insurance may help you with out-of-pocket health care costs, but they do not qualify as Medigap plans.

Standard Medigap Plans

A Medigap policy is a health insurance policy sold by private insurance companies to fill the "gaps" in Original Medicare Plan coverage. There are 12 standardized Medigap plans called "A" through "L." The front of a Medigap policy must clearly identify it as "Medicare Supplement Insurance." Each plan A through L has a different set of benefits. Plan A covers only the basic (core) benefits. These basic benefits are included in all of the plans, but Plans K and L also include hospice care.

When you buy a Medigap policy you pay a premium to the insurance company. As long as you pay your premium a policy bought after 1990 is automatically renewed each year. This means that your coverage continues year after year as long as you pay your premium. This premium is different from the Medicare Part B premium. You must also pay your monthly Medicare Part B premium.

However, in some states, insurance companies may refuse to renew Medigap policies that you bought before 1990. The law in these states did not say these policies had to be automatically renewed each year (guaranteed renewable) at the time these policies were sold.

Medigap policies help pay health care costs only if you have the Original Medicare Plan. You don't need to buy a Medigap policy if you are in a Medicare Advantage plan. In fact, it is illegal for anyone to sell you a Medigap policy if they know you are in one of these plans.

If you have Medicaid, it is illegal for an insurance company to sell you a Medigap policy, except in certain situations.[8]

As you can see from *Figure 3-5*, eight plans offer some coverage for skilled nursing care and four plans offer coverage for some care at home. Contact your State Department of Insurance to find out which plans your state offers.

Overview of Medigap Plans K and L

In 2005, Medigap Plans K and L (also sold as Medicare SELECT) became available. These new Medigap policies can be sold only as standardized plans. *Figure 3-6* gives you a quick look at the Medigap Plans K and L and their benefits. *Figure 3-7* explains how Medigap Plans A through J differ from Medigap Plans K and L. These charts do not apply if you live in Massachusetts, Minnesota, or Wisconsin.

Medigap Benefits and Medicare Part D

Beneficiaries who already have prescription drug benefits at least as good as Medicare's may be able to keep it without the risk of paying a higher Part D premium if they later decide to enroll in Part D. People with a Medigap plan with prescription drug benefits were allowed a choice between their Medigap benefits and the new Medicare Part D benefit. Beneficiaries who decided to sign up for Part D can keep

MEDIGAP STANDARD MEDICARE SUPPLEMENT PLANS

Figure 3-5

CORE BENEFITS	A	B	C	D	E	F	G	H*	I*	J*	K**	L***
Hospital co-insurance: Days 61 to 91	●	●	●	●	●	●	●	●	●	●	●	●
Hospital co-insurance: Days 91 to 150	●	●	●	●	●	●	●	●	●	●	●	●
Hospital Payment in full: 365 additional days	●	●	●	●	●	●	●	●	●	●	●	●
Part A and Part B blood deductible: First three pints of blood	●	●	●	●	●	●	●	●	●	●	50%	75%
Part B 20% co-insurance: Physician and other services	●	●	●	●	●	●	●	●	●	●	50%	75%

ADDITIONAL BENEFITS	A	B	C	D	E	F	G	H*	I*	J*	K**	L***
SNF co-insurance: Days 21 to 100 – $114 per day in 2005			●	●	●	●	●	●	●	●	50%	75%
Part A Hospital Deductible: $912 in 2005		●	●	●	●	●	●	●	●	●	50%	50%
Part B Annual Deductible: $110 in 2005			●			●				●		
Part B Excess Charges: Coverage for up to 115% percent of Medicare's approved charge (Medigap policy will either pay 80% or 100% of excess charge)						100%	80%		100%	100%		
Foreign Travel Emergency: $250 deductible, 80% of the cost of emergency care during the first two months of the trip, $50,000 lifetime limit			●	●	●	●	●	●	●	●		
At-Home Recovery: Maximum benefit of $1,600 annually				●			●		●	●		

*Effective 1/1/06, plans H, I, and J can no longer be sold with prescription drug benefits. Beneficiaries who purchased these plans before 1/1/06 are allowed to renew them and to retain the plans' prescription drug benefits.

** Plan K covers 100% of cost sharing for Medicare Part B preventive services and 100% of all cost sharing under Medicare Parts A and B for the balance of the calendar year once an individual has reached the out-of-pocket limit on annual expenditures of $4,000 in 2006.

*** Plan L covers 100% of cost sharing for Medicare Part B preventive services and 100% of all cost sharing under Medicare Parts A and B for the balance of the calendar year once an individual has reached the out-of-pocket limit on annual expenditures of $2,000 in 2006.

Copyright © Center for Medicare Advocacy, Inc. 03/22/06. Website: http://www.medicareadvocacy.org/FAQ_Medigap.htm.

(View Online at www.longtermcarebooks.com)

Plan K		
Basic Benefits	Skilled Nursing Facility Co-insurance (50%)	Medicare Part A Deductible (50%)

Plan L		
Basic Benefits	Skilled Nursing Facility Co-insurance (75%)	Medicare Part A Deductible (75%)

Figure 3-6 ^   (View Online at www.longtermcarebooks.com)   ∨ Figure 3-7

Comparing Medigap Policies

	Plans A through J	Plans K and L
Premiums	Higher premiums	Lower premiums
Out-of-pocket Costs	Lower (or no) out-of-pocket costs	Higher out-of-pocket costs, but subject to out-of-pocket annual limits
Basic Benefits	Includes ● Medicare Part A co-insurance and hospital benefits ● Medicare Part B co-insurance or co-payment ● Blood	Includes ● Medicare Part A co-insurance and hospital benefits ● Medicare Part B co-insurance or co-payment ● Blood ● Hospice care
Extra Benefits	May include ● Skilled Nursing Facility Co-insurance ● Medicare Part A and B Deductibles ● Part B Excess Charges ● Foreign Travel Emergency ● At-Home Recovery ● Preventive Care	May include ● Skilled Nursing Facility Co-insurance ● Medicare Part A Deductible

their Medigap policy without the prescription benefit or they can switch to another Medigap plan. They can't, however, have both a Medigap benefit for prescription drugs and the Medicare Part D benefit at the same time. Most Medigap prescription drug benefits won't be considered at least as good as Medicare's.[9]

A Physician's Story

My patient, Sam, was 70 years old when he started developing Alzheimer's disease. He had a gradual decrease in memory and tended to wander. His wife, Diane, found that taking care of her husband took all of her time. They had two children living nearby who helped at times. Sam needed full-time supervision. A private home health insurance agency supplied full-time home health care workers at a cost of $18 per hour. Between Sam and Diane's savings, and financial support from their children, the family was able to pay for this help.

About one year later Sam needed custodial care in a nursing home. This was not considered "skilled" care and therefore was not covered by Medicare. Overall, this family spent more than

$50,000 each year out-of-pocket. As in the above cases, long-term care insurance might have covered most or all of Sam's needs if taken out when he was in good health.

The Licensed Clinical Social Worker (LCSW) at my local hospital told me that she never met a patient in over 20 years of clinical practice that had actual "long-term care insurance." I found this incredible, but I believed it was true. She sees the physical disability and resulting financial deprivation that can follow many types of illnesses. She told me that she purchased long-term care insurance for her own mother last year.

During an interview for this chapter the local LCSW stated, "I wish more people would have long-term care insurance so that they would have more choices when they so desperately need them." She added, "I would like people to have policies that would allow them to remain at home with their family and loved ones as long as possible. All of us who work in the hospital have seen what can happen to any one of us. Long-term care insurance is now available and should be a part of everyone's financial planning review."

Obtaining Medicare Benefits

There are two very important people who work in a hospital. The first is the Medical Case Manager (MCM). He/she is an experienced clinical nurse who, on behalf of his/her patients, interacts and advocates with insurance companies, physicians, and possible placement facilities and agencies. He/she reviews utilization of hospital services to make sure that they are in line with Medicare and other insurance regulations and obtains authorization for needed hospital stays and procedures. He/she may ensure that all needed medical tests are done before discharge. He/she contacts skilled nursing facilities, custodial care homes and home health agencies to set up treatment that will keep patients healthy and out of the hospital. Each case is reviewed early in the hospital stay. He/she informs the family about what their "realistic" options may be. He/she educates them about what they really need. He/she knows what insurance coverage exists. As he/she acts as a guide to and for the family, he/she becomes a creative problem solver.

The other person is the licensed clinical social worker (LCSW). He/she works closely with the case manager. He/she is at the center of every crisis. He/she deals with death in the emergency room where an automobile victim may die, or a battered wife may be treated. He/she is on the hospital ward where a family is told that their father has terminal cancer. He/she is at the center of family conferences that discuss the withdrawal of life support. He/she helps patients with the disability forms, finding community resources, providing forms related to adoption and durable power of attorney forms for health care. The social worker also runs the breast cancer support group.

Physicians work with these people to help their patients in the worst situations. Choices are often limited, not only by medical circumstances, but also by financial limitations and concerns, as well as poor planning.

Jane

Jane was 52 when she was diagnosed with an incurable lung cancer. Chemotherapy might have been able to extend her life, but she was unable to handle the side effects. She required 24-hour pain-control management.

Jane had private health insurance, but no secondary insurance. Her insurance covered a short stay in a skilled nursing bed until her pain management was stabilized.

Since her life expectancy was six months or less, the MCM referred her to the local hospice, which assisted her with pain management and offered ongoing emotional support. The LCSW worked with Jane and her daughter to help them make good choices while coping with the awful realization that Jane would die very soon.

Jane was divorced. Her daughter, 25, was very willing to help, but lived in a tiny apartment. Jane could not receive care at her daughter's apartment. She was referred to a local nursing home for custodial and hospice care. Jane's expenses were about $3,800 per month. Other homes in the area ran as high as $6,000 monthly, plus medical costs. Whatever savings Jane had put aside had to be used for outstanding medical bills and the custodial home care before she became eligible for Medi-Cal.

The Medi-Cal application was incredibly complex (it is over one inch thick!). Her daughter was overwhelmed. The LCSW helped her wade through it.

In California, once Jane's resources had shrunk to less than $2,000, she became eligible for Medi-Cal (this is the California Medicaid program). The nursing home that Jane was admitted to knew that she would soon be on Medicaid so Jane did not have to switch to another facility. Once you have a medical need you cannot transfer property to your relatives or others to become eligible for Medicaid. In fact, transfer of property cannot be made for up to 36 months before eligibility. Jane was not eligible. If Jane had long-term care insurance, many or all of these expenses would have been paid.

If you need help with placing a relative or friend in a long-term care facility, or have questions about eligibility, please realize that you have many resources to assist you. In California the statewide resource number for senior services information is 1-800-510-2020. In addition, there is an Area Agency on Aging in every county, which has developed a comprehensive system to administer federal, state, and local resources. A part of this agency provides counseling on insurance coverage. It is called HICAP, the Health Insurance Counseling Advocacy Program. Their toll-free number is 1-800-434-0222.

Each area has an Ombudsman's office, which keeps a list of citations and complaints concerning nursing homes. In California, the California Advocates for Nursing Home Reform (CANHR), a patient advocacy "watchdog" group, will provide listings and other information to help those who need custodial or home care. Contact them at 1-800-474-1116, or at their San Francisco office (650 Harrison Street) at 1-415-974-5171.

Family Involvement and Medi-Cal Issues

(As reported to freelance writer Maureen Dixon by Patricia White, Social Services Director, Villa Scalabrini Retirement Center, Sun Valley, CA)

"At the facility where I am Social Services Director, more than 90 percent of our patients are on Medi-Cal. When people are forced to go on Medi-Cal it's a huge shock for them. Some families argue about who is going to be responsible for the family member. Many are afraid that if they sign the paperwork they will be financially responsible for their loved one, even after I tell them that's not the case.

"Other people thought they planned adequately for retirement. They may have a 401(k) plan or a pension, and they expect it to last for their lifetime. They are shocked when they need to move into a skilled nursing setting, either because of an injury or because of age and frailty, and their money begins to run out. 'What happened to my money?' they want to know. People don't realize that any kind of accident or illness that requires rehabilitation, medication, operations, medical tests or lab work will cost, and costs a lot if you are paying privately.

"Applying for Medi-Cal has its own set of challenges. There is a huge packet of forms to fill out, and it has to be done perfectly. Medi-Cal wants to know everything about you. They ask about your bank accounts, property, stocks and bonds, jewelry, and burial plans. They want to know your whole life story. An individual can only have $2,000 in non-exempt assets to qualify ($3,000 for a couple), so Medi-Cal carefully reviews their financial history. If they see a check written for $1,500 they may ask what that was for and ask to see a receipt. The families find it difficult and frustrating to complete the forms; I have to help a lot of them with it. Some families come to me in hysterics because they are so stressed and scared that the facility will put the family member out on the street for lack of funds.

"It takes up to 45 days for Medi-Cal to process the application. If anything is not completed correctly, or even if Medi-Cal loses the form, you have to start all over. And you can't just send in a copy. An entire original new form has to be resubmitted. Each year Medi-Cal does a redetermination on each patient. You have to send in paperwork for that as well and if the person's assets have built up to more than $2,000, he or she will be denied.

"Medi-Cal does let the person keep $35 a month for personal expenses. At Villa Scalabrini, if you are a woman, $35 will pay to have your hair done every two weeks.

"My primary advice to anyone who has to put a spouse, parent or relative in a long-term care facility is to visit regularly. Come to the care plan meetings. Visit and get involved. It can make all the difference for that person. People whose relatives just drop them off and never come by to see them, can easily get depressed or even become ill. I see people in their rooms crying. 'My family doesn't care,' or 'I don't have anyone' are the saddest things I hear. A little attention goes a long way.

"And make surprise visits. A facility that looks nice when you are on a scheduled visit may not always look that good. Drop in unexpectedly. Smell the place. Listen carefully to the staff. If they say they have to medicate your relative or restrain them, find out what the 'problem' really is. Lesser measures can and should be taken before restraining or giving psychotropic medications to the residents. Make sure their doctor will continue to see them. Some doctors will not follow their patients to a skilled nursing facility. You want to make sure your loved one is getting cared for properly.

"It is really important that people plan ahead and it's best if you can do it without having to rely on Medi-Cal. Many people get depressed when they have to go on Medi-Cal. Most people don't want to be a burden on their families either.

"Long-term care insurance is a good idea. We put money away for retirement or life insurance; we should put money away in case we need care. Every day I see the headaches that families endure when they put their loved ones on Medi-Cal. Things can go more smoothly with less worry and concern when people plan for this need, just as they do for other needs in their lives."

The following information was provided by Professor Jeff Kramer at the University of Connecticut School of Business Administration:

- 10% of Connecticut's budget is for expenses for nursing homes under Medicaid;

- 5 nursing home chains filed for bankruptcy in the 6 months before November 2002;

- 70 percent of all nursing home patients are on Medicaid and, therefore, it is a losing business for the nursing home;

- State budgets will skyrocket as "boomers" start accessing benefits under Medicaid;

- Connecticut is fearful for the future and there is now a moratorium on new nursing homes in the state.

What are Medicaid and Medi-Cal?

Medicare is a federal medical insurance program that covers any citizen or legal resident 65 years or older (*see Chapter 3*). Medicaid is a joint program of the federal and state governments supported by the taxpayers, and it is available to those with little income and few assets. Within the state of California, this joint program is known as Medi-Cal and it is supported equally with both federal and state funding. Medi-Cal pays for health care and also provides long-term nursing care for residents of California who meet the strict criteria and eligibility requirements.

Medi-Cal does not have any restrictions as to marital status, age, disability or veteran's status. It also does not discriminate as to sex, religion, race, color or national origin. Recipients must be residents of California, or have legal immigration status within the state borders. The program is supervised at the federal level by the Department of Health and Human Services and by various agencies at the state level, including the Social Services Office in any given county. Medi-Cal eligibility rules must be completely satisfied to qualify for benefits. Many individuals do not qualify because of assets or investments they have. Because the rules, regulations and funding of this program are constantly being adjusted to meet federal and changing state regulations, this publication will simply give an overview at the date of publication.

The asset and property tests that apply to Medi-Cal specify that a single individual cannot have more than $2,000 of available, non-exempt real and personal property; for a couple, that amount is $3,000. Exempt property is property that does not count as an asset under the property tests. Differences between exempt property and non-exempt property are shown in *Figure 4-1*.

People on public assistance or Supplemental Security Income (SSI) are automatically eligible for Medicaid. In order to prevent a spouse of an SSI recipient from becoming impoverished, the limits for couples are different, but are still quite low.

More than 40 percent of long-term care costs in the United States are paid for by Medicaid/Medi-Cal.[1] People in the lowest income brackets have their long-term care costs paid by Medicaid/Medi-Cal, though they may still have co-payments to make, depending on their income.

Figure 4-1	(View Online at www.longtermcarebooks.com)
NON-COUNTABLE (EXEMPT) PROPERTY	**COUNTABLE (NON-EXEMPT) PROPERTY***
A home** Business property & real estate Household goods A car Life insurance*** *Total non-exempt property cannot exceed $2,000 **Subject to lien ***An individual may have combined face value of life insurance of $1,500 or less, plus accrued interest and dividends. Amounts in excess of that will be included in the property reserve.	Cash over $2,000 (California) Vacation homes Investment property Second vehicles Single premium deferred annuities Whole life insurance*** Stocks/Bonds Certificates of Deposit IRAs and Roth IRAs Keoghs Savings bonds T-Bills/Notes

Many middle-class individuals have begun turning to the Medicaid programs as their personal assets become depleted from paying for long-term care. The average middle-class American has enough assets to cover long-term care costs for approximately one year, after medical expenses and other incidental costs are factored into the equation. Many individuals consider Medicaid a last resort for financing long-term care. People would prefer to have the government pay their long-term care expenses if it becomes necessary. When the actual benefits are provided the recipient may realize too late that the bargain was not all it appeared to be. As we will see, there are good reasons it should be considered a *last* resort.

What Do Medicaid & Medi-Cal Cover?

Medicaid/Medi-Cal pays for physician-approved hospital, medical, prescription drug and nursing home charges. All states are required to cover:

● Inpatient hospital services (except for tuberculosis or mental diseases);

● Outpatient hospital services and rural health clinic services;

● Laboratory services and X-rays;

● Physicians' services provided in a doctor's office, hospital, skilled nursing facility, at the patient's home; or medical and surgical services furnished by a dentist where state law permits either doctors or dentists to perform such services;

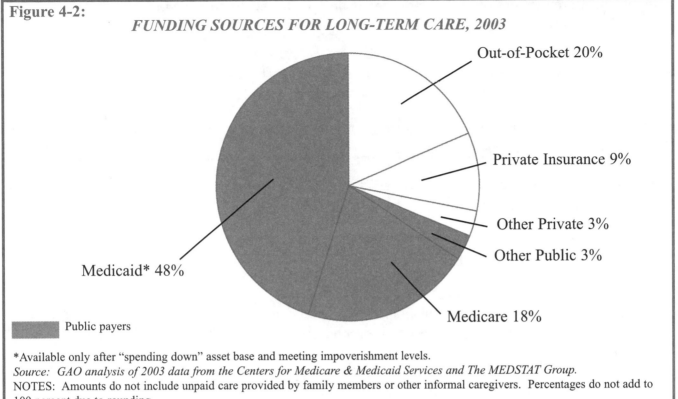

Figure 4-2:

FUNDING SOURCES FOR LONG-TERM CARE, 2003

Out-of-Pocket 20%

Private Insurance 9%

Other Private 3%

Other Public 3%

Medicare 18%

Medicaid* 48%

Public payers

*Available only after "spending down" asset base and meeting impoverishment levels.
Source: GAO analysis of 2003 data from the Centers for Medicare & Medicaid Services and The MEDSTAT Group.
NOTES: Amounts do not include unpaid care provided by family members or other informal caregivers. Percentages do not add to 100 percent due to rounding.

- Skilled nursing facility (SNF) care for individuals 21 or older (except for tuberculosis or mental disease);

- Limited home health-care services; and

- Transportation to medical facilities.

Some states allow Medicaid benefits to pay for Medicare Supplement policies.

Medicaid/Medi-Cal and Long-Term Care

Medicaid does not cover custodial home care, personal care, or community-based services. Eligibility for long-term care in a skilled nursing facility is generally covered under Medicaid/ Medi-Cal when the individual:

- Has personal income and assets under the Medicaid/Medi-Cal financial limits; and

- Cannot perform at least two of six activities of daily living (ADLs), not including ambulation (walking). The six activities of daily living are bathing, dressing, toileting, mobility (commonly called "transferring"), continence and eating by oneself.

In addition, having to take medications on a daily basis can, at times, be considered an activity of daily living if the above factors prevent an individual from taking these medications on their own.

These activities are different from the "instrumental" activities of daily living (IADLs), which include the preparation of individual meals, shopping by oneself, using the telephone, paying one's bills, managing one's money, doing light housework and the ability to take medications. An individual who cannot carry out these functions may be deemed unable to provide for his or her own care.

These activities are also known in the long-term care industry as "homemaker" services and are normally the measurement or criteria for providing home-care services under long-term care policies from most reputable companies.

Medicaid/Medi-Cal has limits on how much of one's assets and income may be kept by the individual and how much the person must spend on long-term care. The government requires that people spend whatever assets they have in excess of the allowable assets, on their long-term care.

Medicaid/Medi-Cal Assets

(Each state has some variations on these asset categories. For more information contact your state's Medicaid/Medi-Cal office or an ElderLaw attorney.[2])

As described in the earlier chart, Medicaid/Medi-Cal divides assets into two classes:

- Countable assets (also called non-exempt or available assets); and
- Non-countable assets (also called exempt assets).

Countable assets include any personal financial property owned or controlled by the individual who needs long-term care. These countable assets must be used to pay for the person's care. Individuals must "spend down" until they reach the qualifying financial limits for their state. Of the items listed, one that is constantly being confused in the industry is the subject of deferred annuities if not annuitized (i.e., if the annuity is paid out in a lump sum). Regulations and rules for qualifications are constantly changing in this area and are interpreted differently depending in which county the recipient lives. Suffice it to say that before any action is taken to change the status of a deferred annuity to a fully paid out annuity, with payments to the spouse or other named beneficiary, it should be reviewed with an attorney or a competent financial advisor.

There is a special rule for an individual's primary residence. Even though it is not "countable," in the case of a primary home it may be subject to a lien to repay the state. A lien will be placed on an individual's home in the amount the state has spent for that individual's care, unless:

- The person intends to return home and has a physician's statement of that fact;
- His or her spouse lives in the home; or
- A dependent child who is under 21, blind or disabled lives in the home.

People who have more assets than Medicaid/Medi-Cal allows *must spend those assets down on their own care before they can qualify*. In the past, many people gave their assets away or transferred title to family members so that they would not have to spend virtually everything they had on long-term care. The government severely restricts this practice and has become very vigilant in tracking such transfers down. There are also severe penalties for people who intentionally transfer assets to fraudulently collect these government benefits.

On February 8, 2006, President Bush signed the Deficit Reduction Act of 2005, a major legislative development affecting the long-term care industry. This is a very important piece of legislation, which will provide Americans with a new tool to protect their nest eggs and plan for financially secure retirements.

The first major provision of this law makes it much more difficult for Americans with significant assets to use estate planning techniques to qualify for long-term care services. Specifically, the new law changes Medicaid's transfer-of-assets rule by extending the look-back period from three to five years and by denying Medicaid coverage of nursing home care to any person with home equity exceeding $500,000 (states may elect an amount up to $750,000). This law also specifies that the date the penalty period for asset transfer begins is the date that one becomes eligible for Medicaid, instead of the date the transfer of assets took place (which was the case in the original law). The message to the public is clear. Take personal responsibility for planning and funding your long-term care needs and don't rely on Medicaid unless you are truly impoverished.

The Deficit Reduction Act also allows for the expansion of the public/private LTC partnership product beyond the four states in which it is currently available (Connecticut, California, Indiana and New York as of January, 2007). The American Council of Life Insurers (ACLI) helped shape the provisions of the partnership product expansion included in the law. These provisions will allow a new qualified long-term care insurance contract to qualify as a partnership if it includes minimum inflation protection and meets other standards identified in the law. Owning a partnership policy will allow the policyholder to qualify for Medicaid, once partnership policy benefits are exhausted, without needing to spend down all of his or her assets. The policyholder will be able to keep assets equal to the total amount of LTC benefits paid by the partnership policy (dollar-for-dollar asset protection). The national partnership provision has now moved to the Department of Health and Human Services (HHS) to set some parameters. While this portion of the law is still evolving, each state that plans to participate must file a Medicaid plan amendment that authorizes the state to adopt "qualified state LTC partnerships."

Spousal Income and Assets

Medicaid/Medi-Cal allows the spouse who does not need long-term care to keep a certain amount of income and assets to keep that person from becoming impoverished. In the year 2007 that person (called the "community spouse") could keep half of the couple's combined assets, from a minimum of $20,328 (called the "floor") to a maximum of $101,640 (called the "ceiling"). Assets that exceed the ceiling must be spent down on the institutionalized spouse's care.

All countable assets in a marriage are considered jointly held and available for the person's long-term care costs. The community spouse's assets are countable even if there is a premarital agreement stating that the assets belong only to the community spouse and/or the assets were never contributed to the spouse needing long-term care.

All income earned by the individual who needs long-term care (regardless of how it is earned) must be spent on his or her own care, except:

- An allowance for personal needs (usually between $30 and $60 per month for someone in a nursing home) for clothing, toiletries, medical expenses and other personal needs not covered by Medicaid;

- Medicare Part B and Medicare supplement insurance premiums; and

- A deduction for federal or state income tax, in some states.

The non-institutionalized community spouse is allowed to keep a minimum amount of income (called a "minimum monthly maintenance needs allowance"), which varies by state but ranged nationally from $1,650 (through June 30, 2007) to a high of $2,541 a month (in 2007). For a listing of income cap states go to *www.elderlawanswers.com*. There are various ways in which the community spouse can get this income. There are differing rules for couples who both bring in income (whether from a business, employment, pension, etc.). In California, the person whose name is on the check is considered the person earning that income. If the check is made out in both names the income is considered to belong in equal proportions to both spouses. There are some exceptions to these limits and states may raise the income floor. For more information, consult with an eldercare attorney or other qualified advisor.

Medicaid/Medi-Cal can and does make changes in the income and eligibility requirements each year, or changes the limits on income and countable and non-countable assets, so be sure to verify these amounts based on your particular situation. In short, the advantage of qualifying for Medicaid is that your long-term care costs will be paid by Medicaid. Disadvantages include:

- Accepting Medicaid benefits opens your estate to state recovery of benefits at your death;
- Eligibility for Medicaid by divesting assets means loss of control of your assets;
- Depending on the method of qualifying, additional tax liability or other undesirable consequences may follow; and
- As of 1997, knowingly disposing of assets to qualify for Medicaid is a federal crime.

California Partnership Plan

In California, an innovative partnership has been developed between the state and private insurance companies to provide middle-income wage earners with private insurance to help them preserve their assets, and to receive a wider range of care than Medi-Cal will allow. It also allows them to retain more of their assets if they do need to apply for Medi-Cal. (*See Chapter 17 for more information on the California Partnership Plan.*)

Medi-Cal Programs for In-Home and Community Care

Several programs for in-home and community care are available to Medi-Cal beneficiaries. These include the Personal Care Services Program, In-Home Supportive Services and the Multipurpose Senior Services Program.

Personal Care Services Program

Medi-Cal covers in-home services through the Personal Care Services Program (PCSP). PCSP uses Medi-Cal benefits to provide choreworker and personal care services at home for those who are eligible. Personal care includes assistance with bodily hygiene, personal safety and activities of daily living.

In-Home Supportive Services

In-Home Supportive Services (IHSS) provides non-medical services to eligible aged, blind and disabled people who are unable to remain in their homes safely without this assistance. Services include menu planning, meal preparation, cleanup, laundry, heavy cleaning and shopping. A person may be eligible for this program when he/she meets specific criteria related to eligibility for the Supplemental Security Income/State Supplementary Program for the aged, blind and disabled. (SSI/SSP). For more information on this program, contact your county Department of Social Services.

Multipurpose Senior Services Program

The Multipurpose Senior Services Program (MSSP) is a case management program that links older people who are eligible for Medi-Cal and who need placement in a nursing home with various health and social services in their community. For more information on the MSSP Program, call 1-800-510-2020 if you live in California. If you live outside California, call the toll-free Eldercare Locator service at 1-800-677-1116.

For more information on Medi-Cal, including eligibility guidelines, specific income and asset limits, and special programs, contact your county Department of Social Services.

5 Long-Term Care Insurance

The Freedom to Choose

Long-term care insurance is one of the most significant products that people can purchase to protect their assets. It is important that people get the kind of care they need and want during one of the most difficult times of their lives. The fact that so many people today have to spend their remaining days in facilities where they have no choice of services or benefits is a national tragedy. In order for individuals to receive the kind of care that they want after a disabling illness or injury, or in the latter days of their lives, it is critical to plan ahead. Once a problem has been formally diagnosed, it may not be possible to get insurance that will cover that condition, or any other conditions in the future.

The most common misconception about long-term care is that "it will never happen to me." The following examples clearly show that it can happen to anyone. By purchasing long-term care insurance, or making other arrangements to take care of this huge potential cost, you can dramatically reduce the risk of completely depleting your assets and losing your freedom to choose the type of care you desire.

History

Long-term care insurance has evolved as care-related services have evolved. The first long-term care insurance plan was developed more than 30 years ago. At that time, Medicare was the only other payer for long-term care. Home health care services were very basic and there were very few private services available.

The first policies had limited benefits and usually only paid for skilled nursing care, with minimal home-care benefits. People had to meet very specific requirements to collect benefits. Even as late as the early 1990s these policies primarily covered stays in skilled nursing facilities. Additional coverage for other types of care was still rudimentary. Medicare and other government programs (i.e., Medicaid / Medi-Cal) paid higher benefits for long-term care than the first private plans. This was how most people financed their long-term care needs. However, Medicaid / Medi-Cal now pays for little, but low-skilled custodial care, so you must be prepared to pay for these expenses (*see Figures 5-1 and 5-2*).

In the late 1980s and early 1990s, Medicare and the other government programs dramatically cut back their reimbursements to facilities and organizations that provided long-term care. At the same time insurance companies were improving their policies to meet more of a person's long-term care needs.

In 1990 most policies sold by insurance companies only covered skilled nursing care if provided immediately after a hospital stay. They required a minimum three-day hospital stay, even though seven out of ten seniors never go to a hospital first. Policies written since 1991 **cannot** require a three-day minimum hospital stay for access to benefits in most states (but read your policy carefully).

There are three major kinds of long-term care insurance: nursing home only, home health care only, and a comprehensive plan that covers both.

Figure 5-1　　　　　　　　　　　　　　　　　　　(View Online at www.longtermcarebooks.com)

Medicare: Levels of Care Received by Nursing Home Residents

<u>Type of Care</u>　　　　　　　　　　　<u>Percentage of Residents Who Qualify for Care</u>

1. Skilled 05%

To qualify for Medicare coverage for skilled nursing facility care you must:

1. Have been in a hospital at least three consecutive days (not counting the day of discharge) before entering a Skilled Nursing Facility.

2. Be admitted to the Skilled Nursing Facility for the same condition for which you were treated in the Hospital; generally the admission must be within thirty days of your discharge from the hospital.

3. Have your physician certify that you need, and receive, skilled nursing or skilled rehabilitation services on a daily basis.

2. Intermediate 4.5%

Medicare provides no benefits for intermediate care (nursing home care requiring occasional medical treatment during recovery from an illness or injury that required hospitalization).

3. Custodial 95.0%

Medicare provides no benefits for custodial care (care which is primarily for the purpose of meeting personal needs provided by non-professional persons).

Figure 5-2　　　　　　　　　　　　　　　　　　　(View Online at www.longtermcarebooks.com)

Cost of Stay in a Skilled Nursing Facility

Reason for Admission	Average Cost		
	Average Stay	Private @ $158/Day	Semi-Private @ $112/Day
Cardiovascular (e.g., stroke)	21 mos.	$99,540	$70,560
Cancer	3 years	$170,640	$120,960
Congestive Heart Failure	16 mos.	$75,840	$53,760
Chronic Obstructive Pulmonary Disease (heart, lungs)	3 years	$170,640	$120,600
Organic Brain Syndrome (e.g., Alzheimer's)	8 years	$455,040	$322,560
Diabetes	4 years	$227,520	$161,280

Current nursing home policies cover skilled care, intermediate care, custodial care and assisted living care. There are also policies exclusively for home health care, personal care, hospice, and adult day care and respite care — services that did not exist in the early 1990s. The policies are more expensive than they were several years ago, but they do cover much more.

Comprehensive plans cover both the nursing home and home health-care requirements. The policies structure the benefits so that care is provided where the insured is most comfortable.

Inflationary Pressures on Nursing Home Costs

In the late 1980s, it was common for nursing homes to charge a patient $15,000 to $25,000 per year. By 2000, average costs around the United States were running between $35,000 and $50,000 per year for basic care. Additional benefits that are usually required bring the average total cost to $60,000-$80,000 per year. Based on their assets, most Americans would be unable to cover such costs for more than one or two years. The difference in cost between the 1980s and 1990s shows how pervasive inflation has been in the cost of monthly care for nursing homes and home-health care.

As an example of long-term care cost inflation, policy riders of two general types are normally provided. The first is a simple inflation rider that provides a 5% simple yearly increase in the benefits provided for both nursing home and in-home care, with a level initial premium that reflects the 5%. A second alternative is a compounded inflation rider, that is also set at 5%, but has a substantially different benefit as it increases over the years. Those benefits are shown in the following table (*Figure 5-3*).

Figure 5-3   (View Online at www.longtermcarebooks.com)

BENEFITS PROVIDED BASED ON PROJECTED INFLATION

YEAR	5% SIMPLE INFLATION	5% COMPOUNDED INFLATION
2006	$ 52,500	$ 52,500
2007	$ 55,000	$ 55,125
2008	$ 57,500	$ 57,881
2009	$ 60,000	$ 60,775
2010	$ 62,500	$ 63,814
2015	$ 75,000	$ 81,446
2020	$ 87,500	$104,144
2025	$100,000	$132,665

Even if costs only rise 5% a year, ten years from now, <u>a two-year stay in a nursing facility will cost more than $160,000</u> (calculation based on the daily nursing facility private pay rate for each year multiplied by 365).

With nursing home costs averaging inflation-adjusted increases of 7% to 8% per year, it is clear that even a 5% compounded increase will become inadequate in the future. In addition, even with a 5% inflation factor, consideration should be given by the insured to increasing the base daily coverage (instead of $100 per day the policy should start out at $150 per day with the 5% compounded factor). This would at least provide benefits at the current levels that are being charged nationally, with the possibility of keeping up with inflationary costs. To assume a 7% to 8% per year factor in the future may be inaccurate as more nursing home facilities are built to increase competition. Benefits may also be provided at different levels, depending on needs, at lower overall costs.

In 1993, the National Association of Insurance Commissioners (NAIC) provided model legislation governing long-term care policies. The program was called "Long-term Care Insurance Model Regulation". It provided a model by which insurance policies could be compared, based on the types of benefits being offered, to ensure that those benefits were consistent from company to company. (*See Figure 5-4 for more details and a comparison of different companies. Information provided by StrateCision of Needham, MA.*)

POLICY COMPARISON
Information supplied by StrateCision

	Company 1	Company 2	Company 3	Company 4	Company 5	Company 6
Policy I.D. #	Product 1	Product 1	Product 1	Product 1	Product 1	Product 1
Elimination Periods, NH	0,100 days	0,90 days	30,90 days	20,60,100,180,365, 730 days	0,90 days	0,30,60,90,180, 365 days
NH Premium waiver wait, in days	90	90	0	0	90	0
Bed reservation days	30	30	21	10*	30	21
Surviving spouse paid up	No	Yes	Yes	No	rider	Rider
Care by Family/Friends	No	See Comments	No	See Comments	No	No
Caregiver Training	5 X HCDB lifetime max	5 X HCDB longtime max	5 X DB lifetime max	No	No	2 X DB lifetime max
Paid from care benefit pool	Yes	Yes	Yes	N/A	N/A	Yes
Other Home Care Benefits	Emergency medical Response System. $50 a month, for as long as you continue to receive HC benefits.	Rental of Emergency Response System up to $50/month when receiving at least 5 days per week HHC benefits.	In home safety devices; home delivered meals.	Personal care to provide assistance with Instrumental activities of daily living	None	Medical Alert System Up to policy limit of 50% MDB @ $50/month. Home modification up to 50% MDB.
ADLs needed for NH benefits	2/6	2/7	2/7	2/7	2/7	2/7
ADLs needed for HC benefits	2/6	2/7	2/7	2/7	2/7	2/7
Compound inflation % per year	5%	5%	5%	5%	5%	5%
Restoration of benefits	No	No	Rider	Rider	Yes	Yes
Care outside U.S.	Territories, Canada	No exclusions	Territories/Possessions	No	Possessions	Territories, Canada

* See Comments. Information as of 1/1/2002.

WARNING: premiums of different policies may not be comparable, because benefit levels may differ. All options not available in all states, or over age 79. California requires 7 ADL limitations in non-TQ policies. In Pennsylvania and Minnesota, ADLs must include bathing. Mental illness is covered in Massachusetts and Washington. Policy information is believed accurate as of the above date. Policy issuers are asked to review their data in all cases. However, no warranties of accuracy or completeness are made by StrateCision and the policy issuer should be consulted for final determination of features and premiums.

6 Long-Term Care Policy Purchase Considerations

With long-term care, as with any contractual agreement, it is essential that you fully understand the terms of your agreement. What may seem like small details can make a difference in many thousands of dollars in anticipated benefits.

Sarah and Paul

In 1996, Paul required hospitalization for a leg amputation due to diabetes. Three days after the surgery the hospital called Sarah to take Paul home. She was 73 years old, he was 75, and she knew there was no way she could care for him at home. She needed help trying to find out if the long-term care policy they had would cover this situation. When she called me, I advised Sarah to call the hospital back and tell them, under the three-day rule that applies to Medicare benefit recipients, she wanted him transferred at the hospital's expense to a skilled nursing facility of their/her choosing.

The hospital reluctantly agreed to do it. Paul was transferred to a local nursing home, where he lived for about 45 days until his death. Thus, the hospital paid all of the expenses for the nursing home, saving Sarah approximately $9,000. In addition, her long-term care policy paid approximately $4,500 in benefits.

Medicare payment for hospital services is governed by a Prospective Payment System (PPS) that requires hospitals to discharge patients as soon as possible. PPS pays hospitals a fee for each general diagnosis (Diagnostic-Related Group, or DRG) which is based on specific medical criteria. The applicable DRGs are identified when the patient is admitted and/or when complications or new medical conditions are diagnosed. The hospital keeps the difference if it can stabilize the condition for less than what the hospital receives from Medicare. However, the hospital often absorbs the overage if the treatment is more costly. This system provides strong economic incentive for the hospital to discharge a patient as soon as his condition is stabilized, whether or not he is actually well enough to leave the hospital.

These discharged patients are then directed to a skilled nursing home or other subacute care center. The increased demand for nursing home beds resulted directly from the PPS system.

From this example you can see how crucial it is that you understand what your insurance policies provide in benefits. Most medical insurance policies, including most employer-sponsored medical plans and all Medicare supplemental policies, specifically state that you must spend a minimum number of days (three to five days are most common) in a hospital (not counting the day of discharge). You must then be transferred directly to a participating skilled nursing facility (SNF) before they will cover the cost of the skilled nursing care.

Nationwide, the demand for skilled nursing care beds in nursing homes is far greater than the supply, with a six-to-nine-month wait to enter one of these facilities not at all uncommon. A Harvard University study also found that less than 1 percent of residents in nursing homes was receiving skilled nursing care. The rest were receiving custodial care (personal care for activities of daily living, including bathing, dressing, transferring, toileting). It is important to note that Medicare does not pay for this personal care.

To qualify as skilled nursing care, the care must be "restorative" and physician-ordered. If it is not, the individual must pay all costs for any care that is provided at the skilled nursing facility. The average time that individuals are covered by Medicare for skilled nursing home care is two weeks or less.[1]

If you do not have long-term care insurance, or have not stayed in a hospital at least three days, then care in intermediate, custodial, or assisted-living facilities must generally be paid for by the individual. After minimal payments from personal health insurance or Medicare, individuals pay most home health care expenses out of their own pocket.

Skilled nursing care, intermediate care and custodial care can all be provided in a nursing home. At the time of this publication, on average, the cost for skilled care runs from $150 to $300 per day, for intermediate care from $100 to $200 per day, and for custodial care $100 per day or more, depending on how many services the individual needs.[2]

Select a Company with Staying Power

When you are purchasing long-term care insurance it is extremely important that you find a strong and financially sound company that will be there for the long term. You are purchasing care that you anticipate you may not need for many years into the future, so you want to make sure the company will still be around when you need it. Look for companies that have some flexibility in the policies that they issue and ask about how these policies will adapt to the changes that will arise in the years to come.

The kinds of policies to look for include the following basic features:

- A great deal of flexibility in the coverage so that all forms of care as they exist today are covered and will continue coverage as the definitions of care and benefits change in the future;

- A wide variety of benefit choices so that you can select coverage that meets your expected individual needs, and also addresses unexpected circumstances that may arise in the future;

- Benefit levels high enough to protect your assets, while providing the type of care you want for the length of time you think you may need it, with the flexibility to accommodate changes in long-term care services.

Bruce and Amy

In 1993 Bruce and Amy, both retired schoolteachers, needed long-term nursing coverage. A friend had noticed Bruce beginning to fail and strongly recommended they seek insurance. Bruce and Amy did purchase long-term care insurance. Fortunately, they chose a good strong insurance carrier that had a solid history and paid its bills on time.

Approximately three years after they purchased long-term care insurance it became evident that Bruce had Alzheimer's disease. He was eventually placed in a facility that specialized in Alzheimer's patients. The facility continued to meet his needs for more than six years as his Alzheimer's progressed, until his death in 2002.

By that time, Bruce and Amy's insurance company, under its lifetime contract provision, paid approximately $3,000 per month for over six years (over $215,000) to take care of Bruce in the nursing facility. This preserved their assets and allowed both Bruce and Amy to live comfortably. Amy was not forced to sell the family home or to give up her lifestyle during Bruce's illness.

How Much Long-Term Care Insurance Should You Buy?

There are two financial factors to consider when purchasing long-term care insurance: how much coverage you need and how much you can afford. Most people have fixed incomes in retirement and usually can't keep up with inflation. Consequently, it's important to buy insurance that has premiums you can comfortably afford.

In most cases, the earlier you buy a policy the better. Assuming the premiums did not increase, the following chart will show you how much a long-term care policy would cost if you didn't need to enter a nursing home until age 81.

Figure 6-1   (View Online at www.longtermcarebooks.com)

Policy purchased at age:	Yearly premium	Years to pay until age 81	Total premiums paid by age 81
45	$ 900	36	$ 32,400
50	$1,169	31	$ 36,239
55	$1,488	26	$ 38,688
60	$2,081	21	$ 43,701
65	$2,938	16	$ 47,008
70	$4,575	11	$ 50,325
75	$8,688	6	$ 52,128

As you can see, the older you are when you first purchase a policy the more you will pay for having it. Also, it is important to remember that you must be healthy at the time of purchase. By waiting until you are older you not only risk paying more for the policy, but also risk being denied due to failing health.

When deciding on the amount of insurance to purchase consider the following four things:

- Benefit amount: the maximum fixed dollar amount of benefits available, either on a per-day or per-type-of-service basis;

- Inflation adjustment: the increases in the benefit amount to compensate for inflation; this continues to increase as long as you hold the policy;

- Benefit period: the length of time the policy will pay for covered services, usually ranging from two years to an unlimited period. *Note*: With an average length of stay in a nursing home of two to two-and-a-half years, the benefit amount is generally more important to consider than the benefit period;

- Deductible period: the number of days that you pay for covered services before the policy begins paying benefits. The insurance industry recommends a deductible period of no more than 100 days. (*See the worksheet, "Tailoring Benefits to Your Own Needs," included later in this chapter.*)

On the following page is a sample of a form required to be given to you for purchasing long-term care insurance in California.

Services Covered by Long-Term Care Insurance

The most important service that a policy should cover is custodial, or personal, care. A good policy covers all levels of care in all settings: facility care, community adult day care, assisted-living facilities and skilled nursing facilities. Policies usually differentiate between a skilled nursing facility and facility care, and sometimes pay a different benefit amount for each. Many policies will offer equal benefit amounts or the option to choose a benefit amount.

Figure 6-2   (View Online at www.longtermcarebooks.com)

— IMPORTANT NOTICE —

This Company offers two types of Long-Term Care policies in California:

1. Long-term care policies intended to qualify for federal and state of California tax benefits; and

2. Long-term care policies that meet California standards and are not intended to qualify for federal or state of California tax benefits, but which make it easier to qualify for benefits.

POLICIES INTENDED TO QUALIFY FOR TAX BENEFITS — Eligibility for Benefits	POLICIES **NOT** INTENDED TO QUALIFY FOR TAX BENEFITS — Eligibility for Benefits
You will not be paid for a level of care services you need until you are unable to do **2 out of 6** ADLs (Activities of Daily Living), which include: • Bathing • Dressing • Continence • Toileting • Transferring • Eating	You will not be paid for care services you need until you are unable to do **2 out of 7** ADLs, which include: • Bathing • Dressing • Continence • Toileting • Transferring • Eating • Ambulating (this added ADL may make it easier to qualify for home care benefits)
You need help due to **severe** Cognitive Impairment. (Please see outline of coverage for definition of each of the above ADL terms.)	You need help due to Cognitive Impairment. (Please see the outline of coverage for a definition of each of the above ADL terms.)
A health care practitioner must certify that the insured will need assistance with Activities of Daily Living for at least a period of 90 days.	No 90-day certification requirement. Some policies may provide benefits for serious illnesses of less than 90 days. (Please see the outline of coverage for your policy provisions.)
In general, no policy benefits can be paid for services covered by Medicare or be applied to pay for Medicare deductibles or co-payments.	In general, there are **no** limitations regarding the use of policy benefits for Medicare related services.

Services *Not* Covered by Long-Term Care Insurance

All long-term care policies (like any other insurance policies) have some exclusions. Generally, the following conditions are NOT covered:

- Health problems diagnosed before purchasing the policy, unless issued with no pre-existing conditions clause;

- Mental and nervous disorders or diseases other than Alzheimer's disease and related dementia (usually limited benefits, e.g., 2 years of coverage);

- Alcohol and drug addiction;

- Illnesses caused by an act of war;

- Illnesses resulting from intentional self-inflicted injury;

- Attempted suicide;

- Treatment already paid for by the government (such as Veterans Administration benefits).

Premium Increases

The premiums cannot increase with increased age or changing health of an individual policyholder. However, the company can raise the premiums for an entire class of people after review by the state insurance commissioner.

Policy Cancellation

The best kind of long-term care policy is one that is guaranteed renewable. This means that the company cannot cancel the policy for any reason unless you do not pay the premium. Some policies provide continuation of the policy for individuals who develop dementia and become unable to manage their affairs, forgetting to pay the premiums. All must now offer to notify a third party if a premium is not paid on time.

Contract Terminology (Definitions of Contract Terms)

Accelerated Death Benefits: Some life insurance companies offer life insurance policies with a special feature that allows payment of a portion of the death benefit while the insured person is still alive. Such payment is usually limited to situations in which the individual is terminally ill. The benefits become available to cover the costs of long-term care services, as well as other needs.

Activities of Daily Living (ADLs): The physical functions necessary for independent living. These include bathing, dressing, continence, using the toilet, eating and moving about (transferring and/or ambulating). Some long-term care policies only pay benefits when an individual needs assistance in two or more ADLs.

Bed Reservation System: Most adequate long-term-care policies have a bed reservation benefit that will pay for the rental of the bed while the insured has additional hospitalization, surgery or other medical care. Companies will provide this benefit anywhere from 14 days up to 30 days in a calendar year.

This simply ensures that the individual will not lose his or her space in the nursing facility while recovering at the hospital and then needing to return to the nursing facility.

Benefit Triggers: The right of the insured to access the financial benefits of the policy upon loss of any of the following:

- Cognitive capabilities (senile dementia or Alzheimer's disease) or severe cognitive impairment (as described under the tax-qualified policies);

- Medical necessity (as defined by the insured's physician);

- Two out of six activities of daily living (ADLs) or two out of seven ADLs, depending on the type of policy issued. ADLs include these seven categories:

  - Toileting,
  - Dressing,
  - Transferring (such as from chair to bed),
  - Continence,
  - Bathing,
  - Eating,
  - Ambulation.*

Care Coordination: Some companies provide for coordinated benefits through their claims offices to insureds who are seeking benefits, but would like to keep costs down during the period of convalescence. Some companies will also provide a policy that, even with a 90-day waiting period, if the insured chooses to use the "care coordination" benefit, they will assume a zero-day waiting period. This means that an insured could basically buy a less expensive policy because of the 90-day waiting period, but using the care coordination benefit of the company the insured would not have to wait 90 days for benefits to begin.

Case Management: A system in which a trained person such as a hospital discharge planner or a social worker helps the insured person and his or her family determine which services are necessary and the best setting for those services.

Cognitive Impairment: A diminished mental capacity, such as difficulty with short-term memory.

Custodial Care (also called Personal Care): Board, room and other personal assistance (including assistance with ADLs, taking medicine, and other personal needs) that do not include a health-care component that may be provided by people without medical skills or training.

Deductible or Elimination Period: The number of days before benefits are paid by the insurance company. Most policies offer a choice of waiting periods, ranging from 0 to 365 days, during which policyholders pay for needed services out of their own pocket.

It has been estimated that more than 60 percent of all claims for nursing home care and/or home health care costs are resolved within six weeks, or 42 days. For a person to take out a 90-day waiting period on a policy would mean that he or she would not have received a single dollar of benefit for that 42-day period. The individual would have received whatever Medicare benefits are available, but only after a three-day hospital stay and immediate transfer to a skilled nursing facility or for home care provided under a physician's direct orders. ***The benefit of longer waiting periods is that the premium cost is usually substantially less.***

---

*The newer tax-qualified policies recognize six of these ADLs and do not consider ambulation as one of the categories to qualify for benefits.

It is also important to understand how the elimination period is actually computed. Determine whether 90-day periods apply to both the nursing home and home care in concert, or whether they are separate computation periods for qualification. As an example, with a 90-day period of elimination for a person in a nursing home, benefits are provided after the 91st day. The first check should arrive within 30 days after that. So, 120 days would go by before the first check would be received for the 30-day period after the 90-day waiting period. If a person had a zero-day waiting period, he/she would have received checks beginning from the first day of coverage, with the first check arriving after the first 30-day period. It is also important to note that some policies consider the 60-day or 90-day wait a cumulative amount over the lifetime of the insured for different illnesses or injuries and for stays in nursing facilities, or required home care.

Dementia: A progressive mental disorder that affects memory, judgment and cognitive powers with a physical cause. One type of dementia is Alzheimer's disease.

Diagnostic-Related Group (DRG): This refers to each generalized diagnosis for which the hospital receives a flat fee from Medicare. The DRG is determined by a set of specific medical criteria (see "Prospective Payment System," or PPS).

Exclusion: Any condition or expense for which a policy will not pay.

Facility Care: Health services rendered to an individual in a facility. Facility care includes a wide range of services, such as part-time skilled nursing care, speech therapy, physical or occupational therapy, facility health aides and care coordinators.

Free-Look Period: After purchasing a policy you usually have 30 days to review it. You may cancel the policy for a full refund during this time. Be sure to procure a dated policy delivery receipt to ensure the 30-day review.

Guaranteed Renewable: With this policy provision an insurance company cannot cancel a policy unless you fail to pay premiums when due. Premiums cannot be raised unless there is a rate increase for all policyholders in a particular group.

Indemnity Benefit: A type of health insurance product characterized by reimbursement on a fee for service basis, freedom of choice in selecting providers and fewer managed care rules and regulations. (Compare with *Per Diem Rates*).

Inflation Protection: One of several mechanisms that can be built into insurance policies to provide for some increase of the daily benefit over time to account for inflation. This feature raises the price of the policy.

Lapse: To allow insurance coverage to expire by not paying premiums.

Level Premiums: The Company cannot raise the premiums due to age or medical condition. The company may raise the premium rates for an entire class of insureds with permission from the state insurance commissioner.

Outline of Coverage: A description of policy benefits, exclusions and provisions that makes it easier to understand a particular policy and compare it with others.

Out-of-Pocket Payments or Costs: Costs for care or services that the policyholder pays, or payments required under insurance savings provisions.

Per Diem Rates: The daily cost or amount reimbursed for providing services in a specific location. Per diem rates are paid without regard to actual charges and may vary by level of care, such as medical, surgical, intensive care, skilled care, psychiatric, etc. Per diem rates are usually flat all-inclusive rates.

Period of Confinement: The time during which you receive care for a covered illness. The period ends when you have been discharged from care for a specified period of time, usually six months.

Pre-existing Conditions: Medical conditions that existed, were diagnosed, or were under treatment before you took out a policy. Long-term care insurance policies may limit the benefits payable for such conditions for a specified period of time.

Prospective Payment System (PPS): A system put in place by Medicare that provides a strong economic incentive to discharge patients as soon as possible. The system reimburses hospitals a flat fee for each generalized diagnosis (see "Diagnostic-Related Group," or DRG).

Post Claims Underwriting: A practice whereby a claim is denied on the basis of the individual's health status at the time the policy was purchased. Most reputable companies do medical underwriting at the time a policy is sold rather than at the time a claim is submitted. (This is not permitted in most new policies now sold, but check your state requirements for policies written in your state.)

Restoration of Benefits: Some companies provide for a restoration of the policy if the insured has left the nursing facility for a minimum of 180 days and required no services during that time. For example, an insured had used two years of a four-year long-term care policy and left the nursing home. Under the "restoration of benefits" clause, if the insured remained healthy for at least 181 days, the policy would fully restore itself back to a four-year policy.

Return-of-Premium Rider: Companies offering this rider do so reluctantly and at additional cost. It provides that up to 100% of the premiums are returned to the insured if benefits are not accessed after many years. If benefits are accessed, the returned amount will be reduced or eliminated by the amount of benefits paid. This kind of a rider, while attractive from the perspective of saving on the cost of coverage, may be a bad option if chosen by an older person who may require these services in five or ten years, since claims could consume the rider benefit.

Severe Cognitive Impairment: This is a loss or deterioration in mental capacity that is comparable to Alzheimer's disease and similar forms of irreversible dementia. It is documented by clinical evidence and standardized tests of memory, orientation as to people, places and time, and deductive or abstract reasoning.

**Tax-qualified policies must require that cognitive impairment be "severe"
in accord with this definition.**

Skilled Nursing Care: Nursing and rehabilitative care that can be performed only by or under the supervision of skilled medical personnel.

Skilled Nursing Facility (SNF): An institution (or a distinct part of an institution) that provides 24-hour-a-day skilled nursing care and related services for patients who require daily medical, nursing, or rehabilitative services.

Unintentional Lapse of the Policy: When a person, due to cognitive impairment, loses the ability to keep track of the payments on the policy. Most companies have a provision that allows the insured to make up the missed premiums for a 30-day or 60-day period after missing the due date. Under tax-qualified policies the insured must be allowed at least a five-month period if it can be shown that there was cognitive impairment or Alzheimer's involved in not making the premium payment on a timely basis. Companies now provide assistance for the insured by naming a third party to receive a copy of the premium notice, such as a child or caregiver, that provides an overview of the insured's finances to make sure the premiums are paid.

Waiver of Premium: This says that after a certain number of days in a nursing facility, or receiving home-care benefits, the insured does not have to pay premiums during the period that benefits are being paid.

Choose a plan that:

- Does not require a stay in a hospital as a qualification for benefits to begin;

- Covers care at home as well as in an institution;

- Does not require home health care to be administered by a professional health care worker or by a certified home health care agency (if it does, benefits may not be paid);

- Covers custodial, or personal, care as well as intermediate care;

- Covers adult day care;

- Does not exclude pre-existing conditions, or at least not for more than six months;

- Does not require payment of premiums (after the waiver period) once you begin to receive benefits until your health is restored and you are able to take care of yourself;

- Requires you to satisfy the elimination period only once no matter how many times you need to access your benefits;

- Does not increase premium levels unless it is for everyone who carries the same plan;

- Is guaranteed renewable (some states, including California, require all plans to be guaranteed renewable);

- Offers a grace period during which your policy continues if a premium is missed;

- Provides you an "Outline of Coverage" that summarizes important plan features;

- When comparing "Outlines of Coverage," compares favorably with other plans you are considering;

- Qualifies as a tax-qualified, or non-tax-qualified, policy with a right to change between the two;

- Allows you a "free look" period in which to review the policy;

- Pays your nursing home stay on an indemnity basis, not a reimbursement basis. In other words, it pays the total benefit amount rather than reimbursing for actual expenses;

- Has a feature called "restoration of benefits" if it does not include a lifetime benefit (if you recover and leave the nursing home and are not readmitted for at least 180 consecutive days your original benefit period will be restored).

In addition, consult a professional advisor about any questions you have and any conditions you do not understand. To ensure that no misunderstandings arise be sure you:

- Keep the signed and dated receipt of the policy from the company or agent;

- Pay with a check written to the insurance company;

- Be candid and accurate about your medical history so no claims will be refused or policies cancelled;

- And take the time to choose the policy that is right for you.

Tailoring Benefits to Your Own Needs*

Five questions to answer before purchasing long-term care insurance:

1. Seven percent of my annual income is approximately $_____.
   (This is the maximum amount experts advise spending on a premium.)

2. The cash value of my non-housing assets is $_____.

3. The total amount of my non-housing assets would last for _____ years if I needed care today. (This is the approximate number of years of coverage you might consider buying.)

4. I can afford to pay $_____ a day towards the cost of my own care. The difference between the amount I can pay and the cost of care today is $_____ a day.

5. I can afford to pay for the first _____ days of care in a nursing home. I will need an elimination period of no longer than 30 days, 60 days, 90 days or (other).
   _____.

Non-housing assets are things you own that don't include your house. When you apply for Medi-Cal the value of your house is generally not counted. The value of your other assets, like stocks, bonds, and investments, will be counted. Contact your Department of Social Services for more specific information.

The answers to the questions above will help you determine what benefits you need:

1. The premium range I can afford is $_____. (Your answer to #1)

2. The total lifetime benefit I can afford is $_____. (Your answer to #2)

3. The number of years a policy should pay is _____. (Your answer to #3)

4. The daily benefit amount I need is $_____. (The 2nd amount in #4)

5. The elimination period I can afford is _____ days. (The answer to #5)

* *Source:* Taking Care of Tomorrow: A Consumer's Guide to Long-Term Care.
California Department of Aging, pg. 44. October 2001.

Durable Power of Attorney for Health Care (DPAHC)

The Durable Power of Attorney for Health Care (DPAHC) is a document created while you are still capable of expressing your desires regarding medical treatment and life support. It designates someone who may authorize taking you off life support if there is no hope you will ever live without the assistance of machines, or to make other health care decisions if you are unable to make them yourself. If you do not have this written authority it is virtually impossible to take your loved one off life support, even if you know that is what that person wanted. Go to the website called *www.uslivingwillregistry.com* to get more information. When you visit you can also register for one copy for free. The service is called an advance directive, which updates annually at no cost to you.

Joan & Lou

It was hard enough knowing she was losing her husband, but the last thing Joan wanted was to keep him hooked up to machines against his wishes.

Lou had a 12-year history of heart disease and had already undergone one bypass surgery eight years before. He was scheduled for a second surgery in the next few days and was beginning to worry about whether he would make it through. He made several comments to Joan about not wanting any life-saving machines if anything were to go wrong. He and Joan agreed that they should sign the durable power of attorney for health care papers that they had prepared many months ago.

Unfortunately, Lou collapsed the next day – before the scheduled surgery and before they had a chance to sign the papers. Additionally, he was revived and hooked up to life support before Joan had a chance to express his wishes to the doctor. Though he showed no sign of brain activity, she was powerless to have him removed from the machines because there was no written durable power of attorney for health care. It would be several days and many dollars later before Joan (with the help of an attorney) would be able to have Lou removed from life support.

If Lou had been conscious he might have been able to decide for himself whether he wanted to terminate any life support systems. Although there is such a thing as a right to die, you cannot exercise this right unless you put your wishes in writing. The person you choose to become your agent with a DPAHC should be someone whose judgment you trust and who knows what you want and agrees with your philosophy. Be sure that you consult with a professional advisor about your specific situation and for obtaining necessary forms.

DPAHC vs. Living Will

A living will and a durable power of attorney for health care are not the same! A living will expresses your general wishes about critical care — it does not authorize anyone to make decisions on your behalf. A living will is interpreted by the doctors as a directive and does not handle the matter of "right to die" as efficiently and effectively as a DPAHC. At the website *www.uslivingwillregistry.com*, you can get more information and register free.

The DPAHC is the most important document you will have because it affects you and your *life* directly. A will and a trust deal only with money matters after you have died. A DPAHC provides documentation you can count on to carry out your wishes, and to emotionally and financially protect your loved ones in the event of a tragedy.

7 Association Plans and Health Savings Accounts

Financial Crises: Medical Insurance and Long-Term Care

Medical insurance for most Americans is a benefit provided from their employer, or they have personal coverage due to self-employment. Medical insurance coverage, whether you are a working person or a retiree, provides basic coverage for hospital visits.

Few Americans realize that unless very strict rules are followed, most medical insurance at any age provides very little coverage, if at all, for long-term care, whether in a nursing home or at home. Today, over 40% of all nursing home residents are under the age of 65. Most residents are paying for the care out of their personal assets since their medical insurance does not usually pay for any coverage. Unless the need is for skilled care and immediately follows a hospital stay of at least 3 days, no coverage is available.

Long-term care costs in the United States run over $183 *billion* per year and are estimated to reach $379 *billion* by the year 2050. The U.S. government pays less than 2% of all nursing home costs annually. The annual cost for a nursing home stay in the United States averages approximately $57,700 per year, while much higher costs are not uncommon for more complicated needs.[1] That number is projected to increase to $190,600 per year by 2030.[2]

Two of my clients, a married couple, both needed care, one at home and one in a nursing home, at a yearly cost of more than $170,000. Approximately one half of that cost was paid by quality insurance coverages. The savings to the estate exceeded $450,000 due to the insurance coverage providing payments when most needed.

The best course of action for clients to take regarding this urgent need is to talk with an insurance professional about their specific needs to protect themselves and their loved ones from these astronomical costs. Premiums can be quite affordable for different coverages depending on age and health considerations. Securing policies at younger ages ensures that costs are reasonable and should an accident or health condition occur the policies will protect the estate and net worth of the individual for retirement purposes.

Association Plans

There is a critical difference between types of long-term care insurance offered to groups such as employees, professional organizations and retiree associations, and association plans with individual policies issued to members (the last usually being the best alternative if available).

Group insurance is a contract with the group itself rather than with the individuals in the group. Certificates of coverage are issued rather than individual policies. It has the serious disadvantage of being cancelable by the insurance carrier – some carriers have pulled out of markets with less than 90 days' notice when the cost of benefits paid out exceeded the carrier's premium income. Of greater concern to the consumer is that when an insurance carrier terminates coverage, the consumer immediately also loses coverage and may not be able to replace the contract at any cost due to failing health.

Association plans, on the other hand, are contracts with individual members through the association. These contracts cannot be cancelled as long as the premiums continue to be paid. The individual may leave the association and still continue the coverage with the insurance carrier. Usually, the criteria for qualifying for coverage are less stringent than in the open marketplace. Individuals can tailor benefits to their specific needs and budget. Coverage is often available to members or their extended family, by blood or by marriage, whether older or younger. Premiums are not subject to annual adjustment, but may be increased if the increase applies to the entire class of insureds. The disadvantage is that members do not automatically qualify for coverage.

Association plans may be tax qualified or non-tax qualified, indemnity, or expense based, depending on the individual member's desires. In this way, the association provides significant protection to its membership along with lower costs for benefits.

In most cases, association plans will cover both working individuals and retirees if they are members. If the retirees are not members, but are related by blood or marriage, then coverage may be provided to them using less stringent criteria than in the open market and at a lower cost.

Types of organizations that provide such benefits include educational and professional organizations, nursing associations, medical associations, agricultural groups and state retiree associations, in addition to municipalities, unions and industry associations of employers.

A large extended group will normally reduce the cost of insurance coverage for everyone in the group. In some cases, association policies will also provide additional benefits not normally provided in a long-term care policy. These benefits may include an accidental death benefit, ambulance service, prescription drug benefits for nursing home stays, substantial spousal discounts and the ability to increase the amount of the benefit at a later date without evidence of insurability.

While the policy benefits are greater it is very important to review carefully the exclusions and limitations of those policies. In some cases, they are more restrictive than the individual policies that are issued outside of associations.

> NOTE: Any association that is created for a purpose other than to buy insurance benefits may offer group long-term care insurance plans to its members.
> Associations cannot be created for the express purpose of buying insurance at a discount.

Programs That Help with Medical Expenses and Long-Term Care

Federal Long-Term Care Program

Approximately 20 million individuals nationwide will be targeted to join the Federal Long-Term Care Insurance Program (FLTCIP), creating what some may see as an increase in competition, and what others may see as an opportunity for the long-term care message to reach a greater population.

The Long-Term Care Security Act (PL 106-265), which passed on September 19, 2000, led to the FLTCIP, which is sponsored by the United States Office of Personnel Management (OPM).

Metropolitan Life Insurance Company and John Hancock Life Insurance Company were chosen by OPM for the long-term care insurance offering. Together, they formed a jointly-owned entity called LTC Partners, LLC, to operate this new program.

Available as of October 2002, the FLTCIP is expected to become the nation's largest employer-sponsored long-term care insurance program, with an estimated 20 million people eligible to apply. The policies offered are expected to have lower premiums than those available in the private market.

Those eligible include:

- Federal and postal employees (excluding employees of the District of Columbia government);

- Members and retired members of the uniformed services;

- Qualified relatives (current spouses and adult children of employees and annuitants, and parents and parents-in-law of living employees but not annuitants). Since the FLTCIP does not provide self and family coverage under one application, each eligible person must apply for coverage separately. And, in meeting with the requirements of the Health Insurance Portability and Accountability Act (HIPAA), once a person applies for insurance the coverage will continue as long as the premiums are paid.

The FLTCIP program may undergo further changes as the LTC Partners continues to conduct research. For the latest information on this new program visit the OPM Web site at *www.opm.gov/insure/ltc*.[3]

Health Savings Accounts: The Basics

If you hold a Health Savings Account (HSA), you can deposit money to save for future medical expenses. There are certain advantages to adding funds into these accounts, including favorable tax treatment. HSAs were signed into law by President Bush on December 8, 2003.

Who Can Have an HSA

To be eligible to contribute to an HSA, a person must:

- Have coverage under an HSA-qualified "high deductible health plan" (HDHP);

- Have no other first dollar medical coverage (other types of insurance, like specific injury insurance, or accident, disability, dental care, vision care, or long-term care insurance, are permitted). First dollar coverage begins as soon as covered medical expenses are incurred. Without first dollar coverage, the insured must pay specified "deductible" amounts first. When that amount of expenses incurred has been paid by the insured, the policy begins reimbursing;

- Not be enrolled in Medicare;

- Not be claimed as a dependent on someone else's tax return.

Contributions to your HSA can be made by you, your employer, or both. However, the total contributions are limited annually. If you make a contribution, you can deduct the contributions (even if you do not itemize deductions) when completing your federal income tax return.

Contributions to the account must stop once you are enrolled in Medicare. However, you can keep the money in your account and use it to pay for medical expenses tax-free.

High Deductible Health Plans (HDHPs)

You must have coverage under an HSA-qualified "high deductible health plan" (HDHP) to open and to contribute to an HSA. Generally, this is health insurance that does not cover first dollar medical expenses. Federal law requires that the health insurance deductible be at least $1,000 for self-only coverage or $2,000 for family coverage. In addition, annual out-of-pocket expenses under the plan (including deductibles, co-pays and co-insurance) cannot exceed $5,100 for self-only coverage or $10,200 for family coverage. These amounts are adjusted annually for inflation.

In general, the deductible must apply to all medical expenses (including prescriptions) covered by the plan. However, plans can pay for "preventive care" services on a first dollar basis (with or without a co-pay). "Preventive care" can include routine pre-natal and well-child care, child and adult immunizations, annual physicals, mammograms, pap smears, etc.

Finding HDHP Coverage

Any company that sells health insurance coverage in your state may offer HDHP policies. You should be able to find a qualified policy by contacting your current insurance company, an agent or broker licensed to sell health insurance in your state, or your state insurance department.

HSA Contributions

You can make a contribution to your HSA each year that you are eligible. You can contribute up to the amount of your HDHP deductible but no more than $2,850 for self-only coverage or $5,650 for family coverage (2007 figures). The following table illustrates how this works.

Figure 7-1					(View Online at www.longtermcarebooks.com)
	Single Coverage				
HDHP Deductible	$1,100	$1,500	$2,000	$2,500	$3,000
Maximum HSA Deposit (2007)	$1,100	$1,500	$2,000	$2,500	$2,850
	Family Coverage				
HDHP Deductible	$2,200	$3,000	$4,000	$5,000	$6,000
Maximum HSA Deposit (2007)	$2,200	$3,000	$4,000`	$5,000	$5,650

Source: "Health Savings Accounts", Department of the U.S. Treasury, www.treas.gov.

Individuals age 55 and older can also make additional "catch-up" contributions. The maximum annual catch-up contributions are: $800 (2007); $900 (2008); $1,000 (2009 and thereafter).

Determining Your Contribution

Your eligibility to contribute to an HSA is determined by the effective date of your HDHP coverage. If you do not have HDHP coverage for the entire year, you will not be able to make the maximum contribution. All contributions (including catch-up contributions) must be pro-rated. Your annual contribution depends on the number of months of HDHP coverage you have during the year (count only the months where you have HDHP coverage on the first day of the month). Contributions can be made as late as April 15 of the following year.

Using Your HSA

You can use the money in the account to pay for any "qualified medical expense" permitted under federal tax law. This includes most medical care and services, and dental and vision care, and also includes over-the-counter drugs such as aspirin.

You generally can **not** use the money to pay for medical insurance premiums, except under specific circumstances, including:

- Any health plan coverage while receiving federal or state unemployment benefits;
- COBRA continuation coverage after leaving employment with a company that offers health insurance coverage;
- **Qualified long-term care insurance;**
- Medicare premiums and out-of-pocket expenses, including deductibles, co-pays, and co-insurance for:
  - ❖ Part A (hospital and inpatient services);
  - ❖ Part B (physician and outpatient services);
  - ❖ Part C (Medicare HMO and PPO plans);
  - ❖ Part D (prescription drugs).

You can use the money in the account to pay for medical expenses for yourself, your spouse, or your dependent children. You can pay for expenses of your spouse and dependent children even if they are not covered by your HDHP.

Any amounts used for purposes other than to pay for "qualified medical expenses" are taxable as income and subject to an additional 10% tax penalty. Examples include:

- Medical expenses that are not considered "qualified medical expenses" under federal tax law (e.g., cosmetic surgery);
- Other types of health insurance unless specifically described above;
- Medicare supplement insurance premiums;
- Expenses that are not medical or health-related.

After you turn age 65, or if you become disabled, the 10% additional tax penalty no longer applies.

Advantages of HSAs

Security – Your high deductible insurance and HSA protect you against high or unexpected medical bills.

Affordability – You should be able to lower your health insurance premiums by switching to health insurance coverage with a higher deductible.

Flexibility – You can use the funds in your account to pay for current medical expenses, including expenses that your insurance may not cover, or save the money in your account for future needs, such as:

- Health insurance or medical expenses if unemployed;
- Medical expenses after retirement (before Medicare);
- Out-of-pocket expenses when covered by Medicare;
- Long-term care expenses and insurance.

Savings – You can save the money in your account for future medical expenses and grow your account through investment earnings.

Control – You make all the decisions about:
- How much money to put into the account;
- Whether to save the account for future expenses or pay current medical expenses;
- Which medical expenses to pay from the account;
- Which company will hold the account;
- Whether to invest any of the money in the account;
- Which investments to make.

Portability – Accounts are completely portable, meaning you can keep your HSA even if you:

- Change jobs;
- Change your medical coverage;
- Become unemployed;
- Move to another state;
- Change your marital status.

Ownership – Funds remain in the account from year to year, just like an IRA. There are no "use it or lose it" rules for HSAs.

Tax Savings – An HSA provides you triple tax savings:

- tax deductions when you contribute to your account;
- tax-free earnings through investment; and
- tax-free withdrawals for qualified medical expenses.

Opening Your Health Savings Account

Banks, credit unions, insurance companies and other financial institutions are permitted to be trustees or custodians of these accounts. Other financial institutions that handle IRAs are also automatically qualified to establish HSAs. If you cannot locate a local institution willing to establish your account, check links under "Resources" on the U.S. Treasury website (*www.treas.gov*).[4]

Health Savings Accounts: Questions & Answers

What happens to my HSA when I die?

If you are married, your spouse becomes the owner of the account and can use it as if it were his or her own HSA. If you are not married, the account will no longer be treated as an HSA upon your death. The account will pass to your beneficiary or become part of your estate (and be subject to any applicable taxes).

How much does an HSA cost?

An HSA is not something you purchase. It's a savings account which enables you to pay for current health expenses and save for future qualified medical and retiree health expenses on a tax-free basis. The only product you purchase with an HSA is a High Deductible Health Plan (HDHP), an inexpensive plan that will cover most of your medical expenses should your expenses exceed the funds you have in your HSA.

Can I get an HSA even if I have other insurance that pays medical bills?

You are only allowed to have auto, dental, vision, disability and long-term care insurance that pays medical bills at the same time as an HDHP. You may also have coverage for a specific disease or illness as long as it pays a specific dollar amount when the policy is triggered. Wellness programs offered by your employer are also permitted if they do not pay significant medical benefits.

Does the HDHP policy have to be in my name to open an HSA?

No, the policy does not have to be in your name. As long as you have coverage under the HDHP policy, you can be eligible for an HSA (assuming you meet the other eligibility requirements for contributing to an HSA). You can still be eligible for an HSA even if the policy is in your spouse's name.

My employer offers an FSA ("cafeteria plan"). Can I have both an FSA and an HSA?

You can have both types of accounts, but only under certain circumstances. Generally, Flexible Spending Arrangements (FSAs) will probably make you ineligible for an HSA. If your employer offers a "limited purpose" (limited to dental, vision, or preventive care) or "post-deductible" (pays for medical expenses after the plan deductible is met) FSA, then you can still be eligible for an HSA.

My employer offers an HRA. Can I have both an HRA and an HSA?

You can have both types of accounts, but only under certain circumstances. Generally, Health Reimbursement Arrangements (HRAs) will probably make you ineligible for an HSA. If your employer offers a "limited purpose" or "post-deductible" HRA, then you can still be eligible for an HSA. If your employer contributes to an HRA that can only be used when you retire, you can still be eligible for an HSA.

My spouse has an FSA or HRA through an employer. Can I have an HSA?

You cannot have an HSA if your spouse's FSA or HRA can pay for any of your medical expenses before your HDHP deductible is met.

What happens to the money in my HSA if I lose my HDHP coverage?

Funds deposited into your HSA remain in your account and automatically roll over from one year to the next. You may continue to use the HSA funds for qualified medical expenses. You are no longer eligible to contribute to an HSA for months that you are not an eligible individual because you are not covered by an HDHP. If you have coverage by an HDHP for less than a year, the annual maximum contribution is reduced. If you made a contribution to your HSA for the year based on a full year's coverage by the HDHP, you will need to withdraw some of the contribution to avoid the tax on excess HSA contributions. If you regain HDHP coverage at a later date, you can begin making contributions to your HSA again.

Where can I get more information about HSAs?

The U.S. Treasury's website has additional information about Health Savings Accounts, including answers to frequently asked questions, related IRS forms and publications, technical guidance, and links to other helpful websites. Treasury's HSA website can be found through *www.treas.gov* (click on "Health Savings Accounts") or directly at the following address:

http://www.treas.gov/offices/public-affairs/hsa[5]

Medical Reimbursement Plans

A Medical Reimbursement Plan is set up by an employer to reimburse employees for medical expenses not covered by their regular medical insurance. Reimbursable expenses include dental expenses and expenses in excess of policy limits. Payments are generally received by the employee income-tax-free.

Uninsured or Self-Insured Plans

These are plans which reimburse employees for medical expenses from the general funds of the business. When the corporation pays premiums to an insurance company and thereby shifts the risk to an unrelated third party, it is called an insured plan.

Qualifying Events – Qualifying events are certain events that would cause an individual to lose health coverage. The type of qualifying event will determine who the qualified beneficiaries are and the amount of time that a plan must offer the health coverage to them under COBRA. A plan, at its discretion, may provide longer periods of continuation coverage.

Qualifying Events for Employees:

- Voluntary or involuntary termination of employment for reasons other than gross misconduct;
- Reduction in the number of hours of employment.

Qualifying Events for Spouses:

- Voluntary or involuntary termination of the covered employee's employment for any reason other than gross misconduct;
- Reduction in the hours worked by the covered employee;
- Covered employees becoming entitled to Medicare;
- Divorce or legal separation of the covered employee;
- Death of the covered employee.

Qualifying Events for Dependent Children:

- Loss of dependent child status under the plan rules;
- Voluntary or involuntary termination of the covered employee's employment for any reason other than gross misconduct;
- Reduction in the hours worked by the covered employee;
- Covered employees becoming entitled to Medicare;
- Divorce or legal separation of the covered employee;
- Death of the covered employee.

Qualified beneficiaries must be offered coverage identical to that available to similarly situated beneficiaries who are not receiving COBRA coverage under the plan (generally, the same coverage that the qualified beneficiary had immediately before qualifying for continuation coverage). A change in the benefits under the plan for the active employees will also apply to qualified beneficiaries. Qualified beneficiaries must be allowed to make the same choices given to non-COBRA beneficiaries under the plan, such as during periods of open enrollment by the plan.

Beneficiaries may be required to pay for COBRA coverage. The premium cannot exceed 102 percent of the cost to the plan for similarly situated individuals who have not incurred a qualifying event, including both the portion paid by employees and any portion paid by the employer before the qualifying event, plus 2 percent for administrative costs.

COBRA establishes required periods of coverage for continuation health benefits. A plan, however, may provide longer periods of coverage beyond those required by COBRA. COBRA beneficiaries generally are eligible for group coverage during a maximum of 18 months for qualifying events due to employment termination or reduction of hours of work. Certain qualifying events, or a second qualifying event during the initial period of coverage, may permit a beneficiary to receive a maximum of 36 months of coverage.

Coverage begins on the date that coverage would otherwise have been lost by reason of a qualifying event and will end at the end of the maximum period.[6]

Cafeteria plans (formally called health care flexible spending accounts) are employer-established benefit plans that reimburse employees for specified medical expenses as they are incurred. These accounts are allowed under section 125 of the Internal Revenue Code and are also referred to as "125 plans." The employee contributes funds to the account through a salary reduction agreement and is able to withdraw the funds set aside to pay for medical bills. (*See Figure 7-2 for examples of covered items.*) The salary reduction agreement means that any funds set aside in a flexible spending account escape both income tax and Social Security tax. Employers may contribute to these accounts as well.

There is no statutory limit on the amount of money that can be contributed to health care flexible spending accounts. However, some companies place a limit of $2,000 to $3,000. Once the amount of contribution has been designated during the open enrollment period that occurs once each year, the employee is not allowed to change the amount or drop out of the plan during the year unless he or she experiences a change of family status.[7]

In May 2005 the Treasury Department said employers can extend the time workers have to spend money in the accounts by 2½ months. Employers, however, must amend their plans.

Examples of Expenses Eligible for Reimbursement as Part of a Cafeteria Plan

Acupressure/acupuncture
Alcoholism/drug/substance abuse treatment
Ambulance hire
Anesthesia
Artificial limbs, teeth and devices
Attendant to groom, bathe, change, feed, give Rx

Bio-feedback
Birth control pills with an Rx number
Blood tests, X-rays and laboratory fees
Braces, crutches and wheelchairs
Braille – books and magazines

Car controls for the handicapped
Care for mentally handicapped child
Child care expenses
Chiropractic care, physical therapy
Christian Science practitioners' fees
Clinic and hospital services
Co-insurance amounts you pay
Condoms (for prevention of disease only)
Contact lenses and cleaning solutions
Co-payments for medical, dental and vision care
Cosmetic surgery (non-elective)
Cost, care of trained animals for impaired persons
Cost of operations and related treatments
Counseling, psychotherapy, psychiatry
Crutches

Day care expenses for eligible dependents as necessary due to caregiver's employment
Deductibles for medical, dental and vision insurance you pay
Dental treatments, dentures and orthodontia
Diabetic supplies, insulin, needles, test strips
Diagnostic fees
Drug and medical supplies

Electrolysis (non-elective)
Employment taxes, meals for an attendant

Eye examinations, treatments, eyeglasses

Fees of practical nurse
Fees for healing services

Guide dog and its upkeep
Gynecology and obstetrics

Handicapped persons' special schools
Health insurance (including Medicare Part B payments, but Part A coverage is not deductible unless person is 65 or over and is not entitled to Social Security benefits)
Hearing exams, aids and batteries
Home improvements necessitated by medical considerations
Homeopathic, naturopathic office visits
Hospital bills
Hospitalization insurance
Hypnosis for treatment of an illness

Infertility services/in-vitro fertilization
Insulin
Invalid care

Laboratory fees
Laetrile by prescription
Legal operations and surgery
Licensed medical practitioner

Maintenance and repair of eligible equipment
Meals, lodging and care in a nursing home
Medic Alert jewelry
Medical care provided by school or college
Medical computer data bank fees
Membership fees in association with furnishing medical services, hospitalization, and clinical care
Midwife services and Lamaze (birthing)

(continued on page 61)

Figure 7-2 (*continued*)　　　(View Online at www.longtermcarebooks.com)

Nurses' fees and services (including nurses' board and Social Security tax where paid by taxpayer)

Obstetrical expenses
Operations
Organ donor or possible donor expenses
Orthopedic shoes
Oxygen and oxygen equipment

Patterning exercises for mentally retarded
Physical exams, preventive/routine care
Physician fees
Physician-prescribed swimming pool or spa equipment costs and maintenance
Physician-prescribed weight loss or smoking cessation programs
Prescribed medications with an Rx number
Psychiatric care
Psychologist fees
Purchase of medical equipment

Radial keratotomy
Removal of breast implants
Rental and repair of medical equipment
Retarded persons' cost for special home/ home care
Routine physicals and other diagnostic services or treatments

Sales tax on eligible expenses
Sanitarium charges
Smoking cessation program (if prescribed by a physician)
Special diets (if prescribed by a physician)
Special education for the blind
Special plumbing for the handicapped
Speech therapy
Sterilization fees
Surgical fees

Telephone, special design for deaf
Television audio display equipment for the deaf
Therapeutic care for drug and alcohol addiction
Therapy treatments

Transportation expenses, primarily in the rendering of medical services; e.g., railroad fare to hospital or to recuperation home, cab fare in obstetrical cases
Tubal ligation and vasectomy
Tuition at special school for handicapped
Tuition fee (part), if college or private school furnishes breakdown of medical charges

Vitamins by prescription

Weight loss program if prescribed by a doctor
Wheelchair
Wigs (non-elective)

Figure 7-3 (View Online at www.longtermcarebooks.com)

The "Alphabet Soup" of Consumer-Driven Health Plans[8]

FSA = Flexible Spending Account   HRA = Health Reimbursement Account   HSA = Health Savings Account

Question	FSA	HRA	HSA
Does the employee own the money in the account?	NO	MAYBE	YES
Can the money be invested and the employee earn interest?	NO	NO	YES
Can the employee use the funds for things other than medical expenses?	NO	NO	YES
Can employees take the money with them if they leave?	NO	MAYBE	YES
How can an employee access funds?	Generally claims reimbursement. Employee provides receipt for services.	Generally claims reimbursement. Employee provides receipt for services.	Individual has direct access to funds with debit card, checks, or withdrawal form.
Who can contribute to the account?	Employers and/or individuals.	Employers.	Employers and/or individuals.
Who is eligible?	Any size group. Not available to partners in a partnership, shareholders who own more than 2% stock in an S-Corp. or LLC.	Any size group. Not available to partners in a partnership, share-holders who own more than 2% stock in an S-Corp. or LLC.	Individuals/ employers of any size who have established a Qualified High Deductible Plan and are under 65.
Does the account need to be paired with high deductible insurance?	NO	NO, but it is recommended.	YES, plans must meet certain requirements determined by the IRS each year.

8 Alternative Ways to Fund Long-Term Care

Long-term care insurance is not the only means available to meet the financial obligations associated with residential or home care. Other alternatives for providing long-term care insurance include the following:

Life Insurance Policies with Special Riders

- Policies with long-term care riders may include a rider that prepays the death benefit to cover expenses of convalescent care.

  1. The amount of death benefit selected is the amount available to cover convalescent care.

  2. If the death benefit for convalescent care is never or only partially used, it will be available at death to help provide income to the survivor, to pay off a mortgage, for estate settlement costs or for any other purpose.

- Policies with accelerated-benefit riders: reduce the death benefit by any amounts paid as long-term care benefits. If long-term care benefits are unused, the death benefit remains in full. The contract is designed to pay a benefit for either long-term care, or death, or both. Accelerated-benefit riders are available in the case of chronic or terminal illness.

For terminal illness the policy owner/insured has the option of receiving up to 100 percent of the death benefit early. All or a part of the death benefit may be requested early (in a lump sum) for any purpose needed by the policy owner/insured.

For chronic illness (depending on the individual policy) the policy owner has the option of receiving the death benefit in periodic payments (subject to meeting the federal guidelines):

- After a 90-day waiting period;

- When unable to perform two of the six ADLs; or

- When the insured has severe cognitive impairment.

The maximum monthly amount under the accelerated rider is 4% of the death benefit. The total benefit can be up to two times the death benefit through the utilization of an optional additional rider added at the time of policy issue.

Be sure to carefully check benefit eligibility and conditions of the policy you purchase.

Critical Illness Policies

What critical illness policies may cover:

- Policies with a benefit payable for certain diseases will pay the death benefit early to meet the needs of long-term care or medical necessity;

- Critical illness policies pay out in the event that the person is stricken with one of the major diseases or disabilities outlined in the policy;

- Most products have a 100% one-time payout in the event of cancer that has spread, and for all heart attacks, strokes, major organ transplants and kidney failure;

- Richer policies also cover Alzheimer's, blindness, deafness, multiple sclerosis, paralysis and death;

- Most critical illness policies offer a portion of the benefit (usually 25 percent) for serious medical conditions such as angioplasty, bypass surgery and certain contained cancers (the remaining benefit is paid at a later date, if needed).

- Policies with multiple coverages may include:

    - Life insurance;

    - Disability income protection;

    - Terminal illness protection; and

    - Chronic illness protection.

Annuity Contracts

These provide a certain income for life after a qualifying event, such as 90 days in a nursing facility or hospital.

Immediate payment contracts can be purchased that will guarantee a certain income upon an event requiring institutionalization. However, any funds not paid out before death are lost to the insured's estate. For example, you take out a contract for lifetime coverage at age 65, but die in a car accident five months after benefits begin. The contract payments stop immediately.

- Private annuities between parent and child: Assets are given to the children, who then guarantee and provide the parent a life income. This guarantees that the principal will not be lost to an insurance company upon the parent's death. The risk is that the parent outlives the expected payments and the children have to make up the difference.

- Variable annuity contracts: In the past twenty years, annuity contracts have been created by most major insurance companies which are categorized as variable annuity contracts. They are variable because they have separate accounts into which the insured can choose to place capital for investment. Investments can include mutual funds with stock portfolios, bond portfolios, international investments, real estate, natural resources, money market accounts and guaranteed rate contracts.

These contracts have no front-end sales charges. There is normally a contract charge of $30 to $35 per year and the expenses of the contract vary greatly. You need to review this with your financial advisor to determine if these contracts are in keeping with your needs. These contracts allow complete

Figure 8-1   (View Online at www.longtermcarebooks.com)

OPTIONS FOR SETTING UP A CONTRACT

Owner, Beneficiary

O	JO*	A	B	First Death	Contract Disposition
H	W	H	H/W	H	Wife may take lump-sum death benefit or continue contract.
W	H	W	W/H	W	Husband may take lump-sum death benefit or continue contract.
H	—	H	W	H	Wife may take lump-sum death benefit or continue contract.
H	—	W	W	H	Wife may take lump-sum death benefit or continue contract.
H	—	H	W	W	Contract remains intact. Name new beneficiary.
H	—	W	W	W	Contract remains intact. Name new annuitant and beneficiary.
H	—	W	C	H	Child must take lump-sum death benefit, annuitize within one year or receive contract value within five years.**
H	—	H	X	H	"Other person" must take lump-sum death benefit, annuitize within one year or receive contract value within five years.**
T	—	H	T	H	Revocable trust must take lump-sum death benefit, annuitize within one year or receive contract value within five years.**
T	—	H	W	H	Contract remains intact. Name new annuitant.

O = Owner/Participant	A = Annuitant (insured)	B = Beneficiary
H = Husband	W = Wife	C = Child
T = Revocable Trust	X = Other	JO = Joint Owner

The beneficiary must provide a written election to the company within 60 days of the company's receipt of due proof of death of the participant.

*Joint owners must be spouses except in Pennsylvania.

The above information may differ for each individual. You are advised to consult with a professional advisor about your specific situation.

**Annuitize – to contractually agree to an irrevocable set of payments over a specific period of time (months, years, etc.)

removal of the original invested capital and all growth to pay for long-term care expenses or medical expenses without back-end surrender fees.

The only consequence of taking out the funds is that taxes are applicable to the growth of capital. There are other conditions and terms of the contracts which should be carefully reviewed prior to purchase.

Figure 8-1 shows the many choices available regarding ownership of annuity contracts. Beneficiary designations can be equally important as to final income and estate tax consequences.

When you consider an annuity contract, ownership is critical as to tax consequences to the owner and beneficiary, as the preceding graph points out. Ownership determines liability for taxes.

Veterans Administration (VA) Benefits

Long-term care in VA or private nursing homes may be provided for veterans who are not acutely ill and not in need of hospital care. If space and resources are available, the VA may provide VA nursing home care. Veterans with a compensable, service-connected disability are given first priority for nursing home care and may not need an income eligibility assessment. Service-connected disabilities are determined by the VA. Care authorized by the VA normally may not be provided in excess of six months, except for veterans who need nursing home care for a service-connected disability or veterans who were hospitalized primarily for treatment of a service-connected disability.

This is possible only if it is available in your local area AND only if there is space. (Currently, the VA believes it will need to increase its operations to meet these needs by at least 175 percent). For a non-service-connected disability that lasts more than six months the veteran must have some other source of benefits.

What the VA will pay for:

- Home improvements necessary to provide disability access to the home and essential facilities; and

- Domiciliary care: rehabilitative and long-term health maintenance care for veterans who require minimal medical care, but do not need the skilled nursing services provided in nursing homes.

Eligibility for VA benefits depends upon individual circumstances. For more information, you can either contact them at 800-827-1000 to speak with a representative, or go to *http://www.vba.va.gov* (Veterans Benefits Administration Index Page includes links to all their regional offices).

Continuing Care Retirement Communities

Continuing Care Retirement Communities (CCRCs) provide a guaranteed residence regardless of the level of care eventually needed. The resident pays for lifetime care and the costs are known in advance. However, there are a number of disadvantages to this arrangement:

- These facilities may have upfront costs ranging from $25,000 to $450,000 or more, plus fees ranging from a few hundred dollars to a few thousand dollars per month. There may be no rebate of upfront costs in the case of early death.

- The actual costs may vary from the original contract for several reasons:

   1. The resident may be dissatisfied with the facility benefits that are provided and have no recourse but to go to a different facility.

   2. The costs of care are increasing at 8% to 10% around the country. It is unrealistic for these facilities to be able to project fifteen to twenty years into the future what their costs will be, for those individuals who might live that long.

   3. The facility may not qualify for Medi-Cal/Medicaid benefits, so costs could be substantially higher than anticipated. (Check how much the facility charges for incidental expenses such as adult diapers, medical appliances, clothing and other special needs – are these charges reasonable?)

- The contract should be reviewed as to the different levels of care that are provided once a person requires nursing or home health care. Is the entire cost covered? Are there additional charges that apply?

- There may be restrictions on the sale of the benefit you have purchased in this facility, whether it is the purchase of a unit, or simply a guaranteed residence for all levels of care.

  If you choose to move on, is it possible to sell your interest to someone else? Is it possible for your beneficiaries to receive any funds back? What kind of requirements are there to qualify for the sale of the property or the return of the funds invested if you died two months after moving in?

- The level of medical care that is being provided today may not be guaranteed into the future.

- The original owners of the facility may have to claim bankruptcy and sell the facility to a debtor, which could void the contract signed by the original insured person moving into the facility.

Warning! Because of the significant investment required to enter a CCRC, it is extremely important that a CPA, attorney, and/or a financial advisor, as well as medical personnel familiar with such facilities, thoroughly review the contract. In addition, the circumstances of a person contracting with a CCRC, and the CCRC itself, including the reputation of the facility management, years in business, number of facilities and past relationships with insureds, are vitally important questions that need to be asked.

Self-Insurance Using Personal Assets

An individual who chooses to self-insure needs both substantial capital, in excess of $500,000 to $750,000, and expert professional tax and income advice to maximize that capital, and not suffer the diminution of the benefits that they have worked so hard to achieve during their lifetimes. Most people who decide to rely on investment funds usually think "it will never happen to me," or think public programs should pay for their care so they do not have to deplete their assets. In addition, the use of investments can lead to serious income and capital gains tax consequences, as well as major estate planning problems.

For example, *Figure 8-2* shows the financial impact on a couple who bought an apartment house in 1954. In 1996 they had to sell the property to help pay medical expenses. (They needed the care in 1996 and had no other assets to use.) Because of the forced sale and because they neglected to obtain professional advice regarding the tax implications, they forfeited a possible gain of more than $500,000. That gain could have paid a substantial portion of their medical and long-term care nursing bills, as well as kept them comfortable during the remaining years of their lives.

If the original owners had considered using a Charitable Remainder Trust (CHRT), they could have controlled the tax costs of the transaction. If the property had been properly transferred into a CHRT prior to sale, there would have been no recapture of depreciation or capital gains taxes to pay. Estate taxes would have been eliminated and a substantial income tax deduction would have been generated

Figure 8-2	(View Online at www.longtermcarebooks.com)
Cost of apartment house in 1954	$ 27,000
Sale price in 1996 – Buyer's market, forced sale	850,000
Taxes paid on capital gains	(260,000)
After-Tax Gain	**$ 583,000**
Sale price of the same building by new owners in 1999 in a seller's market	$ 1,400,000
Taxes paid	**420,000**
Total of sale price difference, less taxes paid	**980,000**

by the transaction. The sale would have allowed for an income to be paid out of the trust for their remaining lives so that they could pay for long-term care expenses and personal household expenses, possibly to buy a long-term care policy or policies. They would have had a continuous flow of income. (*See Chapter 12 for more information*).

Thus, an individual who chooses to self-insure needs both substantial capital and expert professional tax and income advice to maximize that capital.

Viatical Settlements

During the past 10 years, it has become increasingly common for insureds to consider viatical settlements, which provide income to the individual in return for the sale of their life insurance contract to a third party. Viatical Settlements involve, in most cases, several different groups of people:

- The Company (the buyer of the contract);

- The Viatical Investor (a person funding through the company the purchase of the contract, or several people buying a piece of the contract);

- The Viatical Agent (representing the seller of the contract – normally an insurance agent); and

- The Policyholder (the insured).

Viatical settlements are, in many cases, funded by corporations, by individuals or by institutional money. There may be a combination of all of these parties to the transaction. The viatical company buys the contract from the insured. If a person is considering this type of arrangement to provide substantial cash for an emergency, it would be wise to shop the market through an advisor who is technically competent in this area. There are many types of offers that can be made and solutions are not always what they seem.

> ***Warning***: The Departments of Insurance in many states severely limit the use of this arrangement because of the large amount of improper activity in this market. Until you have 100 percent of the money in your hands, you have the possibility of losing not only the money, but the contract itself, or the control of it.

As to tax consequences, the Federal Health Insurance Portability and Accountability Act (HIPAA) states that the proceeds from a Viatical Settlement and also the settlement from an accelerated-death-benefit rider to an existing policy are to be tax-free for a terminally or chronically ill person. Under HIPAA, the viatical company must be a qualified "Viatical Settlement provider," meaning that the company is licensed to do business in the state in which the policyholder resides. If not, the tax-free status is lost.

The major disadvantage of viaticals is that the insured is giving up a death benefit and also possibly the cash value of the policy. If the insured dies in a year or two, he or she will have given up 50% to 75% of the value of the death benefit, and his estate, spouse and offspring could suffer substantial financial loss – when other alternatives might have provided a solution. Example: It might be possible to borrow money using the insurance contract as collateral. When the insured dies, the policy would pay the full death benefit to the estate, or named beneficiary, less the amount of the loan taken on the policy during the insured's lifetime.

Family or Private Foundations

Many individuals can create a tax-planning trust vehicle to provide substantial benefits to themselves, their spouses and their offspring, while at the same time taking care of long-term care needs and estate planning.

Advantages:

- If properly structured, contribution amounts are not limited;

- The foundation can be in addition to any other existing retirement plans;

- The plan does not require participation by employees, co-workers or any person other than the donor if created during a working person's life;

- Trust assets cannot be reached by creditors and will not be included in the donor's estate;

- Income for the foundation manager is available without penalty before age 59-1/2;

- The gains in a private foundation are taxed at 2 percent if the trust has properly filed for tax-exempt status and made proper yearly charitable contributions to recognized 501(c)3 organizations.

Disadvantage:

- The funds are not liquid (a donor cannot withdraw funds for personal use except for reasonable compensation).

Reverse Mortgages (Home Equity Conversion Programs)

A reverse mortgage is an increasing-balance, declining-equity home loan that pays an elderly homeowner tax-free income but requires no monthly payments. This is sometimes called a reverse annuity mortgage. The reverse-mortgage lender can never demand repayment until the borrower:

- Permanently moves out of the home;

- Sells the home; or

- Dies.

The residence is the only loan security; other assets never become liable for repayment, so the loan is non-recourse in nature. Also, since the reverse mortgage must be a first lien on the residence, any existing mortgage balance must be paid off with a lump sum advance from the new reverse mortgage.

Reverse mortgages should be considered only by a qualified senior-citizen-homeowner with no mortgage or a small mortgage balance, who could use:

- Additional monthly, tax-free, lifetime income; or

- A credit line or lump sum amount for paying major expenses such as home repairs, property improvements and property taxes; or

- For pleasure or investment purposes such as travel or college education for the grandchildren since there are are no restrictions on the use of the funds.

The use of a reverse mortgage could disqualify the homeowner from Medicaid / Medi-Cal benefits. If you choose this alternative, in essence, you could be declining your rights to Medicaid / Medi-Cal benefits, so be sure to get competent legal and tax advice.

For example, if you own your house free and clear and meet the other Medi-Cal requirements, you can immediately go on Medicaid. But if you have taken a loan from your house and are receiving income or a large lump sum, then you cannot go on Medicaid unless you spend the income within the month it is received. For more information, contact your local office of the Federal Housing Administration (FHA), or Federal National Mortgage Association (FNMA).

Sale-leaseback: Owners can sell their homes and receive a specified income for the duration of their lives, with the balance on the indebtedness passing to their estate or beneficiaries. In a sale-leaseback, the owner stays in the house and basically pays rent, even though the owner received all of the cash proceeds at the time of the sale. As an example: If you had a $100,000 home, sold it and received the cash, you might have to pay an investor $500 to $700 per month to rent the house should you choose to remain in the home for your lifetime.

Deferred payment loans: An owner sells the residence to a relative, who may not require payments for rent for five to ten years. The relative would be receiving the house at a price commensurate with the deferral of any rental payments being due. This takes the home out of the individual's estate, so he or she is not disqualified for Medicaid / Medi-Cal. While it sounds good, be sure to review with competent legal advice.

The risk here is that there is no guarantee of what the relative might do with the property. Example: The house is sold to the owner's child and the child agrees to pay the parent the value of the house at some future date, or agrees to share it with siblings. Technically, that child (with ownership of the residence) could either encumber the house with substantial debt, sell it, or possibly end up in divorce proceedings or litigation settlements that would cause the loss of the home.

See Appendix A for additional information on reverse mortgages.

Pioneers Set to Change Nursing Homes

When you think of pioneers, perhaps the Gold Rush, covered wagons or John Wayne-type cowboys come to mind. Nursing home reform and societal attitudes toward aging are probably not among your thoughts. Well, heads up, because the Pioneer Network aims to transform skilled nursing facilities into "places for living and growing, rather than declining and dying." And the Pioneers' goals reach beyond nursing home reforms to changing the culture of aging in America.

The Pioneer Network grew out of the nursing home reform movement of the 1970s and evolved into its current structure as a national resource center in 2000. The Pioneers are eldercare professionals, advocates and researchers who champion change in nursing homes, congregate independent living, in-home care, adult day care and assisted living facilities.

Nursing homes were the starting point for the Pioneers because they showcase the devaluation of our elders and of those who care for them. Aware that 30 percent of elders would rather die than enter a nursing home, the Pioneers seek to change conventional nursing home culture. The group would like to reorganize traditional nursing home structure so that medical and nursing care support — rather than dominate — residents' daily routines. The Pioneers propose:

● Moving away from a hospital-based model of care where routines are inflexible and staff dictate when to get up, sleep, eat, bathe and dress;

● Creating a homelike environment and a "resident first" philosophy;

- Viewing residents in terms of their strengths and individuality rather than their illnesses and problems;

- Restoring a sense of control to residents and those closest to them, the certified nursing assistants.

To order publications, be on the mailing list, access speakers or learn of future Pioneer Network activities, call 585-271-7570 or go online to *www.PioneerNetwork.net.* You can also write to the Pioneer Network, PO. Box 18648, Rochester, NY 14618.[1]

Tax Implications

> The information provided in this chapter is based on rules and regulations which are in final revision with the Department of the Treasury and the Internal Revenue Service. Please be sure to review the rules and regulations regarding your particular situation with your CPA or tax advisor for actual application to your situation.

If you obtain a long-term care policy through your employer, whether the employer pays for it or you do, or if the cost is shared, there are serious tax implications you should understand. If you have a "tax-qualified" policy, the amount your employer pays in premiums is not reported as taxable income on your income tax return. (It may be deductible for your employer.) If you pay the full or partial cost of premiums, then the portion you pay is tax-deductible for you under certain rules and categories we will see later in this chapter.

Ordinarily, the employer deducts the premium amount from your paycheck before deducting taxes, so the premiums are paid with "before-tax" income. You cannot then take a deduction for the amount of your premiums on your tax return, since you have not paid taxes on the money used for the premiums in the first place.

Policies Purchased Before 1997

In 1996, Congress passed the Health Insurance Portability and Accountability Act (HIPAA) to clarify some of the issues of health care coverage and taxation of benefits. HIPAA mandated that policies purchased and issued before January 1, 1997, would be "grandfathered" (covered by HIPAA) so benefits would be paid out tax-free to the insured.

The Act also changed the way insured individuals would qualify for benefits under policies issued after January 1, 1997, in order to qualify for tax benefits.

Most of the pre-1997 policies required three "eligibility benefit triggers" (any one trigger qualified the insured) to qualify for benefits. The table (Figure 9-1) on the following page shows how HIPAA changed that requirement, making it more difficult to qualify for benefits with the newer policies (Tax-Qualified after 1/1/97). The number of Activities of Daily Living (ADLs) was changed from seven to six, dropping "ambulation," the first activity in which people are most likely to need assistance.

It is still possible to obtain non-tax-qualified policies (issued after 1/1/97), but the IRS and the United States Treasury have declined to state their positions on the tax status of benefits paid under the non-qualified policies. It is therefore imperative that you seek professional advice on this topic. A page available on our website (*www.longtermcarebooks.com*) called Tax Regulations Affecting Long-Term Care Policies provides information your financial advisor may wish to review in order to evaluate this issue.

Eligibility Benefit Triggers for LTC Policies

Policies written prior to 1/1/97	HIPAA Act of 1996
Medical Necessity – a physician determines the person needs to go to a nursing home	Medical necessity no longer qualifies as a condition for accessing benefits
Cognitive Impairment – physician's determination	Proof of **severe** cognitive impairment or need for **substantial supervision**
The inability to perform **two of seven** **Activities of Daily Living (ADLs)**	Inability to perform **two out of six, or three out of six** depending on the insurance company

There are situations where non-tax-qualified policies are appropriate. Be sure to have your advisor explain the differences with the new regulations. Some insurance companies allow their clients to switch from a non-qualified to a tax-qualified policy to best meet their needs when a claim is imminent. As an example from one company's stated policy, *"I do hereby understand, acknowledge, and declare the following: . . . That I may exchange any long-term care policy issued by . . . Insurance Company in response to my application with the other policy type (whether it be exchanging a non-qualified policy to a tax-qualified policy or a tax-qualified policy for a non-qualified policy) without any increase in premium at any time after the effective date of the policy by making a written request for such exchange."*

Figure 9-2 shows the deduction allowed if you itemize on Schedule A of your tax return. When considering the purchase of a tax-qualified policy, it is important to understand how the actual deduction for the long-term care premium is calculated. In the case of most tax-qualified policies in 2007, IRS regulations stated that for a person age 40 or under, the premiums that are eligible for medical expense deduction on Schedule A of the tax return total $290.

Long-Term Care Premium Deductions*

Attained Age Before Close of Tax Year	Tax Year Ending in 2006	Tax Year Ending in 2007
40 or under	$ 280	$ 290
41 - 50	$ 530	$ 550
51 - 60	$ 1,060	$ 1,110
61 - 70	$ 2,830	$ 2,950
71 and older	$ 3,530	$ 3,680

*These amounts are adjusted yearly for inflation.

The amount of the deduction listed above is not the amount that you get to deduct from your tax return. This is simply the amount that is added to your Schedule A eligible medical expenses that exceed 7-1/2% of adjusted gross income. Only 4% of all eligible seniors over 65 itemize their expenses on Schedule A. The other 96 percent file a simple E-2 income tax return, so the deduction for this coverage is not a tax benefit for 96 percent of all seniors purchasing long-term care insurance. For people under 65 the amount of the deduction is relatively small. When calculated with the normal amount of medical expenses that most people under 65 have, the likelihood of seeing this benefit as a real tax deduction is remote.

Consider this example: Judy, age 71, was a CPA for many years. Prior to retiring, she had an annual gross income of $35,000. In order to save taxes on the purchase of a long-term care policy, her deduction for medical and long-term care expenses must exceed $2,625 (7.5 percent of the $35,000 income). She pays $5,000 a year for her tax-qualified LTC premium, but only the $3,530 maximum deductible (changes yearly) for 2006 can be taken as a tax deduction. She also has unreimbursed medical expenses of $200 for eyeglasses. Adding $3,530 for the premium deduction allowed and $200 for eyeglasses totals $3,730. That total exceeds her required 7.5 percent threshold by only $1,105. Since her income tax rate is 28%, these deductions save her $309.40 ($1,105 times 28%).

A $309.40 saving is roughly 6% of her premium with the expense of the eyeglasses. Her tax-qualified LTC policy would have saved her **6%** of the maximum premium deduction of $3,530.

Judy might have been better advised to have a non-tax qualified policy, which offers benefits that are more generous and easier to access. After all, access to the benefits is the reason to buy insurance in the first place.

Up to 100 percent of medical insurance costs paid by self-employed individuals, covering themselves, their spouse, and their dependents, may be deducted as an adjustment to income on Form 1040, U.S. Individual Income Tax Return. The deduction is subtracted directly from total income and applies whether or not a taxpayer itemizes.[1]

You may be able to deduct 100% of the amount paid for medical and dental insurance and qualified long-term care insurance for you, your spouse, and your dependents if you are one of the following.

- A self-employed individual with a net profit reported on Schedule C, C-EZ, or F.
- A partner with net earnings from self-employment reported on Schedule K-1 (Form 1065), box 14, code A.
- A shareholder owning more than 2% of the outstanding stock of an S corporation with wages from the corporation reported on Form W-2.[2]

Figure 9-3

2007 TAX IMPLICATIONS FOR THE SELF-EMPLOYED	
Beginning in Calendar Year	**Deductible**
2007	100%

A Sampling of Income Tax Incentives By State

Alabama (Deduction) .... A deduction is allowed for the amount of premiums paid pursuant to a qualifying insurance contract for qualified LTC coverage.

Colorado (Credit) .... A credit is allowed in taxable years on or after 01/01/2000, for 25 percent of premiums paid for LTC insurance or $150.00 per policy. The credit will be available to only individual taxpayers with taxable income of less than $50,000 or two individuals filing a joint return with taxable income of less than $100,000.

Indiana (Deduction) .... For tax years beginning on or after 01/01/2000, an individual taxpayer is permitted to deduct an amount equal to the eligible portion of premiums paid during the taxable year by the taxpayer for a qualified LTC policy (as defined in the Indiana Code, for the taxpayer, the taxpayer's spouse, or both FOR QUALIFIED PARTNERSHIP POLICIES ONLY.

Kentucky (Exclusion).................. Exclusion for tax years beginning on or after 01/01/1999, a taxpayer may exclude from Kentucky Adjusted Gross Income any amounts paid for LTC insurance as defined in the Kentucky code.

Minnesota (Credit) .... For tax years beginning on or after 01/01/1999 a credit is allowed for LTC insurance premiums during the taxable year equal to (1) 25% of premiums paid to the extent not deducted in determining federal taxable income; or, (2) $100. Maximum allowable credit per year is $200 for couples filing jointly and $100 for all other filers.

New York (Credit) .... A credit is allowed equal to 20% of the premium paid during the taxable year for LTC insurance approved by the Superintendent of Insurance provided policy qualifies for such credit pursuant to Section 1117. If the amount of credit allowable under this subsection for any taxable year shall exceed the taxpayer's tax for such year, the excess may be carried over to the following year or years and may be deducted from the taxpayer's tax for such year or years and applies to taxable years beginning on or after 01/01/2004.

Ohio (Deduction) .... A deduction is allowed for individual policy premiums paid for qualified LTC insurance effective for taxable years beginning 01/01/1999. Generally allows a deduction for the amount paid for qualified LTC insurance for the taxpayer, his spouse, and dependents.

Wisconsin (Deduction) .... Allows a person to subtract from federal adjusted gross income a portion of the amount paid for an LTC insurance policy for taxpayer and spouse when computing Wisconsin taxable income beginning on or after 01/01/1998.

Source: *"State Tax Incentives for Long-Term Care Insurance." Copyright 2004 (Updated 8/29/05). American Council of Life Insurers, 101 Constitution Avenue, NW, Washington, DC 20001-2133. All rights reserved.*

Why Does It Matter?

In the world of tax and medical planning, one more important issue that is frequently ignored or misunderstood is ensuring that your IRA (Individual Retirement Account) or your Qualified Plan (such as a pension plan, profit-sharing plan, and/or a 401[k] plan) is properly protected and insured against depletion by medical and long-term care expenses. These expenses can extinguish an entire asset or assets of your estate in as short a time as one to three years. We try to provide our clients with extensive investment and insurance planning in this area to protect them from the potential loss of the valued accounts that they have built up over a lifetime. Thus, we are providing structures that preserve the account for the insured owner, or for future generations, if the assets are not needed by the owner.

As we move through this chapter we will provide visual, as well as written, examples to give you an idea of how these structures can be created to meet your particular objectives. We use actual case examples of clients of our firm, who have done this in the past, and continue to take advantage of the tax code, and the insurance rules and regulations that apply to proper structuring of these kinds of investment and insurance plans.

We will start by explaining the concept of insuring your IRA account. Then we will move into coupling life and long-term care coverages. From there, we will move on to charitable remainder trust strategies and other planning alternatives. Finally, we provide corporate strategies that, in the context of business planning, use C corporations, S corporations, and/or limited liability companies (LLCs), and also partnerships.

Long-Term Care for Your IRA

Insuring Your IRA

There are many ways to prevent the loss of the future purchasing power of an IRA, which is one of the most valuable assets for many Americans. One of the ways to protect an account is to purchase a long-term care (LTC) insurance policy to protect the IRA from loss due to the cost of long-term care. A yearly withdrawal from the IRA to pay for a long-term care insurance policy could protect the account holder and the beneficiaries should an LTC event occur. The cost of the policy will determine the amount of the withdrawal each year, but could insure and protect an IRA account from costs of $150,000 – $200,000 a year for a typical nursing home (*see Figure 10-1*).

The long-term care policy could provide tax-deductible protection for all forms of nursing home and/or home health care needs, and any other forms of services, such as assisted living facility care, that a person may need at any time. A policy for the spouse as additional protection is also highly recommended.

Coupling Life and Long-Term Care Coverage

The same solution can be provided by a life insurance contract with a long-term care rider. A long-

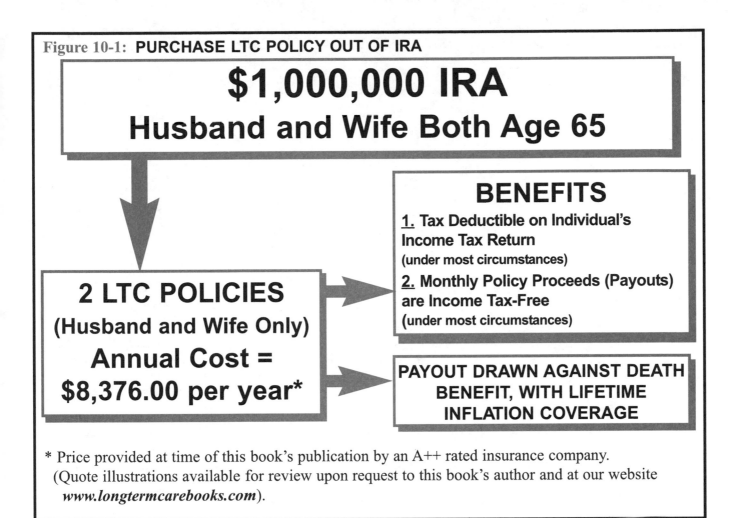

Figure 10-1: PURCHASE LTC POLICY OUT OF IRA

$1,000,000 IRA
Husband and Wife Both Age 65

2 LTC POLICIES
(Husband and Wife Only)
Annual Cost =
$8,376.00 per year*

BENEFITS

1. **Tax Deductible on Individual's Income Tax Return**
(under most circumstances)

2. **Monthly Policy Proceeds (Payouts) are Income Tax-Free**
(under most circumstances)

PAYOUT DRAWN AGAINST DEATH BENEFIT, WITH LIFETIME INFLATION COVERAGE

* Price provided at time of this book's publication by an A++ rated insurance company.
  (Quote illustrations available for review upon request to this book's author and at our website
  www.longtermcarebooks.com).

term care rider provides flexibility in paying monthly expenses using the death benefit of the policy. It also allows the insured to extend the benefits for a significant period of time, up to the limits of the policy (using only what is needed). Depending on the insured's age and the company used, a life insurance policy could be purchased providing $1,000,000 of death benefit and a long-term care rider that could be twice the death benefit. In other words, the long-term care rider could be set at 200% of the death benefit.

Example: John buys a life insurance policy with a $1,000,000 death benefit and a long-term care rider. The rider pays out a maximum of actual expenses each month or 2% of the death benefit ($20,000) if monthly expenses exceed $20,000. The long-term care rider is set at 200% of the death benefit ($2,000,000). The payments received for long-term care expenses would be income tax-free. If John then died after receiving a portion of the LTC benefits, the balance would be paid as a death benefit to the named beneficiary or his estate. Up to $1,000,000 of combined LTC / death benefit would be paid. If John exceeds $1,000,000 in long-term care expenses, then only long-term care benefits continue to pay out, up to $2,000,000, during John's life (*see Figure 10-2*).

Another alternative is to purchase a life insurance policy with an accelerated benefit rider (ABR). Normally the rider will pay out to an insured with a terminal illness and a one-year life expectancy, but some policies have up to five years' life expectancy. The policy would provide up to one-half of the death benefit (DB) to be paid to the insured in a lump sum, or over a very short period of time. The funds could be utilized for various items, such as emergency surgery, taking a trip around the world, paying off old bills and debts before the insured dies, etc. (*see Figure 10-3*).

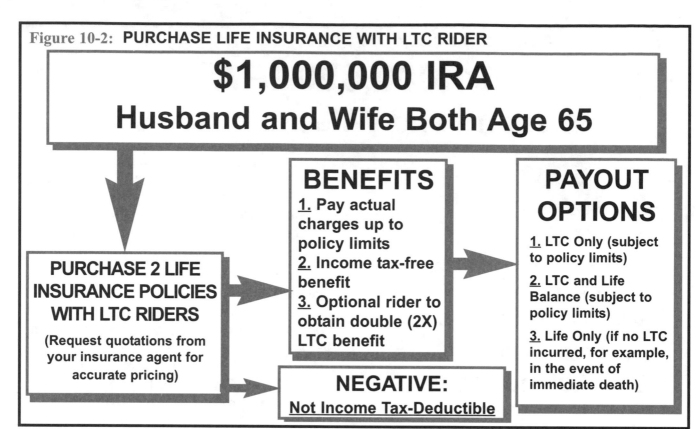

Figure 10-2: PURCHASE LIFE INSURANCE WITH LTC RIDER

$1,000,000 IRA
Husband and Wife Both Age 65

PURCHASE 2 LIFE INSURANCE POLICIES WITH LTC RIDERS

(Request quotations from your insurance agent for accurate pricing)

BENEFITS

1. Pay actual charges up to policy limits
2. Income tax-free benefit
3. Optional rider to obtain double (2X) LTC benefit

PAYOUT OPTIONS

1. LTC Only (subject to policy limits)
2. LTC and Life Balance (subject to policy limits)
3. Life Only (if no LTC incurred, for example, in the event of immediate death)

NEGATIVE:
Not Income Tax-Deductible

(View Online at www.longtermcarebooks.com)

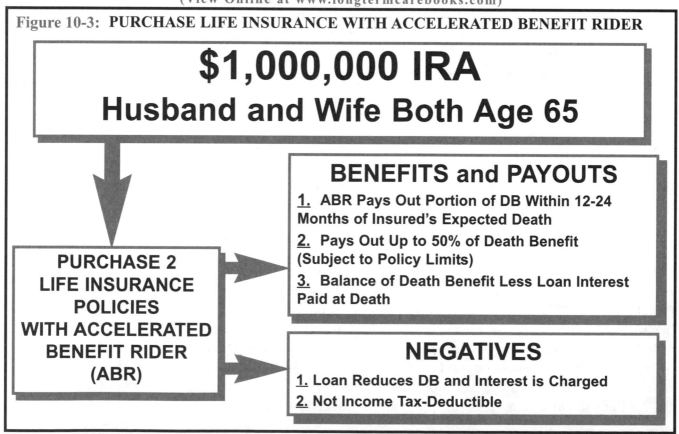

Figure 10-3: PURCHASE LIFE INSURANCE WITH ACCELERATED BENEFIT RIDER

$1,000,000 IRA
Husband and Wife Both Age 65

PURCHASE 2 LIFE INSURANCE POLICIES WITH ACCELERATED BENEFIT RIDER (ABR)

BENEFITS and PAYOUTS

1. ABR Pays Out Portion of DB Within 12-24 Months of Insured's Expected Death
2. Pays Out Up to 50% of Death Benefit (Subject to Policy Limits)
3. Balance of Death Benefit Less Loan Interest Paid at Death

NEGATIVES

1. Loan Reduces DB and Interest is Charged
2. Not Income Tax-Deductible

Placing Life Insurance Outside of the Estate

The life insurance contract can be placed outside of the individual's estate with ownership held by children or other beneficiaries. By setting ownership up in this manner, estate tax would be elimi-

OWNERSHIP ALTERNATIVES

$1,000,000 IRA
Husband and Wife Both Age 65

PURCHASE 2 LIFE INSURANCE POLICIES WITH LTC

(Request quotations from your insurance agent for accurate pricing)

ILIT OWNS

Benefits:
1. Goes To Named Beneficiary
2. May Pay LTC For You

Negatives:
1. May Not Pay LTC (Trustee's Discretion)
2. Tax Consequences (Get Legal Advice)

KIDS OWN

Benefit: No Estate Tax

Negatives:
1. Children Could Go Broke
2. Children Might Divorce
3. Children Could Be Spendthrift(s)
4. Children Could Lose Lawsuit
5. Children May Not Pay LTC
6. Children Could Die First

nated on the policy if the insured died from an immediate event, such as a heart attack. There is a negative side to this arrangement. The beneficiaries, who own the policy, have access to the policy cash values, which could be a problem if they were irresponsible or experience financial difficulties themselves (*see Figure 10-4*).

Another way to place the life insurance outside of the individual's estate is to have the policy owned by an irrevocable life insurance trust (ILIT). Technically the life insurance is not owned by you or your family but by the trustee of the trust, and the trustee determines whether taking money out for long-term care expenses is justified. There is a risk that the IRS may recast the transaction if funds are used for your own benefit. For example, if funds are distributed from the trust to pay for LTC expenses, this could be viewed as an uncompleted gift. The entire policy could be included in your estate, since the gift was not given away entirely. Legal advice is highly recommended regarding these issues before deciding which solution is most suitable for an individual (*see Figure 10-4*).

Figure 10-5: **CHARITABLE REMAINDER TRUST (SCENARIO #1)**

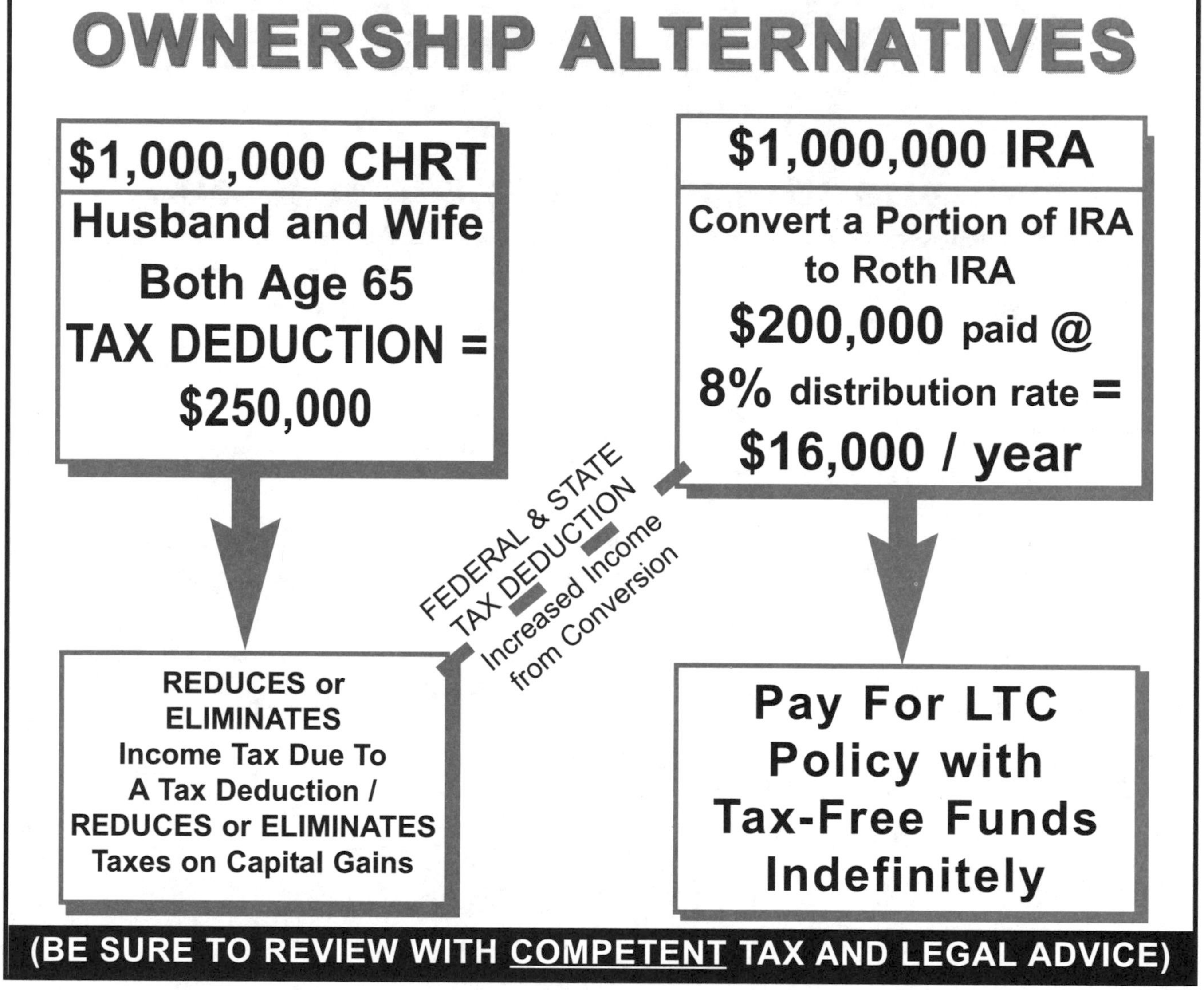

OWNERSHIP ALTERNATIVES

$1,000,000 CHRT

Husband and Wife
Both Age 65
TAX DEDUCTION =
$250,000

$1,000,000 IRA

Convert a Portion of IRA
to Roth IRA
$200,000 paid @
8% distribution rate =
$16,000 / year

FEDERAL & STATE TAX DEDUCTION
Increased Income from Conversion

REDUCES or ELIMINATES
Income Tax Due To
A Tax Deduction /
REDUCES or ELIMINATES
Taxes on Capital Gains

Pay For LTC Policy with Tax-Free Funds Indefinitely

(BE SURE TO REVIEW WITH <u>COMPETENT</u> TAX AND LEGAL ADVICE)

Charitable Remainder Trust Strategy

If you hold highly appreciated assets (real estate, stocks, etc.) you want to protect, and you plan to convert a traditional IRA to Roth IRA, then a charitable remainder trust might be considered. Utilizing a charitable remainder trust (CRT) could provide tax deductions to offset the conversion of the IRA. An appreciated asset worth $1,000,000, that originally was purchased for $100,000 could provide such a solution. The appreciated asset must be placed inside the charitable remainder trust *before* being sold, to properly avoid capital gains tax and recovery of depreciation (if applicable). This would provide a current income tax deduction for the property gifted to the trust. The amount of the deduction would vary, based on the age of the income beneficiary of the charitable remainder trust, whether more than one person was to be an income beneficiary of the trust, and the annual payout percentage of the trust. The income tax deduction can be used in the first year (and for up to five years thereafter) after the creation of the charitable trust (*see Figures 10-5 and 10-6*).

> ...a charitable remainder trust can provide funding for two generations...

In addition, a charitable remainder trust can provide funding for two generations, such as a husband

Figure 10-6: **CHARITABLE REMAINDER TRUST (SCENARIO #2)**

OWNERSHIP ALTERNATIVES

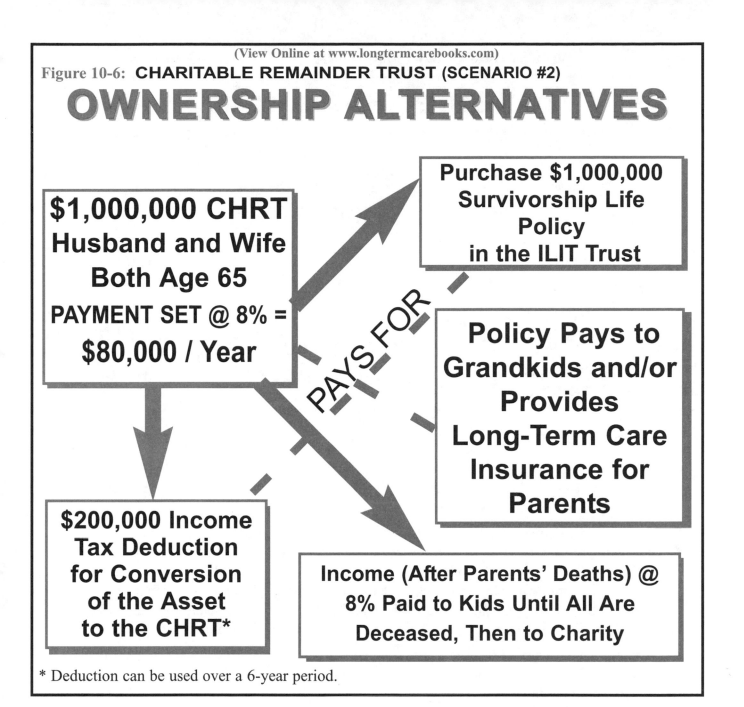

$1,000,000 CHRT
Husband and Wife
Both Age 65
PAYMENT SET @ 8% =
$80,000 / Year

Purchase $1,000,000 Survivorship Life Policy in the ILIT Trust

PAYS FOR

Policy Pays to Grandkids and/or Provides Long-Term Care Insurance for Parents

$200,000 Income Tax Deduction for Conversion of the Asset to the CHRT*

Income (After Parents' Deaths) @ 8% Paid to Kids Until All Are Deceased, Then to Charity

* Deduction can be used over a 6-year period.

and wife, as well as children (*see Figure 10-6*). The trust would stay in existence until all of the family members had died, and would make payouts over all those years. As the last person dies, which could be 50 to 80 years after the original trust was created, the corpus** is then transferred to the charities named in the original document. Because of the income tax deduction it might be possible to have life insurance purchased on the parents or the children (depending on insurability). The death benefits could be payable to grandchildren to replace the gifted asset in the future. The life insurance could be purchased, in full or in part, with the income tax savings realized in creating the charitable trust.

More Planning Alternatives

- Insuring the IRA could be completed by doing a partial Roth conversion of the IRA account, if the account owner qualifies. As an example, after paying the income tax on a partial conversion of an IRA to a Roth IRA, the account owner can take income tax-free

** corpus defined: *capital, as contrasted with the income derived from it*

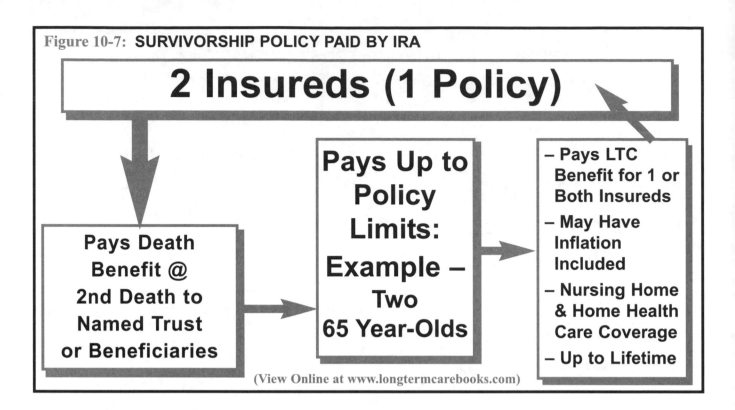

Figure 10-7: SURVIVORSHIP POLICY PAID BY IRA

2 Insureds (1 Policy)

Pays Death Benefit @ 2nd Death to Named Trust or Beneficiaries

Pays Up to Policy Limits: Example – Two 65 Year-Olds

– Pays LTC Benefit for 1 or Both Insureds

– May Have Inflation Included

– Nursing Home & Home Health Care Coverage

– Up to Lifetime

(View Online at www.longtermcarebooks.com)

distributions from the Roth IRA as needed (if he is over the age of 59½ and the account has been open for five years) to pay for the policy(ies) chosen. The balance could remain in the traditional IRA account, or it could also be partially or completely transferred into a Roth IRA, as desired (*see Figure 10-5*).

● Annuities are commonly used investments for the funds in an IRA account. Some annuity products offer a long-term care benefit as an optional rider. Annuities may also have additional income riders, or estate tax riders that would automatically increase the value of the annuity at death. An increase in the value of the contract at death by as much as 50% could be used to recover LTC expenses previously paid for an otherwise uninsurable account holder. However, distributions from an IRA annuity will be subject to income tax.

● Another solution would be to take small payouts from other low tax or non-tax type investments, such as tax-free bonds or annuities. An annuity contract would create a stream of payments (annuitize the contract over a number of years) to minimize income tax consequences (due to the exclusion ratio that might apply). Long-term care policies that could protect the IRA account could then be purchased with those payments.

● Another alternative would be to use a second-to-die life insurance product, also known as a survivorship policy, by having payments made by the IRA account, as mentioned previously. The second-to-die policy could have long-term care benefits as an additional benefit for both insureds. The second-to-die policy could provide life insurance, and also up to lifetime LTC coverage for both insureds. This is especially attractive for people who have widely different ages with different LTC needs in the future. This type of insurance is also available for business insurance needs and domestic partner relationships (*see Figure 10-7*).

Corporate Strategies

Another way to protect an IRA/qualified plan account is to provide LTC insurance benefits through a corporation for the owner or executive of the business. A standard C corporation allows

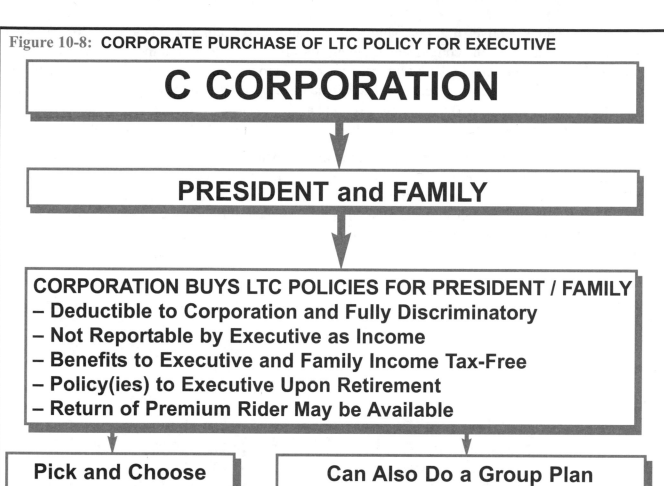

Figure 10-8: CORPORATE PURCHASE OF LTC POLICY FOR EXECUTIVE

C CORPORATION

PRESIDENT and FAMILY

CORPORATION BUYS LTC POLICIES FOR PRESIDENT / FAMILY
– Deductible to Corporation and Fully Discriminatory
– Not Reportable by Executive as Income
– Benefits to Executive and Family Income Tax-Free
– Policy(ies) to Executive Upon Retirement
– Return of Premium Rider May be Available

Pick and Choose Other Executives
– Same Benefits As Above

Can Also Do a Group Plan For All Employees (or Selected Group)
– Same Benefits As Above

(View Online at www.longtermcarebooks.com)

> ...the president of the company could be the only employee to have a long-term care policy completely paid for by the corporation.

for payments for individuals on a discriminatory basis. In other words, the president of the company could be the only employee to have a long-term care policy completely paid for by the corporation. There would be no income tax liability to the president personally. There would be a 100% tax deduction to the corporation for the purchase of the policy, and there would be no taxable effect upon the benefits when paid out to the insured. The president of the company, his/her spouse, and other family members can also be provided benefits on a fully discriminatory basis (*see Figure 10-8*). There would be true tax efficiency at all three levels: the corporation, the insured, and the benefits paid out of an LTC policy. (This will also work with a life insurance policy with an LTC rider, *but there is no deduction for premiums paid*.)

A corporation could also provide a deferred compensation plan to reduce current income of the executive and build up value in the plan that could be used to fund future long-term care needs when the executive is retired from the company. Policies can also be paid for by the corporation as a single payment, or over a five-year or ten-year period. Some policies also have a return-of-premium rider that can be beneficial.

Many highly paid executives find their ability to contribute maximum amounts to their 401(k) accounts are reduced due to the complicated funding rules for all employees in the plan. These excess funds could be used to purchase a long-term care rider, again to protect the assets in qualified plans in place for these executives. In many cases the LTC benefits can be provided on a guaranteed issue basis (no underwriting or qualification) as part of a group plan provided by the employer. The executive would take the policy upon retirement or separation from the corporation at no income tax cost.

Welfare benefit trusts can also be created as an employee benefit within a corporation to provide post-retirement benefits. These benefits can include medical, long-term care, and critical illness coverage. Benefits are provided by the trust after the employee retires from the company. A tax deduction can be taken by the company currently to offset that actual expense in the future. These can be very attractive for highly compensated individuals who are concerned about ways to reduce their income taxation, and to provide significant necessary benefits in the future when retired.

Long-term care and life insurance planning are an important part of an individual's financial, retirement and estate plans. Careful consideration must be given to the needs and goals of the individual.[1]

BE SURE TO SEEK COMPETENT TAX AND LEGAL COUNSEL FOR ALL THESE CONCEPTS AND PROGRAMS TO BE SURE THEY MEET YOUR SPECIFIC NEEDS AS WELL AS LOCAL LAWS, RULES AND REGULATIONS.

11 Proper IRA Distribution Planning

Making Sure Your Heirs Get Your IRA

Now that you know how to protect the value of your IRA (Chapter 10), you may want to pass it on to your children, grandchildren or other heirs after your death. How can you make sure that your hard-earned, well-planned IRA won't be eaten up by inheritance and income taxes?

Losing Out on the Stretch

Inherited IRAs don't work like regular IRAs. So don't assume that rules governing the IRAs you own would apply to any that you inherit.

For example, if you inherit an IRA from anyone other than your husband or wife, you cannot, under any circumstance, roll it into your own IRA. You also cannot withdraw the assets from an inherited account and then deposit them into a new IRA. You cannot consolidate IRAs you inherit from different people into one account.

Inherited IRA Basis

In an IRA, making nondeductible IRA contributions creates basis (the amount of nondeductible IRA contributions made). If the person you inherited the IRA from had basis, you inherit that basis in the IRA. When you withdraw basis, there is no tax because no deduction was ever taken. Most beneficiaries do not know to ask if basis was even created. If you are an IRA beneficiary and taking distributions from an inherited IRA, you should learn if some of those distributions may be tax-free. To find out, you'll have to know if the person you inherited from ever made any nondeductible IRA contributions. You can discover that by looking for Form 8606 (Nondeductible IRAs) attached to any of his or her income tax returns. Form 8606 shows the basis.

If there is basis, then as you withdraw from the inherited IRA, that portion of the withdrawal that is a return of the basis is tax-free, the same as it would have been for the person who created the IRA you inherited. It is rare that even a professional tax preparer thinks to ask if there were any nondeductible IRA contributions made by the person from whom you inherited the IRA. That is why you'll have to find out for yourself.

If no Form 8606 is found, it does not automatically mean that no nondeductible IRA contributions were made. It may mean that the form was never filed. Nondeductible IRA contributions began in 1987, so do not bother checking returns for years prior to 1987.[1]

IRAs that you inherit have one important thing in common with the ones you hold yourself: You can stretch out the withdrawals across your lifetime, rather than taking them as a lump sum. That gives you a chance to postpone the tax bite and lengthen the time that tax-free earnings can accrue, possibly increasing your inheritance by thousands of dollars.

Unfortunately, few heirs realize that's even an option. Until 2001, when the IRS proposed new IRA rules that became final the following year, most people – including all types of financial advisors – assumed that you had to cash out an inherited IRA within five years of the owner's death. That is because the government had made that option the default, as explained by Ed Slott (CPA and prominent expert on IRAs). But the new rules make it easier to stretch those withdrawals across your life expectancy. Even if you successfully get the money into your own account, it's important to recognize the unique way you must withdraw it.

With your own IRA, you have to start taking minimum withdrawals by April 1 of the year after you turn $70\frac{1}{2}$. You determine the minimum amount each year by looking up your life expectancy in the appropriate table and then dividing your prior year-end account balance by that number. (The tables are at *www.irs.gov* in Publication 590 [page 76 of the 2005 edition] or *see Figure 11-6* on page 94 of this book. Make sure any advisor you consult is using the current numbers.)

With an inherited IRA, you first need to re-title the IRA. If you are the primary beneficiary, do the following if you are not disclaiming the IRA:

1. Change the Social Security number on the account to your own Social Security number;

2. Change the account title with the name of the deceased account owner remaining in the account title [*e.g.*, John Smith, deceased, IRA fbo Charles Smith]; and,

3. Name a successor beneficiary (if the account document allows).[2]

The decedent's name <u>must</u> remain on the account. Re-titling helps make clear that the owner died and you are the beneficiary. After doing that, you would look up your life expectancy one time. Each year, you simply subtract a year from your initial life expectancy to figure out how much to withdraw.

What are the distribution options allowed by the custodian? Did the account owner die before or after the required beginning date (RBD)? If the primary beneficiary is a non-designated beneficiary (any beneficiary for whom a life expectancy cannot be determined, such as non-qualified trusts, charities, and the decedent's estate), there are only two payout options (*see Figure 11-1*):

1. If the death occurs before the RBD, the only option is a five-year payout. The account must be emptied by the end of the fifth year after the account owner's death. There are no required annual distributions; or

2. If the death occurs after the RBD, distributions can be stretched over the remaining life expectancy of the account owner, or the beneficiary, whoever is younger (*see Figure 11-1*).[3]

If you inherit an IRA along with other heirs (the custodial documents will list all heirs), typically your siblings, you can split up the account, allowing each heir to spread withdrawals across his or her own life expectancy. Otherwise, you get stuck using the life expectancy of the oldest heir.[4]

Steve, Debra and Victoria

Consider the case of Steve and Debra, a married couple. Steve had accumulated a balance of $100,000 in his Roth IRA by age 50 (assume an 8% rate of return [ROR]). Steve lives to age 85, then dies in 2040. He leaves his Roth IRA to Debra. Debra in turn dies in 2050 at age 92. Debra has arranged for their granddaughter, Victoria, born in the year Debra dies, to inherit the balance of the Roth IRA. Victoria begins receiving Required Minimum Distributions (RMDs) in 2051, when she turns 1 year old. (A guardian would actually take these distributions, or they would be received by a trust set up for her benefit.)

At this point the Roth IRA is worth $3,447,436! If Victoria receives only the RMDs for her full 81.6-year life expectancy, she will have withdrawn $281,570,832, *income tax-free*, by the end of 82

Figure 11-1: INHERITED IRA PAYOUTS – NON-SPOUSE BENEFICIARY

	Account Owner Dies Before RBD	Account Owner Dies After RBD
Non-spouse, Designated Beneficiary	Distributions based on the life expectancy of the beneficiary. Use **Single Life Expectancy Table**, look up attained age in the year after the account owner's death to get factor. Factor is **reduced by one in each subsequent year**.	Distributions based on the life expectancy of the **younger** of the account owner or the beneficiary. Use **Single Life Expectancy Table**, look up attained age in the year after the account owner's death to get factor. Factor is **reduced by one in each subsequent year**.
Non-designated Beneficiary	**5-Year Rule** No annual required distributions but account must be emptied by the end of the fifth year after the year of the account owner's death.	Distributions based on the life expectancy of the **deceased account owner**. Use **Single Life Expectancy Table**, look up attained age account owner would have been in the year of death to get factor. Factor is **reduced by one in each subsequent year**.

The above is a synopsis of options allowed by the IRS final distribution regulations. All distribution options are subject to the terms of the custodian's IRA agreement in effect at the time of the distribution. The 10% early distribution penalty never applies to beneficiaries taking distributions. All beneficiaries generally have the option of taking a lump-sum distribution and paying income tax on the distribution or choosing to use the 5-Year Rule. Roth IRA beneficiaries use the Owner Dies Before RBD rules. *(Source: Slott, Ed.* Ed Slott's Elite IRA Advisor Group, Workshop 3, January 13-15, 2006. *Rockville Centre, NY. Copyright © 2006 Ed Slott, CPA. Page 11 of 13.)*

(View Online at www.longtermcarebooks.com)

years (the "stretch" period). She could buy a small country at that point and name it after her grandpa, Steve, who made it all possible!

You, too, can create this kind of benefit for your loved ones with what is commonly called a Stretch IRA. But there's one thing you _need_ to do first:

Make sure you designate a beneficiary for your IRA (and your pension, if you have one) separately from your will.

Why? Read on. (By the way, it's good practice to update your IRA forms every year, and give copies to other trusted individuals to hold. Above all, please don't leave them in your safe deposit box. It will be sealed at your death, and its contents won't be available for some time.)

Make Your Legacy Last

IRAs were designed to generate retirement income. However, many retirees will never spend their IRA assets in their lifetime if they are taking income from other sources. So they plan to leave them to their loved ones. The problem is that – while IRAs are ideal for retirement – they are poor wealth transfer tools. IRA beneficiaries will face income taxes on the assets. Taxes could be especially high for beneficiaries who are in their 30s, 40s and 50s – their peak earning years.

One way you can soften the tax blow for your loved ones is to help them plan a "stretch" IRA. That way your beneficiaries can take their payments a little at a time, which can help them keep their income tax bracket in check. More importantly, it gives the remaining IRA assets even more time for long-term growth and compounding.

Important Considerations for Stretch IRAs

Will you need the money during your retirement?

Americans are living longer than ever before and life expectancies are rising. Using your IRA assets during your retirement will, of course, reduce the amount that passes to your loved ones.

Will your intermediate IRA beneficiaries need the money?

If beneficiaries need to pay estate taxes on part of their inheritance, or have other expenses to pay, they may need to take the asset as a lump sum, thus ending the "stretch." Plan to discuss your intention to provide a stretch opportunity with your beneficiaries, and also your advisors, to better understand the alternatives.

Will you take the smallest amount possible from your IRA?

Stretch IRAs tend to assume only the required minimum distributions are taken (although you are always free to take more). The smaller the distributions, the longer the IRA may last.

What will happen with tax laws, inflation, and market volatility?

As we all know, past results can never predict the future. Although they are beyond our control, your loved ones will certainly have to pay taxes, deal with inflation, and face significant market volatility. That's why it's so important to seek out financial strength and thoughtful stewardship for the long-term management of your money.[5]

Anne and Bruce Friedman

A story in the *New York Post*[6] on January 31, 2005, reported that when Brooklyn resident Bruce Friedman's wife, Anne, died, he assumed he would inherit her pension, then worth almost $1 million. Not so fast, said the court. Anne had never named Bruce as her beneficiary, although they had been married 20 years (and the annual statements she received from her pension fund indicated there was no beneficiary named). But she had named beneficiaries, several years before she even met Bruce – her mother, uncle and sister. Since her mother and uncle had died, her sister got it all, and Bruce got absolutely nothing. Zero.

If you can't remember who your beneficiary is, or you aren't sure you've named one, stop reading right here and pick up the phone to get a new beneficiary form and fix this. *Now.*

Naming No Beneficiary or the Wrong One

When it comes to your IRA, your will is irrelevant. The way an IRA gets passed along to your heirs is governed by the beneficiary form you are supposed to fill out when you open the account. It is a good idea to review those forms regularly and keep your own copy in an easy access spot because banks and brokerage firms can lose track of the paperwork over time. And make sure you fill out a beneficiary form when you inherit an IRA as well.

You may see a box on the forms to check for a "per stirpes" designation. That means the assets would go to your beneficiary's children if he or she dies before inheriting your IRA. "Per stirpes" is one designation for beneficiaries, the other is "per capita." Consider an example. A father has two children – Joe and Sue. Sue has four kids. Under per stirpes designation, Joe and Sue each get one half of the estate per stirpes. If Sue dies, Sue's children still get half of the assets from Dad. But if Sue was deceased and then Dad died and had used per capita, Joe and each of Sue's children get one-fifth apiece. If per stirpes is not indicated on the beneficiary form, the money will be distributed per capita.[7]

Another example would be to assume that Joe also had two children. Say Joe was driving his Dad to the airport, and both were killed in an accident. Under per capita distribution rules, Joe's children

---

Figure 11-2: INHERITED IRA PAYOUTS – SPOUSE AS SOLE BENEFICIARY

Spouse as Sole Beneficiary	Account Owner Dies *Before* RBD	Account Owner Dies *After* RBD
Remain as Beneficiary	**Spouse** uses **Single Life Expectancy Table** (*see Figure 11-5*) and looks up his/her attained age **each year** a distribution is required (recalculation) to get the life expectancy factor.	
	Spouse can delay taking distributions until account owner would have been 70½.	Spouse must take first distribution by 12/31 of the year after the account owner's death.
	Spouse is not subject to 10% early distribution penalty.	Spouse is not subject to 10% early distribution penalty.
Spousal Rollover	Spouse takes first distribution at his/her RBD or in year after account owner's death if spouse is over age 70½. **Spouse** uses **Uniform Lifetime Table** (*see Figure 11-6*) and looks up his/her attained age **each year** to get the life expectancy factor.	
Take Account as Own	Spouse takes first distribution at his/her RBD or in year after account owner's death if spouse is over age 70½. **Spouse** uses **Uniform Lifetime Table** and looks up his/her attained age **each year** to get the life expectancy factor.	

This graph is a synopsis of options allowed by the IRS final distribution regulations. All distribution options are subject to the terms of the plan agreement in effect at the time of the distribution. The 10% early distribution penalty never applies to beneficiaries taking distributions. All beneficiaries generally have the option of taking a lump-sum distribution and paying income tax on the distribution or choosing to use the 5-Year Rule. Roth IRA beneficiaries use the Owner Dies Before RBD rules. A spouse is considered the sole beneficiary of the plan when he or she is the only designated primary beneficiary on the account as of 12/31 of the year after the account owner's death.

(Source: Slott, Ed. Ed Slott's Elite IRA Advisor Group, Workshop 3, January 13-15, 2006. Rockville Centre, NY. © 2006 Ed Slott, CPA. Page 12 of 14.)

(View Online at www.longtermcarebooks.com)

Figure 11-3: INHERITED IRA PAYOUTS – SPOUSE AND OTHER BENEFICIARIES		
Spouse is NOT Sole Beneficiary	Account Owner Dies *Before* RBD	Account Owner Dies *After* RBD
Spouse Must Remain as Beneficiary	Use **Single Life Expectancy Table** (*see Figure 11-5*), look up his/her attained age in the year after account owner's death to get factor. Factor is reduced by one in each subsequent year. Spouse MUST take first distribution by 12/31 of the year after the account owner's death. Spouse is not subject to 10% early distribution penalty.	
(Source: Slott, Ed. Ed Slott's Elite IRA Advisor Group, Workshop 3, January 13-15, 2006. Rockville Centre, NY. Copyright © 2006 Ed Slott, CPA. Page 12 of 14.) **(View Online at www.longtermcarebooks.com)**		

would get nothing from Dad's estate. Sue would inherit 100% of the estate, and then the distribution at Sue's death would go to her four children. Nothing would go to Joe's children ever. Under a per stirpes designation, Joe and Sue would each inherit 50% of Dad's estate. Because Joe was deceased, his 50% share would go to his children based on his distribution designations prior to death. Sue would receive the other 50% for her benefit, and eventually the benefit of her children.

If you name no beneficiary, or you name your estate, your heirs lose the ability to stretch their withdrawals over their lifetimes, which means they would also lose out on the potential for decades of tax-free growth of your assets. In some cases, naming the estate as the beneficiary could even prevent your spouse from being able to roll the plan into his or her own IRA.[8]

Spouses are allowed to roll over inherited accounts into their own. A spouse should take some time to think through the best strategy for making such a move. You shouldn't do the rollover too fast, and you should keep in mind that you can do a partial rollover at any time. If you're the inheriting spouse, you don't have to do anything with the account until your spouse would have turned $70\frac{1}{2}$ years old. At that point you would have to start taking withdrawals. But if you're younger, you could roll the assets into your own IRA and let it sit there [or continue to grow] until you turn $70\frac{1}{2}$. Either way, when you roll the money into your own account you get to stretch those payments across your life expectancy.

And make sure you don't miss this tax break: You can deduct estate tax already paid on an IRA you inherit from your income tax bill. To do so, get the accountant who handled the estate tax return to calculate what part of the overall bill was due to the IRA (referred to as Income in Respect of a Decedent [IRD]). Then you can deduct that portion from your federal tax bill, offsetting the taxes on the IRA withdrawal you make for the same year.[9] After doing the IRD calculation, you can partially offset the income taxes due on the IRA distribution until the deduction is used up.

Income in Respect of a Decedent (IRD) Checklist

Use the list below to identify the amount of IRD in an estate. IRD is income earned by the decedent during his lifetime, but unpaid (owed to the decedent) at death. IRD items do NOT receive a step-up (increase in value) in basis, but beneficiaries who inherit any of these items may be able to claim an

IRD deduction as they collect the income. [*NOTE*: This is only a partial listing. For further details and assistance, contact the author of this book or speak with your financial advisor.] Examples of IRD might include:

- **Investment Income** such as interest income and interest from U.S. Savings Bonds;
- **Employee Compensation (post-death payments from employers)** such as regular wages, vacation pay;
- **Independent Contractor Income (sole proprietors, professionals, contractors, consultants, etc.)** such as receivables for services, partnership income, etc.;
- **Retirement and Pension Income** such as tax-deferred retirement plans, joint and survivor annuities;
- **Sales Activities** such as sale of a partnership interest, installment sales, etc.;
- **Proceeds of property sales owed to the decedent at death** such as stocks, bonds, mutual funds, land, buildings, equipment;
- **Other income owed to the decedent at death** such as legal claims, lawsuits, damages, alimony.[10]

Converting to a Roth IRA to Benefit Heirs

If you have a traditional IRA, but want your heirs to have a Roth IRA, you must make this conversion yourself. Your heirs are not allowed to do it. If you die and leave them a standard IRA, it's too late to convert it. But why would you make this conversion?

Since contributions to a Roth IRA have already been taxed, your beneficiaries will pay no income taxes when they inherit your Roth IRA. Non-spouse beneficiaries are obligated to take distributions from the account, but the distributions are not taxed. You, the original Roth IRA owner, may also continue making contributions to the account after age 70½ if you have income. You are not obligated to take distributions during your lifetime.

One more caution: If you don't take your annual distribution before you convert to a Roth, you may be double-taxed. Yes, this can be corrected, but why go down that road in the first place?

If you are the beneficiary of a Roth IRA, the following tax breaks apply (*also see Figure 11-4*):

1. If the account has been established for more than five years (counting the time the Roth IRA was held by the deceased IRA owner) then all distributions from the Roth are income tax-free.

2. If the account has been established for less than five years, then distributions of contributions and conversions are income tax-free. Distributions of earnings will be subject to income tax, but never a 10% penalty since the penalty never applies to beneficiaries.[11]

For Non-Spouse Beneficiaries

If you inherit a traditional IRA, you must start taking distributions in the first year after the account owner's death, based on your (the beneficiary's) life expectancy, not the original owner's. That's easy enough – unless you inherited the account jointly with another person. In that case, the distributions are based on the older beneficiary's life expectancy. What does that mean? It means that RMDs will be larger and paid out over a shorter time than if the younger beneficiary inherited alone. Of course, that also means the IRS will take a bigger bite in taxes on the distributions and you will enjoy less tax-deferred growth on the assets.

Figure 11-4 (View Online at www.longtermcarebooks.com)

SINGLE LIFE TABLE FOR INHERITED IRAs

Age = Age of IRA or Plan Beneficiary; Life = Life Expectancy (in years)

Age	Life	Age	Life	Age	Life	Age	Life	Age	Life	Age	Life	Age	Life
0	82.4	16	66.9	32	51.4	48	36.0	64	21.8	80	10.2	96	3.8
1	81.6	17	66.0	33	50.4	49	35.1	65	21.0	81	9.7	97	3.6
2	80.6	18	65.0	34	49.4	50	34.2	66	20.2	82	9.1	98	3.4
3	79.7	19	64.0	35	48.5	51	33.3	67	19.4	83	8.6	99	3.1
4	78.7	20	63.0	36	47.5	52	32.3	68	18.6	84	8.1	100	2.9
5	77.7	21	62.1	37	46.5	53	31.4	69	17.8	85	7.6	101	2.7
6	76.7	22	61.1	38	45.6	54	30.5	70	17.0	86	7.1	102	2.5
7	75.8	23	60.1	39	44.6	55	29.6	71	16.3	87	6.7	103	2.3
8	74.8	24	59.1	40	43.6	56	28.7	72	15.5	88	6.3	104	2.1
9	73.8	25	58.2	41	42.7	57	27.9	73	14.8	89	5.9	105	1.9
10	72.8	26	57.2	42	41.7	58	27.0	74	14.1	90	5.5	106	1.7
11	71.8	27	56.2	43	40.7	59	26.1	75	13.4	91	5.2	107	1.5
12	70.8	28	55.3	44	39.8	60	25.2	76	12.7	92	4.9	108	1.4
13	69.9	29	54.3	45	38.8	61	24.4	77	12.1	93	4.6	109	1.2
14	68.9	30	53.3	46	37.9	62	23.5	78	11.4	94	4.3	110	1.1
15	67.9	31	52.4	47	37.0	63	22.7	79	10.8	95	4.1	111+	1.0

This table will be used by every designated beneficiary to calculate post-death required distributions. It will never be used by IRA owners or plan participants to calculate lifetime required distributions. This is a recalculating table, but only a spouse beneficiary who is the sole beneficiary can go back to the table each year and recalculate life expectancy. A non-spouse beneficiary cannot recalculate and would only use this table to compute the first year's required distribution for the inherited IRA. The life expectancy will then be reduced by one year for each succeeding year. **Under the Final Regulations (issued by IRS in April 2002), this table will also be used by designated beneficiaries to change the distribution schedule by reconstructing life expectancy factors from prior years.** *(Source: Ed Slott's IRA Advisor, 2003.)*

It's even worse if you are a joint beneficiary with a charity. Since only living persons (not organizations) have life expectancies under the law, the charity has a life expectancy of zero. Yes, zero. Can you see where this is going? Bigger distributions, with a very short payout time. In fact, you could be forced to cash out the entire amount of the IRA within five years, and pay an enormous tax bill, to boot!

Clearly, both scenarios can create tax catastrophes. The solution? In both cases, the inherited IRA can be divided into separate accounts. Look at *Figures 11-4 and 11-5* to compare the tax implications.

Never, though, roll the inherited money into your own IRA (only spouses can do this), and don't just start a new IRA on your own. The IRS considers that a rollover, and taxes it as income. Look at the consequences for these beneficiaries:

The June 27, 2005, *Wall Street Journal*[12] reported that two sisters inherited a $212,000 IRA from their mother. They knew they needed separate accounts and, on the advice of an uninformed professional, they each received a check from the IRA trustee and opened their own IRAs. No dice, said the IRS, which hit each sister with a bill for almost $50,000 in taxes, wiping out almost half their inheritance at one stroke. Closing out their mother's IRA terminated it, the IRS ruled, making it subject to income tax.

Figure 11-5 (View Online at www.longtermcarebooks.com)

UNIFORM LIFETIME TABLE

Age = Age of IRA Owner or Plan Participant; Life = Life Expectancy (in years)

Age	Life	Age	Life	Age	Life	Age	Life	Age	Life	Age	Life
70	27.4	78	20.3	86	14.1	94	9.1	102	5.5	110	3.1
71	26.5	79	19.5	87	13.4	95	8.6	103	5.2	111	2.9
72	25.6	80	18.7	88	12.7	96	8.1	104	4.9	112	2.6
73	24.7	81	17.9	89	12.0	97	7.6	105	4.5	113	2.4
74	23.8	82	17.1	90	11.4	98	7.1	106	4.2	114	2.1
75	22.9	83	16.3	91	10.8	99	6.7	107	3.9	115+	1.9
76	22.0	84	15.5	92	10.2	100	6.3	108	3.7		
77	21.2	85	14.8	93	9.6	101	5.9	109	3.4		

This table is only used for lifetime required distributions. Most IRA owners will use this table, but there is one exception. If the spouse is the sole beneficiary for the entire year AND is more than 10 years younger than the IRA owner, do not use this Uniform Lifetime Table. In this case, use the actual ages of both spouses based on the Joint Life Table. This will result in a longer life expectancy and a smaller required distribution. *(Source: Ed Slott's IRA Advisor, 2003.)*

What should they have done? The IRS doesn't like you to handle the account on your own. In their view it is an inherited IRA only if it is a trustee-to-trustee direct transfer into an account designated specifically for inheritance funds, and only if it retains the deceased person's name on the account.

There is a December 31 deadline for starting withdrawals from an individual retirement account that you inherit from someone other than your husband or wife. **But if you are named as one of two or more heirs, mark September 30 on your calendar.** You can divide an inherited IRA into separate accounts – one for each heir – by that date in the year *following* the original owner's death, allowing each heir to spread withdrawals across his or her own life expectancy. Separate accounts must be established no later than December 31 of the year after the account owner's death.

If you decide, instead, to share withdrawals from the inherited account (to avoid the extra paperwork), you get stuck using the life expectancy of the oldest heir. Using the example of the two sisters mentioned above, assume one was 50 and the other was 45. The payment would be based on the life expectancy of the 50-year-old, and that payment would be divided in half.

This means the younger sister would end up with larger withdrawals than necessary, over a shorter time period (given that the 50-year-old sister would have the shorter life expectancy). So, the younger sister would enjoy less tax-deferred growth on the assets than if she were making withdrawals based on her longer life expectancy.

Sharing with a Charity

The September 30 deadline is even more important if you inherit an IRA jointly with a charity, since a charity has a life expectancy of zero. If the charity doesn't take its share of the account by that date, and if the original owner died before starting required distributions (at age 70½), a tax rule kicks in that would force you to cash out the entire account in five years. The clock starts the year after the

Figure 11-6   (View Online at www.longtermcarebooks.com)

ROTH / TRADITIONAL 401(k) COMPARISON

	Roth IRA	Roth 401(k)	Traditional 401(k)
Contribution/ Deferral Limits*	$4,000 for 2007, plus $1,000 catch-up if you are 50 or older	$15,500 for 2007, plus $5,000 catch-up if you are 50 or older	$15,500 for 2007, plus $5,000 catch-up if you are 50 or older
Matching Contributions	None	Personal contributions only	If the plan allows
Income Limits	Yes	None	None
Taxability	Contributions are after-tax	Deferrals are after-tax	Deferrals are pre-tax
Rollovers	Only to other Roth IRAs	Only to other Roth IRAs or Roth 401(k)s	To most other retirement plans, not to Roth IRAs
Required Distributions	None to Roth IRA owner	At age 70½. (If you are still working and are not a 5% owner, distributions are deferred until you are no longer working)	At age 70½. (If you are still working and are not a 5% owner, distributions are deferred until you are no longer working)

* An individual who has traditional IRAs and Roth IRAs can contribute a maximum total of $4,000 a year to his or her IRAs. An employee with a 401(k) and a Roth 401(k) can defer a maximum total of $15,000 a year to both types of accounts. If you are age 50 or older, the catch-up amount is added to your contribution or deferral amount.

** Matching contributions from an employer must go into the traditional 401(k) account.

(Source: Slott, Ed. Ed Slott's Elite IRA Advisor Group, Workshop 3, January 13-15, 2006. Rockville Centre, NY. © 2006 Ed Slott, CPA. Page 33.)

IRA owner's death. To avoid this potential snag, it is advisable that a person planning to give part of his or her IRA assets to a charity set up a separate IRA in the organization's name.

Again, all these rules involve inheriting an IRA from someone other than a spouse. The most basic rule of thumb in such circumstances is: **Never roll the inherited money into your IRA.**[13]

When Rollovers Might Make Sense

Unlike IRAs, employer plans have an entirely different set of rules. Most have no "stretch" provision, and they also have restrictions on who may be named a beneficiary (the law favors your spouse). A beneficiary of an employer plan may be required to take a lump-sum distribution at the time of inheritance, with a correspondingly large tax bill. That's a boon for the IRS but certainly not for your loved ones.

If you have multiple retirement plan accounts, distributions can sometimes be taken from any one or a combination of accounts, for example:

1. Owned IRAs (SEP or SIMPLE, but not Roth IRAs) or IRAs inherited from the same person can be added together. A SEP-IRA (Simplified Employee Pension Plan) is a retirement plan specifically designed for self-employed people and small-business owners. A SIMPLE IRA plan is an IRA-based plan that gives small employers a simplified method to make contributions toward their employees' retirement and their own retirement. Under a SIMPLE IRA plan, employees may choose to make salary reduction contributions and the employer makes matching or non-elective contributions;

2. Any 403(b) plans inherited from the same person can be added together; and,

3. All other employer plans, such as 457s or 401(k)s, can *not* be added together.[14]

Because of these restrictions, some holders of these accounts choose to roll them over into an IRA when they leave the company's employment or retire.

There are two times when you might roll assets into a new IRA: When you retire or otherwise leave a job with a defined-contribution plan, like a 401(k), or when you simply move an IRA from one financial institution to another. In either case, you have 60 days to get the money from one tax-deferred account to another.

Failed Rollovers: Good News, Bad News

Here's the good news: Many people were missing the 60-day deadline, often blaming the investment firm or bank that was supposed to get the money into the IRA for the mistake. To rectify the problem, the IRS set up what it calls an "automatic waiver" a few years ago. In order to use the waiver, you must meet several conditions. They include:

- You moved the money to the financial institution setting up the new IRA within the 60 days, and

- You asked the financial institution to put the money into the new IRA, following all of its procedures for doing so, and

- Even though the financial institution made a mistake, the money was moved into the IRA within a year of the first day of the 60-day period.

The bad news: A lot of would-be IRA investors don't get the money moved within a year, so they don't qualify for the automatic waiver. Many people aren't reading their financial statements, which would alert them to the problem. Instead, the first inkling they have that something went wrong comes the following January when they get a 1099-R form, a statement from the financial institution showing they took a distribution and owe tax on the money.

There is a fix, however. You can request a "private-letter ruling" from the IRS (by filing an application and paying a user fee, plus other fees if you hire an advisor) to get off the hook. See *Figure 11-7* for a listing of some common user fees.

The rulings have been favorable for investors in cases *where there was a real reason beyond their control*, such as being hospitalized or called for military duty in Iraq. But requests are being rejected in which people already had spent the money, demonstrating that they *didn't really have the intent to do a rollover*.

Figure 11-7   (View Online at www.longtermcarebooks.com)

USER FEES FOR IRS PRIVATE-LETTER RULING

	User fee for requests postmarked on or after 2/1/2006
● Computation of exclusion for annuitant under § 72	$380
● Certain waivers of 60-day rollover period	not available
(a) Rollover less than $50,000	$500
(b) Rollover equal to or greater than $50,000 and less than $100,000	$1,500
(c) Rollover equal to or greater than $100,000	$3,000
● Individually designed simplified employee pension (SEP)	$9,000
● All other letter rulings	$2,570

Source: U.S. Internal Revenue Service Website. "Appendix: Schedule of User Fees – TE/GE." December 20, 2005. http://www.irs.gov/pub/irs-news/irs_tege_user_fees.pdf

Another possible pitfall: If you're already over $70^{1}/_{2}$ years old and taking required distributions from your IRA every year, be sure to make your annual withdrawal before doing a rollover. If you're already in pay status, you aren't allowed to roll over that year's minimum distribution.

If you don't know about that rule and move the money anyway, and then take the distribution from the new account, both custodians could wind up reporting your distributions to the IRS – even though you took only one withdrawal. It's not illegal to take twice as much from your IRA as required, but it means you'd have to pay more in taxes. Untangling the mess requires professional help.[15]

Qualified Plans That Contain Company Stock

Property and cash received in a distribution: If you receive both property and cash in an eligible rollover distribution, you can roll over part or all of the property, part or all of the cash, or any combination of the two that you choose. ***The same property (or sales proceeds) must be rolled over.*** If you receive property in an eligible rollover distribution from a qualified retirement plan you cannot keep the property and contribute cash to a traditional IRA in place of the property. You must either roll over the property or sell it and roll over the proceeds, as explained next.

Sale of property received in a distribution from a qualified plan: Instead of rolling over a distribution of property other than cash, you can sell all or part of the property and roll over the amount you receive from the sale (the proceeds) into a traditional IRA. You cannot keep the property and substitute your own funds for property you received.

Example: You receive a total distribution from your employer's plan consisting of $10,000 cash and $15,000 worth of property. You decide to keep the property. You can roll over to a traditional IRA the $10,000 cash received, but you cannot roll over an additional $15,000 representing the value of the property you choose not to sell.

Treatment of gain or loss. If you sell the distributed property and roll over all the proceeds into a traditional IRA, no gain or loss is recognized. The sale proceeds (including any increase in value) are treated as part of the distribution and are not included in your gross income.

Example: On September 2, Mike received a lump-sum distribution from his employer's retirement plan of $50,000 in cash and $50,000 in stock. The stock was not stock of his employer. On September 24, he sold the stock for $60,000. On October 4, he rolled over $110,000 in cash ($50,000 from the original distribution and $60,000 from the sale of stock). Mike does not include the $10,000 gain from the sale of stock as part of his income because he rolled over the entire amount into a traditional IRA.

Note: Special rules may apply to distributions of employer securities. For more information, see Publication 575.[16]

Putting Company Stock in Your IRA

If you have company stock in your qualified plan or 401(k) plan, take a step back before you roll it into an IRA – or before you make any withdrawal, at any age, of any assets from the plan. A little-known tax break for what's known as "net unrealized appreciation" (NUA) allows you to pull out some or all of your shares in the company where you work at the same time you roll the rest of your assets into an IRA.

The big advantage: By taking the stock out of your 401(k), any increase in the stock price after you originally acquired the shares would be subject only to long-term capital gains tax, with a maximum 15% rate (at the time of publication), rather than ordinary income tax, up to 35%. You have to pay income tax on the original purchase amount, or "cost basis," when you take it out of your tax-deferred plan, and you wouldn't owe any capital gains tax until you sell the stock.

Make sure that both parts of the transaction – the withdrawal of the stock and the rollover of any remaining assets into an IRA – are completed in the same taxable year. Otherwise, the IRS could deny the tax break.

One other note: Use the company stock first to fund your retirement needs or make charitable donations. Upon your death, most stock that your heirs inherit get what's called a stepped-up basis, which means they wouldn't owe capital gains tax. But employer stock that already has gotten the favorable treatment described above does not receive the same bump in value.[17]

Mr. Smith Rolls Over

Let's use the following case study to explain this. Mr. Smith, age 65, has a 401(k) plan valued at $500,000. Of this, $250,000 is in mutual funds, and $250,000 is in company stock. The basis on the company stock is $50,000. Assume Mr. Smith is in the 25% federal income tax bracket.

Option 1: The normal rollover approach
Mr. Smith rolls the entire account into an IRA. Any normal distributions he takes will be taxed in the 25% federal income tax bracket. At age 70$\frac{1}{2}$, he will be forced to take RMDs and pay taxes on these distributions in his then applicable (assumed 25%) tax bracket. (*See IRS Publication 590.*)

Option 2: The NUA rollover approach
Mr. Smith rolls the stock out of the 401(k) plan. The basis on the stock is $50,000, and he must pay ordinary income tax in the amount of $12,500 ($50,000 x 25 percent tax rate). The stock is transferred to a non-qualified account. No additional taxes are owed on the stock until he sells it. Assume he does sell the stock. He pays capital gains tax on the sale versus ordinary income and is thus taxed at 15% (current maximum capital gain tax rate), not 25%. This creates an immediate tax savings of 10%. Shares sold under this technique are taxed at long-term capital gains tax rates up to the NUA, regardless of the length of time between the roll-out and the sale of the stock and short- or long-term gains on any additional gain beyond the NUA based on the time of sale. All other remaining funds are rolled into an IRA.[18]

Advisor errors in dealing with IRA distributions and especially inherited IRAs are rampant today, and this is just the tip of the iceberg for this problem. The fact is, most people with large IRAs simply have not died yet.

Advisors are quick to take over IRA rollovers, but few realize the depth of the professional responsibility that comes along with those assets. It is not enough just to help clients invest on the front end; when it comes to taxes, it's what you keep in the long run that counts. The end game is protecting IRAs from the excessive and often needless taxation that consumes them when the account holders die. As an advisor, you would want this protection for yourself as well. Following are some of the questions consumers should ask financial advisors before handing over their retirement assets.

- **What resources or publications do you use to keep up to date with changing IRA distribution rules?**

  Ask to take a look at them and see how long it takes advisors to find them. If they are not within arm's reach or close by, that's a bad sign. If advisors show you a company brochure on inherited IRAs or other company IRA literature, that's also a bad sign. It means they know of no other resources. When advisors do show you the publications, check to see whether they have opened them before, made notes, or highlighted any sections. You are looking for signs that they have actually used the publications to research IRA distributions. Also ask them how often they go to IRA training seminars and when they went to the last one. You can really put them on the spot if you ask to see the course manual for that last seminar they attended.

- **What is the last new IRA ruling or tax law change you are aware of?**

  Ask to see a copy of anything written on the subject. Competent advisors should be able to pull out the backup material quickly, if they have the resources. Once they do, check the date to see how current it is. Changes and new rulings are coming out at least once a month in this area. If your advisor shows you the new IRA rules from April 2002, for example, it's old news already. There have been many new twists in this area since then.

- **What factors should I consider before deciding what to do with my company retirement plan?**

  There are four choices: rolling the money into an IRA, leaving it in the plan, rolling it to a new plan, or taking the money and paying the tax. Often the best move is a direct IRA rollover, but a good advisor will ask questions first. There are good reasons to choose any of the four options. Advisors should be able to present the advantages and disadvantages of each choice in a clear, precise way.

- **Whom should I name as my IRA beneficiary?**

  Should you name your spouse? A trust? When advising clients on naming IRA beneficiaries, what factors do your advisors take into account? Do they know the distribution options that are available to each type of beneficiary? For example, do they know how to do a post-death IRA rollover when the spouse is the beneficiary? This should be simple, yet financial advisors mess it up often.

  Do they know how to integrate this decision with your overall estate plan? In other words, what effect would naming a certain beneficiary for your IRA have on other beneficiaries and the distribution of other estate assets?

  Actually, an advisor's first answer to the IRA beneficiary question should be, "To whom do you want to leave your IRA?" Not everything is about taxes. But once advisors know what the client wants, they should be able to explain both the tax and estate planning advantages and disadvantages of each beneficiary choice, as well as how the inherited IRA will be distributed.

This is a common question, so advisors should have information prepared to answer it, especially the question on naming a trust. A common – and expensive – mistake is for a client to name a trust as the IRA beneficiary when it was unnecessary to do so.

Advisors should also know the difference between a designated beneficiary and other types of beneficiaries. A designated beneficiary is a living person who is named on the IRA beneficiary form. Designated beneficiaries are permitted to stretch inherited IRAs over their life expectancies. In addition to knowing the IRA distribution rules, they have at least a basic knowledge of estate planning in order to answer questions properly about selecting IRA beneficiaries.

- **How do you keep track of IRA beneficiary forms?**

Where does the advisor keep them? Who has a copy of them? How often are they updated? How will you know when your IRA beneficiary form needs to be updated? Will the advisor call you, or should you call the advisor?

The IRA beneficiary form is the key to the stretch IRA concept, which allows IRAs to be tax-deferred (or tax-free with a Roth IRA) for decades if the form is available, filled out correctly, and updated. Advisors should always ask their clients to keep them informed about any major life changes – birth, death, marriage, divorce – so they can make any appropriate changes and keep IRA beneficiary forms current at all times. Good financial advisors will also be proactive and call their clients when there are changes in tax laws or new IRA rules that might warrant a change to beneficiary forms.

Advisors should keep track of their clients' IRA beneficiary forms. At a minimum, the advisor should have a copy in his or her files and make sure that copy agrees with the copy on file with the financial institution.

(An excellent service available for this purpose is provided by a California firm headquartered in Walnut Creek called Video Inventory Services. They can provide video documentation of your vital records and store them on CD or videotape so you can store them, access them, and review them whenever necessary and at your leisure. The company will also keep a separate copy in a secure location in backup storage if you desire. You can contact this company toll-free at 1-866-791-3144 for more information or to place an order.)

- **Can you show me the IRS life expectancy tables you use to calculate required IRA distributions for both IRA owners and beneficiaries?**

These tables should be close at hand. If they are not, chances are an advisor doesn't do much IRA distribution work. He or she probably just dabbles in the business, and that's a danger sign. The tables your advisor uses appear in Appendix C of the 2005 version of IRS Publication 590.

- **What will happen to my IRA after my death?**

How will it be distributed? How will you know your IRA was set up correctly so that your beneficiary will have every possible option available as allowed under IRS rules?

There are many other questions to ask advisors on this topic. Do they know how inherited IRAs should be titled? Do they know that beneficiaries are subject to required distributions and how to compute those distributions? Do they know that beneficiaries may be entitled to an income tax deduction (Income in Respect of a Decedent [IRD]) when they withdraw from their inherited IRAs? Much of the litigation out there deals with the mishandling of inherited IRAs by advisors who just did not know what to do.

99

- **Whom do you call when you have questions about IRA distributions?**

  An answer like, "I know this stuff like the back of my hand, so I don't have to call anyone" is the wrong answer. You can study IRA distributions full time, and still have questions. Other IRA experts will be the first to tell you the same thing. If your advisor can't name at least a few experts outside of his or her firm, then you have the wrong advisor. Also ask if your advisor works with other advisors in different professions, such as attorneys or accountants. A good advisor will have these contacts.

You may be wondering why one of the questions was not "How long have you been in business?" It's because the length of service is not a critical issue if you know the answers. There are advisors who have been around for years and still don't know what they are doing in this area, so being in business a long time is not a major factor in finding a competent IRA advisor. Some firms have wisely begun to build a specialty in this area, and although they may not have been in business for long, they are already IRA experts.[19]

Help on IRA Withdrawals

Retirees and their baby-boomer children are struggling to figure out the correct ways to take distributions from their own, or inherited, individual retirement accounts. To help lessen the confusion, here are some resources that should prove helpful. The authoritative voice on IRAs is IRS Publication 590, available at *www.irs.gov* or by calling 1-800-829-3676. Some details, though, particularly involving inherited IRAs, are not spelled out. Three books that elaborate on these subjects are: ***IRAs, 401(k)s & Other Retirement Plans: Taking Your Money Out***, by Twila Slesnick and John Suttle, ***Parlay Your IRA Into a Family Fortune***, by Ed Slott, and ***Life & Death Planning for Retirement Benefits: The Essential Handbook for Estate Planners***, by Natalie Choate.

Ask the Pros

To find a professional who can help with IRAs, there's a directory at *www.irahelp.com*, or try *www.fpanet.org.* to find a certified financial planner. As part of the interview process, ask how many clients they have assisted with IRA distributions and how much professional education they have that is specific to such issues.

A word about the customer service departments at big IRA custodians. As with many call centers, readers report mixed results. One problem: The customer is advised of withdrawals that can be made – but is not advised of the tax consequences. For example, a custodian might tell you that you can withdraw all the assets in an inherited IRA right away – but not tell you that you would owe taxes on the money immediately, or that you could stretch withdrawals across your life expectancy to spread out the taxes owed. Before making the call, check the custodian's website. Most have well-researched guides on IRA distributions.[20]

The Roth IRA Alternative and Life Insurance

Roth IRAs are a great way to accumulate dollars for retirement. They are easy to establish and relatively flexible. Often overlooked are the benefits of life insurance as a Roth IRA alternative. Life insurance offers the same tax-deferred growth and tax-free retirement income, but also provides greater flexibility as a financial planning tool. Insurance is most advantageous for people in their forties and fifties because the earlier the policy is established, the greater the potential income that will be generated from contributions and growth of the account. (*See Figure 11-8*)

1 The biggest advantage that life insurance has over a Roth IRA is that the death benefit creates an immediate estate. The death benefit is income tax-free, which survivors can use as income to pay debts or as emergency funding. While the death benefit of a Roth IRA would also be income tax-free, the beneficiary would only receive the accumulated value at death.

2 You must financially qualify for a Roth IRA. You must have "compensation income," but not too much. To contribute the full dollar amount, a single taxpayer's adjusted gross income (AGI) cannot exceed $95,000, and a married taxpayer (filing jointly) cannot have AGI in excess of $150,000. The contribution limits are phased out for AGI levels $10,000 higher than these amounts as of the date of this publication. These contribution limits are decreased by contributions made to traditional IRAs, which have different limits. Life insurance does not have these limitations.

3 Access to accumulated dollars can be critical. With a non-MEC life insurance policy (*see Figure 11-8 footnote*), its cash value is always available. The policy owner can borrow and repay the loan, while the death benefit protection is still there. At retirement, the policy owner can use the policy to supplement his/her income.

4 Life insurance can be used for retirement at any time, but the owner of a Roth IRA must wait until age $59\frac{1}{2}$ to take qualified withdrawals and the Roth account must have been held for five years. With a Roth IRA, some withdrawals made prior to age $59\frac{1}{2}$ are subject to a 10% IRS penalty if the funds are used for anything other than: 1) first-time homebuying expenses up to $10,000 or 2) death or disability.[21]

Figure 11-8   (View Online at www.longtermcarebooks.com)

ROTH IRA vs. LIFE INSURANCE

Feature	Roth IRA	Life Insurance
Non-Deductible Contribution	Yes	Yes
Tax-Deferred Growth	Yes	Yes
Tax-Free Distributions	Yes	Yes, if non-MEC*
Defer Distributions Until Death	Yes	Yes
Income Tax-Free to Beneficiaries	Yes	Yes
Minimum Compensation Requirements	Yes	No
Income Limitations	Yes	No
Unlimited Contributions	No	Yes, subject to insurability limitations
Early Withdrawals Without Penalty	No**	Yes, if non-MEC*
Create Estate	No	Yes

* A MEC is a Modified Endowment Contract. If your cumulative premium payments exceed certain amounts specified under the Internal Revenue Code, your policy will become a MEC. If your policy is a MEC, the tax treatment of any death benefit provided under the contract will still qualify for income tax-free treatment but you may be subject to additional taxes and penalties on any distributions from your policy during the life of the insured.

** Except limited use as previously listed.

(Source: "The Roth IRA Alternative." Cenco Street Journal. © January/February 2004. Sacramento, CA. Vol. 4, Issue 1.)

BE SURE TO SEEK COMPETENT TAX AND LEGAL COUNSEL FOR ALL THESE CONCEPTS AND PROGRAMS TO BE SURE THEY MEET YOUR SPECIFIC NEEDS AND LOCAL LAWS, RULES AND REGULATIONS.

12 Estate and Asset Planning

Jack and Mary

Assume a couple has accumulated assets over their lifetime and they now have more than $2 million of liquid assets (assets that are not pledged against a debt). They have a household income of $75,000 per year.

Then the husband, Jack, age 74, suffers a debilitating stroke. After one month of medical care in a hospital and care in a skilled nursing facility paid by Medicare and his personal insurance, he is released to the care of his wife, Mary, age 75. Jack cannot take care of the activities of daily living (ADLs), so his wife, with minimal help from family and friends, tries to fill the role of homemaker, nurse and medical aide (lifting, bathing and caring for Jack daily).

Since Jack's health does not improve, Mary must continue this regimen of care indefinitely. Because they desire to save their assets for the children, they do not wish to pay for outside services, which are too costly, at an average $150 per day, or $4,500 per month. It would take 60% of their current income to pay for this care that Mary is providing to Jack free. The only problem is that Mary becomes weary and her health deteriorates quickly. She suffers a heart attack and must go to a nursing home. Now, not only can she no longer care for Jack or herself, but the nursing home costs $4,000 a month for her.

Jack must now also be placed in a nursing home, since family and friends cannot provide the around-the-clock care required as his health declines. His costs will run more, since he needs more services as his condition worsens. As we have seen previously, the monthly bill from the nursing home is only the beginning since many other incidental costs for the care must also be paid.

It is decided by the children, who have no real knowledge of their parents' assets, to seek conservatorship of the estate to assure that the bills are paid and proper care is provided for their parents. When the children learn the size of the estate, they seek to conserve the estate to pay the costs their parents are incurring, but also to preserve their future inheritance.

Now the real problems begin. The parents lose control of their assets to the court and to a conservator appointed by the court, incurring potentially enormous legal and accounting fees.

This entire problem could have been avoided through the use of a trust, powers of attorney and other planning mechanisms had Jack and Mary confronted the problem by doing the requisite planning before it was too late.

Long-Term Care as an Estate Planning Tool

Long-term care (LTC) insurance is the most under-utilized tool in estate planning. Changes in tax laws and LTC policies provide opportunities ignored by most estate planning professionals. This chapter discusses the basics of estate planning in general, and details ways to intertwine LTC insurance with the estate planning process.

LTC is different from "acute" care, where doctors and registered nurses provide care for medical conditions such as cancer, broken bones, and sore throats. Health insurance pays for some or all of these costs.

LTC is either custodial or supervisory. *Custodial care* assists individuals in performing the "activities of daily living," (ADLs).

Supervisory care is required because of cognitive impairment (physically-caused dementia). Causes include Alzheimer's, Parkinson's disease, stroke and head injuries. Cognitive impairment does not include purely psychiatric conditions such as depression or schizophrenia.

Contrary to popular belief, Medicare and Medigap insurance do not pay for long-term care.

What Medicare does not pay for, long-term care must pick up. Good quality assisted living facilities charge $53,000+ on average per year. These aforementioned charges are for room and board only. Both nursing homes and assisted living facilities charge extra for other services and supplies such as bandages, laundry, rubber gloves, diapers, oxygen, turning and positioning, hand-feeding, etc. These additional charges typically range from approximately $4,000 to $18,000 per year.

LTC is also frequently provided at home. Care costs at home for 24 hours a day would run anywhere from $100,000 to $150,000 or more per year.

LTC Statistics

The risk of needing LTC increases with age. More than 50% of those over 85 years of age need some form of LTC. Nine percent of Americans who reach age 65 will need more than five years of nursing home care, in addition to any care at home or in assisted living facilities. It is not unusual for someone to need 10 to 20 years of care. For those who have Alzheimer's, statistics tell us that these individuals, from the date of diagnosis, live with the disease from three to 20 years and that the average is eight years. Most or all of these years require some kind of custodial care.

LTC is one of the worst risks to self-insure because of the high incidence of need and the high expense:

- Only one in 1,200 uses their fire insurance, and the average loss is $3,428;

- Only one in 240 uses their automobile insurance, and the average loss is $3,000;

- One in three uses their LTC insurance, and the average cost is $50,000 to $60,000 each year.

The Role of Federal and State Governments

Because of the high incidence and cost of LTC, the federal government offers tax incentives to encourage the purchase of LTC policies. Policies must meet federal standards to qualify for most tax incentives. Policies that meet federal standards are called "tax-qualified."

Tax incentives for purchasing LTC insurance include:

- No federal tax on benefits.

- C corporations can fully deduct LTC premiums paid for employees including owners and their spouses, even if they discriminate in providing coverage. Premiums paid by the corporation are not considered income to employees. Benefits paid are still treated as non-taxable income.

- S corporations, partnerships and LLCs have the same benefits as C corporations for employees owning less than a 2% interest. Owners with more than 2% interest are considered self-employed. Owners treat premiums as income, but can then deduct certain amounts.

- Self-employed individuals can use some of the premium as an above-the-line business expense. The remainder can be added to unreimbursed medical expenses.

- A limited ability to deduct premiums on a 1040 return. A certain amount of premium can be added to unreimbursed medical expenses. Very few individuals benefit from this. At least 21 states provide either a tax deduction or credit for residents who purchase policies.

How can LTC insurance assist in achieving estate planning goals? The six examples below illustrate:

1. Preserving Step-Up in Capital Gains Basis at Death

Wealthy individuals may have assets to pay for their own long-term care without life insurance, but not enough liquid assets. This forces them to sell assets (and incur capital gains taxes) to pay for LTC. Selling assets incurs capital gains taxes. If, however, they buy an LTC policy, the insurance pays their LTC expenses and they need not sell assets. Then, basis is stepped up at death and heirs can sell without capital gains.

2. Transferring Value Out of C Corporations Income Tax-Free

LTC premiums paid by a C corporation for employees, owners and their spouses are a tax-deductible expense in any amount. Premiums and benefits are not taxable income. Discrimination (i.e., providing this for only some employees) is allowed. Some policies can be fully paid in one or ten years, accelerating the tax deductions. This means that the income used to pay premiums of a fully paid-up policy is taken out of the corporation without taxes being due.

3. Providing Comfort Level for Gift-Givers

Without LTC insurance, wealthy donors making lifetime gifts need to worry about retaining enough assets to pay for catastrophic LTC costs. Appropriate amounts of LTC insurance eliminate this concern.

4. Third-Party Ownership of Policies

Some companies allow a trust or heir to own an LTC policy that insures another individual. If the insured needs LTC, benefits can be paid to the policy owner instead of the insured. The insured's own assets must then be used to pay the cost of the care. The insured's estate is reduced, the policy owner's estate increases and there is no income or gift tax.

5. Return of Premium at Death Rider

Some companies offer a rider that returns all paid premiums to heirs at the death of the insured. Since this is a death benefit it should be income tax-free. If the policy is not owned by the insured, it should also be free of estate taxes. This rider is especially useful for third-party ownership.

6. Prenuptial Agreements

There is a big hole in most prenuptial agreements. If one spouse exhausts all assets paying for LTC, the other spouse must begin paying for that care with his/her assets and income. This happens no matter how the assets are titled, regardless of any provision in a prenuptial agreement, because Medicaid requires both spouses to be impoverished for either to be eligible. LTC insurance protects against this risk.

The most commonly cited reasons for purchasing LTC insurance are staying in control, preserving quality of life and quality of care, and preserving assets. In addition, estate planning utilizing long-term care insurance provides a variety of strategies to maximize assets received by heirs after tax.[1]

This chapter focuses on reviewing trusts and the options they can provide. The use of trusts in estate planning to handle estate taxes and to transfer assets has been available to Americans for generations. The need to plan for catastrophic events, such as the need for long-term care for one or both spouses, Medicaid planning and the care of a disabled child, have also become of vital concern to aging Americans in considering trust alternatives in recent years.

WARNING!

Readers should not assume they can tackle this topic themselves using this publication. Currently numerous federal, state and local agencies oversee, or at least review (sometimes in tax court), the more exotic estate planning activities of attorneys, CPAs, financial planners and advisors. This is done to be sure that the proper amount of tax is being paid using these plans and that clients are properly advised regarding appropriate use of trusts and Medicaid eligibility. The Department of the Treasury and the Department of Labor review some trusts, such as qualified retirement plans under ERISA regulations, to assure equality in benefits and proper allocation of the funds. The Internal Revenue Service, under the guidance of Treasury, interprets federal tax regulations after laws have been created by the Congress and signed into law by the President.

Also, the Department of Health and Human Services administers Medicare, Medicaid and other federal programs meant to serve the needs of seniors and the disabled. At the state level, various agencies, such as the Department of Insurance, Department of Corporations and agencies dealing with medical services at the state and local level, review insurance and securities offerings to provide protection for consumers. These government agencies do not automatically endorse, or even try to understand these tax-savings concepts.

It is foolhardy for the layperson to try to tackle this complex area without proper advice and guidance. The "I'll save hundreds of dollars by doing it myself" mentality has been quickly translated into numerous examples of disasters that have cost individuals hundreds of thousands of dollars, in some cases millions of dollars, that could have been completely avoided with proper planning. *Figures 12-1* and *12-2* show some well-known personalities whose estates were reduced substantially by the lack of proper estate planning.

Figure 12-1: Estates of the Wealthy – Using Marital Deductions[2]

The following estates made use of the marital deduction. Under current laws, the costs would be different:

Name	Gross Estate	Settlement Costs	Net Estate	Percent Shrinkage
Stan Laurel	$ 91,562	$ 8,381	$ 83,181	9%
Goodwin Knight	102,049	21,585	80,464	21%
W.C. Fields	884,680	329,793	554,887	37%
Nelson Eddy	472,715	109,990	362,725	23%
Dixie Crosby	1,332,571	781,953	550,618	59%
Franklin D. Roosevelt	1,940,999	574,867	1,366,132	30%
Humphrey Bogart	910,146	274,234	635,912	30%
Clark Gable	2,806,526	1,101,038	1,705,488	30%
Dean Witter	7,451,055	1,830,717	5,620,338	24%
Henry J. Kaiser, Sr.	5,597,772	2,488,364	3,109,408	44%
Henry J. Kaiser, Jr.*	55,910,373	1,030,415	54,879,958	2%
Al Jolson	4,385,143	1,349,066	3,036,077	31%
Gary Cooper	4,984,985	1,530,454	3,454,531	31%
Myford Irvine	13,445,552	6,012,685	7,432,867	45%
Walt Disney	23,004,851	6,811,943	16,192,908	30%
Harry M. Warner	8,946,618	2,308,444	6,638,174	26%
William E. Boeing	22,386,158	10,589,748	11,796,410	47%

Figure 12-2:   Estates of the Wealthy – No Marital Deduction

Estates where the marital deduction was not used or not available:

Name	Gross Estate	Settlement Costs	Net Estate	Percent Shrinkage
William Frawley	$ 92,446	$ 45,814	$ 46,632	49%
"Gabby" Hayes	111,327	21,963	89,364	20%
Hedda Hopper	472,661	165,982	306,679	35%
Marilyn Monroe	819,176	448,750	370,426	55%
Erle Stanley Gardner	1,795,092	636,705	1,158,387	35%
Cecil B. DeMille	4,043,607	1,396,064	2,647,543	35%
Elvis Presley	10,165,434	7,374,635	2,790,799	73%
J.P. Morgan	17,121,482	11,893,691	5,227,791	69%
John D. Rockefeller, Sr.	26,905,182	17,124,988	9,780,194	64%
John D. Rockefeller, Jr.**	160,598,584	24,965,954	135,632,630	16%
Alwin C. Ernst, CPA	12,642,431	7,124,112	5,518,319	56%
Frederick Vanderbilt	76,838,530	42,846,112	33,992,418	56%

*Over $50,000,000 of Henry J. Kaiser's estate went to the Kaiser Family Foundation.

**Most of the estate of John D. Rockefeller, Jr. went to the Rockefeller Brothers Fund, Inc.

Figure 12-3

Estate and Gift Taxes[3]

For Deaths / Gifts Occurring in 2007

If Taxable Estate Is:

Over	But Not Greater Than	The Tax Is:	Of the Amount Greater Than
$ 0	$ 11,000	$ 0 + 18%	$ 0
$ 11,000	$ 20,000	$ 1,800 + 20%	$ 11,000
$ 20,000	$ 40,000	$ 3,800 + 22%	$ 20,000
$ 40,000	$ 60,000	$ 8,200 + 24%	$ 40,000
$ 60,000	$ 80,000	$ 13,000 + 26%	$ 60,000
$ 80,000	$ 100,000	$ 18,200 + 28%	$ 80,000
$ 100,000	$ 150,000	$ 23,800 + 30%	$ 100,000
$ 150,000	$ 250,000	$ 38,800 + 32%	$ 150,000
$ 250,000	$ 500,000	$ 70,800 + 34%	$ 250,000
$ 500,000	$ 750,000	$ 155,800 + 37%	$ 500,000
$ 750,000	$ 1,000,000	$ 248,300 + 39%	$ 750,000
$ 1,000,000	$ 1,250,000	$ 345,800 + 41%	$ 1,000,000
$ 1,250,000	$ 1,500,000	$ 448,300 + 43%	$ 1,250,000
$ 1,500,000	$ 2,000,000	$ 555,800 + 45%	$ 1,500,000
$ 2,000,000	– – –	$ 780,800 + 46%	$ 2,000,000

Subtract applicable credit below from calculated tax:

Year	For Gift Tax Purposes:		For Estate Tax Purposes:	
	Unified Credit	Applicable Exclusion Amount	Unified Credit	Applicable Exclusion Amount
2007, and 2008	345,800	1,000,000	780,800	2,000,000
2009	345,800	1,000,000	1,455,800	3,500,000
2010	Estate tax repealed; gift tax remains			

Annual Gift Tax Exclusion: $12,000 in 2007 / GST Tax Exemption: $2,000,000 in 2007

(View Online at www.longtermcarebooks.com)

The Importance of Planning

A 62-year-old client visited my office to complete some estate planning started three months earlier. Over a four-hour period we discussed these complex issues as they applied to his situation. Estate planning for a single person with a net worth over $2.5 million can be very difficult if there are no family members named as beneficiaries or family members to gift, as was true in his case. With the estate growing at a high rate of return yearly the complexity increases, especially considering the level of taxation on an estate of this size, based on the tax rates shown in *Figure 12-3*.

After the meeting had ended, my client made the observation that he could have done all of the planning that we were able to complete successfully in four hours, but it would have taken him five years to understand it enough to try to do it himself, "if he dared." He pointed out that, if he tried to do it himself, he would be looking at years of study on federal and state tax law, investment planning, insurance rules and regulations. He also believed he would need extensive personal experience of friends and associates for him to feel comfortable with the process, so that he would not feel he had missed important steps in the process. Missing steps can mean paying substantial additional income and capital gains taxes during your lifetime, or denying benefits to those you care about after your passing.

The meeting saved my client over $850,000 in income, capital gains and estate taxes. The maze of rules, regulations and laws makes it nearly impossible for an individual to avoid the obstacles established by the taxing authorities without careful planning. These rules and regulations can subject an estate to more than 80% total taxation, depending on the ownership, disposition and control of assets at the death of the individual. This example is not the exception, but rather the norm that is seen daily in planning offices around the United States. Large estates are not the only ones affected by the regulations. A person with a debt-free home, some life insurance, a few financial assets, an IRA, or pension accounts can lose 15% to 50% of the estate value in income and estate taxes through imprudent planning or neglect.

> *(The following information through page 111 was provided by Steven F. Klamm, Attorney at Law, specializing in Income, Estate and Gift Tax Planning. Telephone 925-934-7300.)*

Issues to Consider

Law of Intestacy (dying without a will): The laws vary considerably in the various states and are affected by your state of residence. If you live in the western United States and you are married, your estate will more than likely fall under the "community property" rules, while most other parts of the country adhere to a more traditional set of rules.

Probate, and the "Simple Will": Many people incorrectly assume that the writing of a will automatically sets up the proper transfer of assets to named beneficiaries and the avoidance of probate fees and expenses for the balance of their estate. In most cases, nothing could be further from the truth.

The following vehicles normally bypass probate, **even with a valid will**:

- Life and annuity insurance policies, IRA and pension accounts, and other accounts with proper beneficiary designations;

- Gifted property to another person, property that has been transferred by trust document, and property held in joint tenancy (probate still applies at the death of the survivor joint tenant). For example, it is entirely possible to unintentionally disinherit a child from a prior marriage if assets are held in joint tenancy since joint tenancy will be given legal precedence over terms of a will. It happens frequently, and creates significant problems for the next generation.

Costs of Probate

- If your estate is subject to probate, your estate will have to pay both statutory fees to attorneys (set by laws of the state where the decedent resided, usually 4 to 7% of the estate value), and extraordinary fees (charged by attorneys or specialists for extra services and approved by the probate court). There are also court costs that can run another 1 to 2 percent of the estate value.

- Probate includes the process of closing the estate. It can lead to substantial delays (sometimes months or years) as various family and business issues are resolved. This can lead to serious additional costs and losses, especially if a business is left to flounder for lack of control and authority.

Probate also makes the estate open to public record and review, since all creditors of the estate must be given complete information about the estate's financial status.

Your estate will also be subject to:

- Estate Taxes: It is critical to remember that some or all of these taxes can be avoided by using the vehicles of credits, deductions, charitable bequests, and the types of trusts noted in this chapter and elsewhere (*see Figure 12-3*).

- State Inheritance Taxes: This definitely requires legal and tax counsel since the various states consider these taxes differently, including the use of matching credits to the federal taxation system. In some cases there is no exemption for transfer to the surviving spouse, and beneficiaries may also be taxed. Check with your personal financial advisor on this issue.

- Generation Skipping Transfer (GST) Tax: If it applies, it is a whopping flat 46% tax (2006), in addition to the other income and estate taxes on any transfers made to certain named beneficiaries. These can include relatives, such as grandchildren or other lineal heirs. Great care must be exercised with planning for this tax since it is so onerous and can be applied on top of the maximum estate tax rate, currently at 46 percent (2006).[4]

Important Terms

- <u>Durable Power of Attorney</u>: A document that provides for decision-making authority when the individual cannot make decisions due to health incapacity or other limiting conditions.

- <u>Durable Power of Attorney for Health Care</u>: A document that allows other family members or medical personnel to act on the wishes of the individual regarding prolonging life by artificial means or at great added cost with no real benefit.

- <u>Conservatorship</u>: A court-ordered process to appoint someone to oversee care for a person no longer able to care for himself or herself when no trust documents were created to deal with the issue. This can tear families apart and drain their estate assets, so it should be carefully weighed if this course of action appears to be the only alternative.

Types of Trusts and Their Benefits

Some of the types of trusts are listed below. The list is not all-inclusive, nor is this meant to be a thorough description of these planning techniques. Again, this is not meant to be legal advice for the reader, but rather a description of some of the trusts commonly available, some of the ways they can be used, and how they can benefit the individual(s).

Revocable Trust Utilizing an A/B Trust:

There are two ways to structure this trust:

- With Marital Deduction: Allows for a complete transfer of all assets at the death of the first spouse to the surviving spouse, without having to pay any estate taxes at the first spouse's death. Certain unintended consequences can occur in later tax planning, so competent counsel should be consulted.

- With Unified Deduction: Allows for the maximum exemption for a couple, currently at $2,000,000 (2007).[5] If an A/B or "bypass" trust is not properly created at the first death, then this can result in loss of the deceased spouse's deduction, resulting in substantial additional estate tax on the surviving spouse's estate.

Irrevocable Life Insurance Trust: Most people are not aware that the personal ownership of life insurance in estates of more than $2,000,000 (including the death benefit of the insurance policy) can subject some, or all, of the policy death benefit to estate tax upon the death of the insured (2006). A simple technique to avoid this is to have the policy owned from inception by an irrevocable life insurance trust, or to transfer policy ownership to the trust at least three years and one day prior to the death of the insured.

Charitable Remainder Trust (CHRT): A CHRT allows for the complete avoidance of income, capital gains and estate tax on appreciated assets (i.e., real estate, stocks or other assets, such as stamp collections as an example) that have grown in value over time in the estate of the donor. The donor receives a tax deduction in the first year, calculated on the value of the asset given, the age of the donor, and the number of years income will be paid to the donor. The deduction can be used in the first year within limitations, to reduce or eliminate personal income taxes, plus up to five more years, depending on the size of the deduction. (*Figures 12-4 and 12-5 show the effect of a CHRT and its structure.*)

Charitable Lead Trust: This is the reverse of a Charitable Remainder Trust. The income generated from assets placed in a trust goes to charity for a number of years. Eventually, what is left in the trust goes back to the donor's children or other named beneficiaries. By using this strategy, large amounts of assets can be transferred with little or no estate or gift taxes.

QTIP Trust – Qualified Terminal Interest Property Trust: Typically, this trust is used to preserve assets for the children of a prior marriage. The trust allows the creator to restrict the surviving spouse's ability to access trust assets, so as to protect these assets until the death of the surviving spouse. Income is provided to the surviving spouse, but the trust principal passes to the creator's children at the second death.

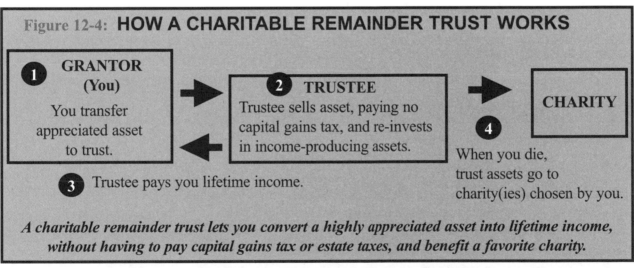

Figure 12-4: HOW A CHARITABLE REMAINDER TRUST WORKS

① GRANTOR (You) — You transfer appreciated asset to trust.

② TRUSTEE — Trustee sells asset, paying no capital gains tax, and re-invests in income-producing assets.

③ Trustee pays you lifetime income.

④ CHARITY — When you die, trust assets go to charity(ies) chosen by you.

A charitable remainder trust lets you convert a highly appreciated asset into lifetime income, without having to pay capital gains tax or estate taxes, and benefit a favorite charity.

(View Online at www.longtermcarebooks.com)

Figure 12-5: COMPARISON OF INCOME AFTER SALE OF ASSETS

	Without CHRT	With CHRT
Current Value of Stock	$ 500,000	$ 500,000
Capital Gains Tax*	- 80,000	0
Balance To Re-Invest	$ 420,000	$ 500,000
7% Annual Income	$ 29,400	$ 35,000
Total Lifetime Income	$764,400	$910,000
Tax Deduction Benefit**	$ 0	$ 45,556

*15% federal capital gains tax only for high income taxpayers. State capital gains tax may also apply.
**$126,545 charitable income tax deduction at an assumed 35% income tax rate.*

The Terri Schiavo case has prompted discussion in homes all over America about whether or not to prolong life-sustaining treatment when there is no hope of recovery. Whatever your personal feelings may be toward this case, there are some lessons for our own end-of-life planning that we can all take away from this woman's struggle.

Terri Schiavo collapsed in her home at age 26 in February 1990. Her husband, Michael Schiavo, delayed calling 911. During this time, Terri experienced a lack of oxygen to her brain causing her to lapse into a persistent vegetative state (PVS). She was able to maintain a heartbeat and blood pressure and breathe on her own, but she was severely brain-damaged. Michael contends that Terri suffered from a cardiac arrest induced by a potassium imbalance from her bulimia. Terri's parents, the Schindlers, argued that Michael strangled Terri, and court testimony from a neurologist suggests this might have been true. From 1990 to 1993, the Schindlers worked together toward progressive rehabilitative therapy.

In 1993, Michael received a $1.3 million dollar settlement in a medical-malpractice lawsuit against Terri's physicians who should have treated her potassium imbalance before it led to cardiac arrest. Less than eight months after receiving the award, Michael tried to establish a Do Not Resuscitate (DNR) order in her nursing home chart. The nursing home challenged this order in court and won. The Schindlers began to repeatedly petition the courts to have Michael removed as Terri's legal guardian on the grounds that he was not acting in her best interests.

Florida state law changed in 1999, making it easier for Michael to remove Terri's feeding tube. Previously, state law required the patient must have a terminal condition with no reasonable probability of recovery. The provisions now include patients who are in an end-vegetative state or who were in a PVS.

In 2000, the court ruled that Terri would not want to be kept alive by artificial means and was in a PVS. The feeding tube was removed but put back in after an appeal. The next two years were spent in appeals. Many nurses and caregivers testified that they secretly provided physical therapy behind closed doors so that Michael would not discover them. In November 2002, the trial court reaffirmed Terri's condition and the feeding tube was again removed, this time for six days during which Terri suffered dehydration and starvation. It was put back in when the Florida state legislature passed "Terri's Law" and Governor Jeb Bush ordered the tube to be reinserted.

On March 16, 2005, the feeding tube was removed for the final time after 40 judges and six courts. Terri died on March 31, 2005.

There are many more details to this case that make this a terrible story for both sides. Terri's legacy should be that no person or family should need to go through this struggle when there are ways to prevent this from happening.

California's Advance Health Care Directives state that each person has a fundamental right to control his/her own health care and to decide whether or not to withhold life-sustaining treatment.

Advance Health Care Directives can be registered online with:

1) The California Secretary of State at no cost. Forms are available at: *www.ss.ca.gov/business/sf/sf_formsfees.htm*; or

2) The U.S. Living Wills Registry, a private online registration site at *www.uslivingwillregistry.com*. This site also provides free forms, free registration of your living will and a great deal of information. The site will contact you once per year to make sure your living will is up to date. You can make changes at any time. The site will make your living will documents available to any health care agency in any state.

The Health Care Agent that you choose can authorize the following decisions:

- Medical treatment
- Medical providers
- Medications and tests
- Food, water and resuscitation

- Personal care
- Access to medical records
- Consent or withdrawal of consent
- After-death decisions

They cannot authorize mercy killings or euthanasia, psychosurgery or commitment to a mental institution, abortion or sterilization.

Factors you should consider when choosing a Health Care Agent include: age, maturity level, health condition, location or proximity, belief system. It should be someone who will not gain from your passing. You should choose someone who will decide the way you would, someone who is familiar with your health history and understands your wishes.

If you feel strongly about euthanasia, you can consider adding a paragraph like this: "I want my agent to utilize euthanasia in the event that California law is changed to permit it. I am a believer in active euthanasia for terminally ill individuals. This language supercedes all other inconsistent language in this document." Currently, Oregon law permits "assisted suicide" while California does not.

An Advance Health Care Directive must grant authority, be signed by the principal or another adult at the direction of the principal, must be dated and must be notarized or have two witnesses.

Eldercare

If you are reading this book, you are taking an important step toward understanding and planning for the issues we will all eventually face. If you are a senior citizen with adult children it will be important for you to sit down and discuss your wishes as to how you would like to live your life if it becomes necessary to accept some help. If you are a child of a senior citizen you may be wondering how you will care for your aging parent or how you will coordinate that care.

Careful planning can prevent changes that a senior did not want. For example, a senior citizen may qualify for a desirable living facility when able to perform most activities of daily living (ADLs) and may be able to be moved into an assisted living area of the facility when the time is needed, but may not have that option if he/she are not already in the facility. A senior citizen may want to live out his or her life in his or her home and, if proper planning and financial resources are in place for in-home care, this may work well for all those involved. However, it takes time to consider these options, and work with those professionals who can help make these options a viable reality.

Though it is difficult to do, the best time for planning is now, while you are in good health and of sound mind. To help you do this, we have included questionnaires and worksheets to get you started.

Estate Planning Questionnaire

Figure 12-6 (*thru page 119*)

Date: _____/_____/_____

Personal Information

Client's Name: _____ _____   Spouse's Name: _____ _____
                 First   Last   First   Last

Date of Birth:___/___/___Age: ___ Sex: M F   Date of Birth:___/___/___Age: ___ Sex: M F

Current Account #s: Primary Account _____
                            Related Accounts _____

Assets / Liabilities / Bequests & Gifts

Assets	Client	Spouse	Joint/ Community
Liquid:	$_____	$_____	$_____
Investments (Tax-Deferred) – IRA/401(k)	$_____	$_____	$_____
Investment (Other) – All taxable securities	$_____	$_____	$_____
Business – closely-held	$_____	$_____	$_____
Real Estate – residence/rental property	$_____	$_____	$_____
Personal – jewelry, artwork, cars, boats, etc.	$_____	$_____	$_____
Insurance – face amount/death benefit	$_____	$_____	$_____
Liabilities – mortgage, auto, credit cards, etc.	$_____	$_____	$_____
Bequests & Gifts	$_____	$_____	$_____

Savings & Assumptions

Administrative Costs: (percentage of gross estate usually 3% - 5%)   _____%

Final Expenses: (funeral/burial costs, medical expenses, etc.) $_____

Final Expenses Inflation: _____%

Asset Growth Rate: _____%

Average Income Tax Rate: (state and federal)   _____%

Pay Estate Taxes on First Death: (must circle Y if spouse is not U.S. citizen):   Y   N

Years (From Today) Until First Death: _____ yrs

Years (From Today) Until Second Death: _____ yrs

Show Reduction Due To Income Taxes   Y   N

Prepared By: _____
                                  Consultant's Name

Information offered as a guideline. As always, refer to counsel for tax and legal advice

(View Online at www.longtermcarebooks.com)

Retirement Planning Questionnaire

Date: _____/_____/_____

Personal Information

Client's Name: _____ _____   Spouse's Name: _____ _____
                    First   Last   First   Last

Date of Birth:___/___/___ Age: ___ Sex: M F   Date of Birth:___/___/___ Age: ___ Sex: M F

Current Account #s: Primary Account _____
                      Related Accounts _____

Retirement Objectives

	Client	**Spouse**
Anticipated Retirement Age:	_____	_____
Annual Before-Tax Salary:	$_____	$_____
Anticipated Pay Raises:	_____%	_____%
% of Income Desired at Retirement (See page 119):	_____%	
Inflation Rate:	_____%	
Age to End Analysis:	_____	_____
Future Legacy to Heirs: Adjust for Inflation Y N	$_____	

Government Programs / Social Security

	Client	**Spouse**
Include Social Security Benefits:	Y N	
Age Social Security Benefits Begin:	_____	_____
Inflation Rate on Social Security Benefits:	_____%	

Retirement Plans / Tax-Deferred

Regular Savings – Profit Sharing, Money Purchase, 401(k), SEP, SIMPLE, IRAs, Regular Savings – Contributions continue every year until retirement.

	Client	**Spouse**
Current Balance:	$_____	$_____
Annual Contributions: (Employee)	$_____	$_____
(Employer)	$_____	$_____
Total Contributions:	$_____	$_____
% Increase in Contributions:	_____%	_____%
Before-Tax Return on Plan Assets:	_____%	

Information offered as a guideline. As always, refer to counsel for tax and legal advice.

Retirement Plans / Tax-Deferred (*continued*)

Periodic Savings Plans (IRAs) – Contributions that can start and stop at a specific age prior to or at retirement.

Annual Contribution:	_____%
% Increase in Contributions:	_____%
Client Age When Contributions Begin:	_____
Client Age When Contributions End:	_____
Before-Tax Return on Annual Contributions:	_____%

Defined Benefit Pensions – Based on final salary and years of service

	Client	Spouse
Expected Annual Benefit:	$_____	$_____
% Increase on Annual Benefit:	_____%	_____%
Age Payments Begin:	_____	_____

Personal Savings / Taxable

Regular Savings – Personal Savings, CDs, Mutual Funds, Money Market Accounts – Contributions continue every year until retirement.

	Client	Spouse
Current Balance: Itemize? Y N , (If "Y" then list on page 117)	$_____	$_____
Annual Contributions:	$_____	$_____
% Increase in Contributions:	_____%	_____%
After-Tax Return on Savings:	_____%	_____%

Periodic Savings / (Withdrawals) - Contributions that can start and stop at a specific age prior to or at retirement. Annual amounts should be in today's dollars.

Annual Contributions / (Withdrawals):	$_____
% Increase in Contributions / (Withdrawals):	_____%
Client Age When Contributions / (Withdrawals) Begin:	_____
Client Age When Contributions / (Withdrawals) End:	_____
After-Tax Return on Annual Contributions:	_____%

Future Receipts / (Expenses) - Supplemental retirement income such as inheritance, part-time work, insurance cash value withdrawals, etc.

	Receipt (Expense)	Receipt (Expense)
Expected Annual Receipt/(Expense):	$_____	$_____
% Increase on Annual Receipt/(Expense):	_____%	_____%
Your Age When Receipt/(Expense) Begins:	_____	_____
Your Age When Receipt/(Expense) Ends:	_____	_____

Prepared By: _____

Consultant's Name

Assets (Personal Qualified Plans, Non-Qualified Plans, etc.)

List tax-deferred retirement plan assets first (i.e., Profit Sharing, Pension Plans, 401(k) Plans, SEPs, SIMPLE Plans, IRAs, 403(b) Plans). Next, list taxable assets (in order of liquidity). See page 10-16 for category types.

* Owner: You (Y), Spouse (S), Jointly-Held/Community Property (J/C).
** Type: Liquid (L), Personal (P), Investment (I), Closely-Held Business (B).
*** Purpose: Use for College (C), Retirement (R), Survivor Income Needs (S). Note: You may circle more than one purpose.

List of Assets	Assumed Value	Rate of Return	Owner*	Type**	Purpose***
1 _____	$_____	_____%	Y S J/C	L P I B	C R S
2 _____	$_____	_____%	Y S J/C	L P I B	C R S
3 _____	$_____	_____%	Y S J/C	L P I B	C R S
4 _____	$_____	_____%	Y S J/C	L P I B	C R S
5 _____	$_____	_____%	Y S J/C	L P I B	C R S
6 _____	$_____	_____%	Y S J/C	L P I B	C R S
7 _____	$_____	_____%	Y S J/C	L P I B	C R S
8 _____	$_____	_____%	Y S J/C	L P I B	C R S
9 _____	$_____	_____%	Y S J/C	L P I B	C R S
10 _____	$_____	_____%	Y S J/C	L P I B	C R S
11 _____	$_____	_____%	Y S J/C	L P I B	C R S
12 _____	$_____	_____%	Y S J/C	L P I B	C R S
13 _____	$_____	_____%	Y S J/C	L P I B	C R S
14 _____	$_____	_____%	Y S J/C	L P I B	C R S
15 _____	$_____	_____%	Y S J/C	L P I B	C R S
16 _____	$_____	_____%	Y S J/C	L P I B	C R S
17 _____	$_____	_____%	Y S J/C	L P I B	C R S
18 _____	$_____	_____%	Y S J/C	L P I B	C R S
19 _____	$_____	_____%	Y S J/C	L P I B	C R S
20 _____	$_____	_____%	Y S J/C	L P I B	C R S

Asset Worksheet

Under Assets (*page 117*) . . . Don't forget to list the following:

ASSET CLASS	SECURITY	DESCRIPTION
Cash	Cash Equivalents	Deposits at savings institutions or banks (savings, checking and money market demand deposit accounts).
	T-Notes / CDs	Short-term government notes, CDs, and commercial paper.
Bonds	Government Bonds	Treasury Bonds, Government Agency Bonds.
	Municipal Bonds	Bonds issued by state and local governments.
	Corporate Bonds	Bonds issued by corporations – Investment Grade (A/AA or AAA credit rating). Include convertibles.
	High-Yield Bonds	Bonds issued by corporations – Non-Investment Grade (lower than A/AA or AAA credit rating).
	Mortgage Backed Securities	Securitized mortgage pools backed by GNMA, FNMA, FHLMC or other government agency. Include CMOs or REMICs.
	International Bond	Fixed income securities issued by companies domiciled outside of the United States.
	Fixed Income Mutual Funds / UITs	Mutual Fund (open-end or closed-end) or UITs which invest primarily in bonds or other fixed income securities.
Equities	Domestic Equities	Individual stocks issued by companies domiciled within the United States. Include REITs.
	International Equities	Individual stocks issued by companies domiciled outside the United States, (includes ADRs or foreign stocks listed on domestic exchanges).
	Equity Mutual Funds / UITs	Mutual funds (open-end or closed-end) or UITs which invest primarily in stocks.
	Options	Option contracts on equities.
	Employee Stock Options	Options on a company owned by an employee.
Insurance Annuities	Life Insurance Annuities	Whole Life, Variable Life, Universal Life, etc. Include any fixed or variable annuity contracts.
Other Investments	Limited Partnerships	Real Estate, Equipment Leasing, Cable TV and Energy programs.
	Real Estate	Investment or Personal real estate or property owned.
	Intangibles	Gold, coins, art.
	Business Interests	Franchise interests, small companies, other ventures.

Retirement Expenses Worksheet

	Amount x	Payments / Year =	Annual Expense
Home Mortgage	$_____	_____	$_____
Property Taxes	$_____	_____	$_____
Utilities	$_____	_____	$_____
Other Housing Expenses	$_____	_____	$_____
Auto Expenses	$_____	_____	$_____
Life and Health Insurance	$_____	_____	$_____
Long-Term Care	$_____	_____	$_____
Food	$_____	_____	$_____
Clothing / Grooming	$_____	_____	$_____
Child Care	$_____	_____	$_____
Travel / Entertainment	$_____	_____	$_____
Family / Charitable Gifts	$_____	_____	$_____
Loan Repayment	$_____	_____	$_____
Income Taxes	$_____	_____	$_____
Social Security Taxes	$_____	_____	$_____
Other Expenses	$_____	_____	$_____
Additions to Savings	$_____	_____	$_____

****

TOTAL $_____

% Of Current Combined Income: _____%

13 Disability Insurance

Disability Insurance Defined

Long-term care insurance is a child of disability insurance. We have chosen to include a chapter on disability insurance, both group and individual coverages, because disability insurance provides for replacement of your individual income during periods in which you cannot earn a living, or you have business expenses which must be paid whether you are at work or not.

As an example, if you were a doctor or dentist and suddenly had an incapacitating injury, the expenses of the office must continue to be paid. Salaries, rent, equipment and other vital services of an office must continue to be covered, or the business will shut down. If the individual returns to work after the illness and cannot start the business again, serious, substantial, long-term loss of income results. Disability insurance can fill the gap.

A second situation where disability insurance is appropriate is the case of an individual hurt in a car accident and unable to work for an extended period. If the employer did not provide disability coverage, and benefits were exhausted under state and federal disability programs, the injured employee would have no income without disability coverage.

Such insurance would also assist someone who developed a debilitating illness and could no longer work at his or her current occupation. The individual would need replacement income to age 65, above and beyond the benefits that might be provided by federal and state disability programs, which are, in any case, minimal at best.

Long-term care insurance is an outgrowth of the concept of disability coverage, which has been available to Americans for more than 80 years. Disability insurance carriers have developed long-term care policies as a result of their experience in the disability insurance market over the years. Long-term nursing care coverages are, in some cases, provided as riders to disability policies.

Some disability policies will provide coverage even after age 65, if the person continues to be gainfully employed. In the alternative, some disability policies can be converted to a long-term care policy, which may avoid the necessity of qualifying for a long-term care policy. Why is this important? By the time a person reaches the late 50s and 60s, he or she may be suffering from illnesses or injuries that could be debilitating and would otherwise bar long-term care coverage. Having a rider attached to a disability policy that allows for issuance of a long-term care policy automatically avoids the issue of qualifying and provides a cost-effective policy.

Sandra

Sandra was a 26 year-old fitness instructor who was involved in a car accident in which she broke her back and nearly died. Her medical bills exceeded half a million dollars, but she had medical coverage that paid those bills. Still, during her rehabilitation, Sandra could not work and had no other source of income. Through her employer, however, she had group disability insurance. This kept her from becoming destitute while she recovered, saved her assets and allowed her to return to her previous lifestyle.

Figure 13-1   (View Online at www.longtermcarebooks.com)

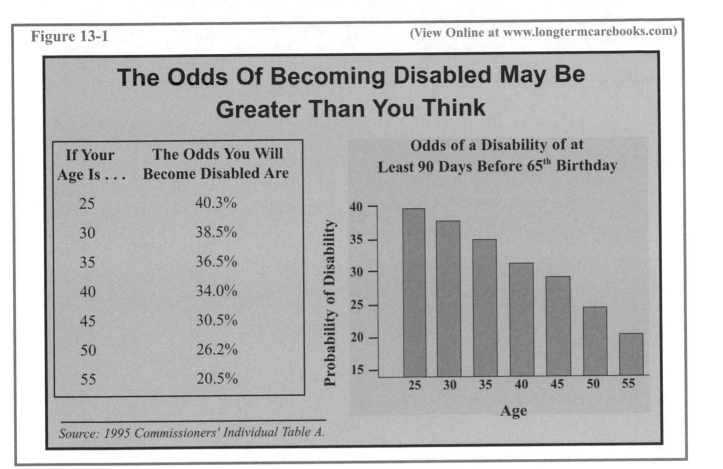

The Odds Of Becoming Disabled May Be Greater Than You Think

If Your Age Is . . .	The Odds You Will Become Disabled Are
25	40.3%
30	38.5%
35	36.5%
40	34.0%
45	30.5%
50	26.2%
55	20.5%

Odds of a Disability of at Least 90 Days Before 65th Birthday

Source: 1995 Commissioners' Individual Table A.

Why Buy Disability Insurance?

Disability insurance (short- and long-term) is designed to replace a portion of your income should you become partially or totally disabled. Your employer may provide a group policy and you may also be able to obtain individual coverage. This provides substantial protection to maintain your lifestyle.

Ask yourself the following questions:

- How long can I survive financially without any income if I become disabled? Even if you saved 10 percent of your income each year, one year of disability could wipe out 10 years of savings.

- How will I pay my rent or mortgage and other living expenses should I become disabled?

Consider these sobering statistics:

- 2 out of 5 workers age 45 and up will be disabled 90 days or longer before retirement.[1]

- Nonfatal workplace injuries and illnesses occurred at a rate of 4.6 cases per 100 equivalent full-time workers among private industry employers in 2005, resulting in a total of 4.2 million nonfatal injuries and illnesses in private industry workplaces.[2]

- 16.9 million working-age Americans, or 10.1 percent of the population who are 16 to 64 years old, have a work disability (a limitation in the amount of work they are able to perform, due to a chronic condition or impairment).[3]

- Only 28 percent of totally disabled workers qualify for Social Security benefits.[4] In order to receive Social Security you must be so severely impaired that you cannot perform ANY substantial gainful work, and this impairment must be expected to last at least 12 months or result in early death.

Group vs. Individual Disability Insurance

Group Disability Coverage – Advantages:

- Can cost less than individual disability coverage;

- Does not require medical questionnaires, as are required for individual coverage;

- Can be provided by your employer, or in some cases can be purchased individually through an employer. In the latter case, each employee can decide the amount of coverage to purchase and it can be automatically deducted each month;

Disadvantages:

- Has more restrictions than individual policies on when benefits will be paid;

- May no longer cover you if you leave that employer, although you may be able to convert to individual coverage;

- Normally can be discontinued on 30-60 days notice to the employer or association sponsor.

Individual Policies – Advantages:

- Provide coverage that cannot be terminated if you change employers, as long as you pay the premiums;

- Provide access to benefits more easily than group contracts, in most cases;

- Can be purchased in addition to group coverage, so that you more fully cover your income;

- Can provide coverage for business overhead expenses, if you as the manager or owner are disabled.

Tax Consequences of Group Policies

Group disability policies have the following tax implications:

- If the employer pays for the coverage, the employee is not taxed on the amount of the premiums, but does pay tax on any benefits collected under the policy;

- If the employee pays for the coverage with a monthly salary deduction, the employee pays taxes on the money used to pay the premiums, but not on benefits collected under the policy.

Tax Consequences of Individual Policies

- Individual disability insurance policies purchased with after-tax dollars by the insured will provide the disability benefits on an income tax-free basis;

- Premiums for business overhead disability policies are normally deductible as an ordinary and necessary business expense and any benefits that are paid out are normally offset by any expenses incurred by the business during a period of disability for the owner of the business, so no tax is due on benefit payments;

- Depending on the structure of the individual disability plan provided for the employees of a small corporation, it is sometimes possible to arrange the payment of the premiums on a tax-free basis;

- Corporations can specify that only certain individuals receive these benefits to the exclusion of other employees, but the corporation will still receive tax benefits.

Wayne and Betsy

In 1987, Wayne and Betsy came to me to review their financial planning needs. During the course of the meetings that we held, it was determined that Betsy's income, which was $3,000 per month, was the main funding source for their mortgage payments. Wayne's income was used to cover the other family expenses and education for their child.

I recommended to Wayne that, since his company provided disability coverage for him, there was no need for a disability policy for him personally. In the case of Betsy, I recommended a disability policy that would protect her income should she become disabled. At that time, Betsy was 43 and Wayne 58, and their child was 5.

Betsy and Wayne were reluctant to make an investment of approximately $2,000 per year for the coverage. Ultimately they did, although Wayne thought it was a poor investment.

Nine months after they took out the policy, Betsy was rear-ended in a car accident and seriously injured. Her ability to sit at a desk, type, do paperwork, or do any type of office work was destroyed, and she was totally and permanently disabled. At age 43, she had no income because federal and state disability benefits ran out in less than one year.

However, after a 30-day waiting period, her new disability policy began to pay benefits. She received, and continues to receive, $1,800 per month, completely tax-free, since the policy was purchased with the couple's personal income. She will receive that income until age 65, when she will then have her IRA accounts and Social Security. The total amount of benefits she will receive will be about $450,000 over the years from age 43 to age 65.

What to Ask About Disability Insurance

Because of the variation among disability insurance policies, you should review coverage with an experienced insurance advisor. Questions you should ask include the following:

- When will the benefits start paying if I am disabled?
- How long will the benefits last?
- Under what circumstances can I access benefits (what kinds of health conditions and how severe)?
- How will the benefits and the premium cost interface with state and federal disability programs?
- Is it possible to extend the coverage beyond age 65 if I continue to work?
- Can I increase the coverage through a guaranteed benefit option later on?
- Does the policy provide an inflation-adjustment rider that I can purchase?
- What kinds of serious health conditions could prevent me from getting coverage? (Some companies will decline certain illnesses and other companies will not. Once a decline shows up on your medical insurance record, it becomes increasingly difficult to get coverage elsewhere.)
- What percentage of my income will the policy pay if I am disabled?
- Will I be covered the same whether disability is due to illness or an accident?
- What is the definition of partial or part-time disability due to an accident or injury, where I am able to work part-time?

- Is the policy directed to my occupation (i.e., if I am a surgeon and can no longer practice surgery, but can teach at a local hospital, will I receive the benefit or a portion of the benefit up to age 65)?

- Is the policy guaranteed renewable as long as I work?

Federal and State Benefits

If you are no longer able to work and are permanently and totally disabled, federal payments can average $700 per month for a single person and up to $1,200 for a married person with dependents. This is based on age at the time of disability, the number of years the person has been gainfully employed and average income over that period of time.

There are two ways to access more specific information. You can go to the government website: *www.ssa.gov*, or call directly: 800-772-1213. It is also important to check with your individual state disability program to find out what is provided based on the payments made by your employer and yourself over the years of your employment.

It is vital that you understand that these programs are not a free lunch. It is very difficult to qualify for benefits and you must be totally disabled for nine to twelve months, in most cases. The definition of total disability is very restrictive.

More than two-thirds of the claims filed for federal and state benefits are declined because the applicants are not severely disabled.

(Determining how much coverage you need)
DISABILITY INCOME

Current coverage provides:

After	____days/ weeks	____days/ weeks	Six months	_____	_____	_____	Age 64
NEED	$_____	$_____	$_____	$_____	$_____	$_____	$_____
Social Security			$_____	$_____	$_____	$_____	$_____
Company Plan(s)	$_____ $_____	$_____ $_____	$_____ $_____	$_____ $_____	$_____ $_____	$_____ $_____	$_____ $_____
Other	$_____	$_____	$_____	$_____	$_____	$_____	$_____
Income	$_____	$_____	$_____	$_____	$_____	$_____	$_____
TOTAL	$_____	$_____	$_____	$_____	$_____	$_____	$_____
NEED	$_____	$_____	$_____	$_____	$_____	$_____	$_____
NEW	$_____	$_____	$_____	$_____	$_____		

FAMILY MONTHLY INCOME

# Years / # Survivors:	____years Surviving spouse & 2+ children	____years Surviving spouse & 1 child	____years Surviving spouse	____Life Surviving spouse age 60
NEED	$_____	$_____	$_____	$_____
Social Security	$_____	$_____		$_____
Co. plan(s)	$_____ $_____	$_____ $_____	$_____ $_____	$_____ $_____
Insurance	$_____ $_____	$_____ $_____	$_____ $_____	$_____ $_____
Other income	$_____ $_____	$_____ $_____	$_____ $_____	$_____ $_____
TOTAL	$_____	$_____	$_____	$_____
NEED	$_____	$_____	$_____	$_____
NEW	$_____	$_____	$_____	$_____

14 Choosing a Nursing Home or Nursing Care Services

Choosing a nursing home for yourself, a loved one, or a friend is an important and difficult decision. Often this decision must be made in a crisis situation, such as when a person is about to leave the hospital or soon after a serious illness or operation. Finding the right nursing home is of utmost importance not only for the well being of the patient, but because it may become that person's home for the remainder of his or her life. A website (provided by Medicare) that may be of significant value is:

http://www.medicare.gov/NHCompare/home.asp

Following are some guidelines to help you select the most appropriate nursing home for your situation:

- Find out what nursing homes are located in your community and learn what you can about them. Ask people you know about any nursing homes they know about. Visit friends or relatives who live in a nursing home to get a first-hand impression. Find out if the nursing home you visit has a list of references of residents' family members;

- Check with the state Department of Health Services' Licensing Field Office and ask to see the latest "Health Facilities Directory." This lists all facilities currently licensed by the state Department of Health Services, by county, including the address, administrator's name, type of facility, number of beds and other information;

- Examine the state Department of Health Services' nursing home inspection records of each nursing home you visit. Every home is required to make such records available. You may also refer to the website previously mentioned;

- Contact your local Ombudsman's office for information about choosing a nursing home in your neighborhood (see the Resource Directory on our website, *www.longtermcarebooks.com*);

- Make a personal visit to each place you have determined appropriate. Pick locations close to home and relatives or friends, if possible. Visit at least three or four to get a better idea of the type of nursing home that fits your needs and preferences. Make an appointment with the administrator, director of nursing or social services director and bring along a list of questions.

Things to Consider When Visiting a Nursing Home

- Note the physical condition of the nursing home – be sure it is clean and well maintained;

- Observe the interactions between the staff and the residents. Does the staff listen attentively and respectfully to residents? Observe the interactions among the residents themselves. Are they relating to each other? Are there visitors? What is the atmosphere – does it appear home-like or institutional?

- Speak with the staff, the residents and their families;

- Try to visit more than once, at different times of the day;

- Visit during mealtimes. Are residents eating in their rooms or in a dining room? Are those who need assistance receiving it? Are residents eating and enjoying the food? Are they talking with one another over the meal?

- Ask about the activities program, and what is offered. Would the activities appeal to you or your family member?

- Ask the director or social services director how decisions are made to provide therapy or rehabilitation to a resident;

- Ask about admissions criteria. Find out if the facility participates in Medicare. Ask if your family member is eligible for it, and if so, how many rooms are certified for Medicare. Does the resident have to move to another room when the Medicare coverage is exhausted?

- Ask about payment requirements and billing procedures. If you will be paying privately, what services does the daily rate cover and what are the charges for extra services? If your family member will be on Medi-Cal, ask whether the facility participates in Medi-Cal and which services are not covered by the Medi-Cal rate;

- Evaluate the quality of the care and the concern for the residents that you see. The staff should show a true interest in each person;

- Ask how many residents, on average, each nurse's aide or direct care nurse is assigned;

- Ask the dietitian for a list of menus for the month and taste a sample of the food being served. How are special diets handled?

- Ask about access to eye doctors and dentists;

- Make sure the special services your family member may require are available, such as physical therapy, or extra guidance and safety for an Alzheimer's patient.

For more information, contact the Licensing and Certification District Office and the Ombudsman Program in your county. (See the Resource Directory on our website, *www.longtermcarebooks.com*.)

Costs of Care

The average daily cost of a private room (single occupant) in a nursing home in the United States increased 2.2% from 2005 to 2006, according to a study conducted by Genworth Financial in 2006.[1] The average daily nursing home cost was $194.28 ($70,912 annually) compared to a rate of $190.20 per day in 2005.

Alaska continued to have the highest average annual cost, at $191,140, for a private room, followed by New York City at $140,708. Louisiana and Missouri (excluding St. Louis and Kansas City) had the lowest average annual costs for a private room, at $42,304 and $43,249, respectively (*see Figure 14-1*).

The average annual cost for a semi-private room (double occupancy) nationally was $62,532 ($171.32 per day), up 2.3% from $167.44 in 2005. These costs are particularly important to families choosing how to care for a loved one. The 1999 *National Nursing Home Survey* conducted by National Center for Health Statistics indicated that the average nursing home stay for patients currently in residence was two and a half years. This makes the cost of an average nursing stay a whopping $156,330.

Researchers in the Genworth study also found that, on average, the cost of care for a private nursing home room in America's urban areas was 17% greater than in non-urban areas. The greatest disparity exists in New York City, where the cost of care was 68% greater than the cost of care in New York's non-urban areas. The cost of care in San Francisco is 45% greater than the cost of care in California's non-urban regions.

Assisted living facilities (ALFs) were surveyed to determine the rates for private one-bedroom units.

All ALFs surveyed were licensed by the state as assisted living facilities or other comparable residential care facilities. Nationally, the average monthly cost for a private one-bedroom unit is $2,691.20 (implying a daily rate of $88.48/day), reflecting an average annual cost of $32,294.40 – a 6.7% increase over 2005 survey rates ($30,265/yr.). These rates exclude any onetime community or entrance fees. Nationally, the average one-bedroom rate increased $2,029 per year ($169/mo.) compared with Genworth's 2005 survey. The highest annual costs for one-bedroom units in ALFs is the Bridgeport area of Connecticut ($57,566.52 excluding community fees) and the state of New Jersey, excluding the Newark and Edison areas, ($51,314.41 excluding community fees). North Dakota ($20,714 excluding community fees) and Arkansas ($20,937 excluding community fees) have the lowest annual cost for a one-bedroom unit in an ALF. Approximately 33% of the ALFs surveyed charge a one-time fee, commonly referred to as a community or entrance fee, ranging from $50 to $8,490 with a national average onetime fee of $1,369.68.

Home care providers were classified into three types, according to certification and license status. The three provider types are:

• Medicare certified home care providers. These providers are also licensed.

• Non-certified but licensed home care providers.

• Non-certified and non-licensed home care providers.

Researchers surveyed all three home health provider types to determine the hourly charge for care provided by certified Home Health Aides. Also, the two types of non-certified providers were surveyed to determine the hourly charge to provide homemaker services. Across all home care provider types, the average hourly rate for home health aides is $25.32, a 13% increase over 2005 survey results. The average hourly rate for homemaker services is $17.09, a 3% increase over 2005 survey results. Certified home care providers charge the most for home health aides, averaging $36.22 per hour (a 17% increase over 2005), compared to $22.15 per hour charged by non-certified but licensed providers (a 19% increase over 2005), and $17.57 per hour charged by non-certified and unlicensed providers (flat compared to 2005). Unlike certified home care providers, the non-certified providers also offer homemaker services. Nationally, non-certified but licensed providers charge $17.73 per hour (a 5% increase compared with 2005 survey results), while non-certified and unlicensed providers charge $16.45 per hour (flat compared to 2005).

"The rise in these long-term care costs of 5% and more constitutes a crisis for many people who have not made the necessary financial preparations," said Sandra Timmerman, Ed.D., director of the MetLife Mature Market Institute and a gerontologist. "As we age, the more likely we are to develop conditions that result in the need for ongoing day-to-day assistance with activities of daily living. Because long-term care services are so costly and the costs will increase significantly over time, planning for long-term care must be an integral part of the retirement planning process."[2]

Figure 14-1 (View Online at www.longtermcarebooks.com)

Average Daily Room Rates for a Private Nursing Home Room – 2006

Alaska $523.67	Kansas $122.04	New York City. $385.50
Alabama $147.46	Kentucky $152.41	Buffalo, New York $255.21
Arkansas $127.22	Louisiana $115.90	New York (rest of state) $230.12
Phoenix, AZ $199.72	Boston, MA. $282.07	Ohio $179.67
Tucson, AZ $175.08	Massachusetts (rest of state). $273.45	Oklahoma. $134.87
Los Angeles, CA $203.95	Baltimore, MD $201.91	Portland, OR $195.13
Oakland, CA. $242.27	Maryland (rest of state) $181.20	Oregon (rest of state) $190.93
San Diego, CA $197.59	Maine $219.43	Philadelphia, PA $249.26
San Francisco, CA $268.40	Detroit, MI. $173.14	Pennsylvania (rest of state). $209.25
Denver, CO. $169.82	Michigan (rest of state). $182.68	Rhode Island $200.82
Colorado (rest of state). $164.89	Minneapolis, MN $155.87	South Carolina. $151.97
Bridgeport, CT $337.70	Minnesota (rest of state) $131.25	South Dakota. $151.97
Connecticut (rest of state) $314.86	Kansas City, MO. $158.49	Tennessee. $151.18
Washington, DC. $219.98	St. Louis, MO $124.90	Austin, TX $139.85
Delaware. $196.70	Mississippi $151.05	Dallas, TX $156.95
Jacksonville, FL $175.42	Montana. $154.96	Houston, TX $270.80
Miami, FL. $224.99	Charlotte, NC. $164.20	San Antonio, TX $144.54
Orlando, FL $187.94	North Carolina (rest of state) $168.74	Texas (rest of state) $129.23
Atlanta, GA. $159.77	North Dakota. $133.75	Utah $165.18
Georgia (rest of state). $134.91	Nebraska $130.90	Virginia. $158.53
Hawaii. $270.92	New Hampshire. $233.10	Vermont $207.55
Iowa. $130.50	Newark, NJ $270.92	Seattle, Washington. $235.60
Idaho $155.25	New Jersey (rest of state) $236.00	Washington (rest of state). $185.72
Chicago, IL. $167.05	New Mexico $151.29	Wisconsin. $199.13
Illinois (rest of state) $155.84	Las Vegas, NV. $188.07	West Virginia $176.02
Indianapolis, IN $176.05	Nevada (rest of state) $184.24	Wyoming $156.64

Average Hourly Rates for Home Health Aide (All 3 Provider Types) – 2006

Alaska. $42.78	Kansas $24.05	New York City. $17.63
Alabama $26.80	Kentucky $21.20	Buffalo, NY $23.44
Arkansas $29.42	Louisiana $25.77	New York (rest of state) $25.32
Phoenix, AZ $19.13	Boston, MA. $22.12	Ohio $20.00
Arizona (rest of state) $22.88	Massachusetts (rest of state). $21.99	Oklahoma. $20.16
Los Angeles, CA $24.57	Baltimore, MD. $19.73	Portland, OR $35.71
Oakland, CA. $34.37	Maryland (rest of state). $22.05	Oregon (rest of state). $49.36
San Diego, CA $33.45	Maine $26.69	Philadelphia, PA $22.93
San Francisco, CA $44.97	Detroit, MI. $22.93	Pennsylvania (rest of state). $20.45
Denver, CO. $23.39	Michigan (rest of state). $18.43	Rhode Island $23.95
Colorado (rest of state) $20.68	Minneapolis, MN $26.32	South Carolina. $21.29
Bridgeport, CT $22.17	Minnesota (rest of state) $31.45	South Dakota. $23.77
Connecticut (rest of state) $26.27	Kansas City, MO. $22.48	Tennessee. $30.14
Washington, DC. $21.26	St. Louis, MO $27.74	Austin, TX $21.93
Delaware. $28.56	Mississippi $37.56	Dallas, TX $26.98
Jacksonville, FL $19.21	Montana. $19.15	Houston, TX $19.72
Miami, FL $15.30	Charlotte, NC. $21.10	San Antonio, TX $25.94
Orlando, FL $17.31	North Carolina (rest of state) $20.60	Texas (rest of state) $20.80
Atlanta, GA $32.78	North Dakota. $29.53	Utah $21.01
Georgia (rest of state) $22.37	Nebraska $26.06	Virginia. $18.49
Hawaii $27.35	New Hampshire. $26.96	Vermont $31.86
Iowa. $22.39	Newark, NJ $19.58	Seattle, WA $34.73
Idaho $21.06	New Jersey (rest of state) $23.74	Washington (rest of state). $28.23
Chicago, IL. $24.56	New Mexico $27.74	Wisconsin. $29.29
Illinois (rest of state). $27.89	Las Vegas, NV. $23.67	West Virginia $32.84
Indianapolis, IN $22.88	Nevada (rest of state) $28.74	Wyoming $30.61

Source: "Genworth Financial 2006 Cost of Care Survey: March 2006 Nursing Homes, Assisted Living Facilities and Home Care Providers." ©2006 Genworth Financial, Inc. and National Eldercare Referral Systems, Inc. (CareScout)..

15 The World of Long-Term Care

World Graying Quickly, Population Study Finds[1]

Feeling old? You're not alone. According to a United Nations study released in 2005, the whole world is getting older — and at a pace that has taken demographers by surprise and presented governments with economic and social challenges.[2] About 10% of the world's population is now older than 60, and by mid-century that will double to 20% — marking the first time that group will outnumber children.

"This is unprecedented in human history," said Joseph Chamie, director of the U.N. Population Division, who supervised the study. The trend is most acute in advanced industrial nations, where the working-age population is shrinking as the number of older citizens steadily increases — a development with profound implications in a world where fewer and fewer workers will be supporting more and more older dependents, Chamie said.

Yet ultimately, U.N. experts stress, these statistics depict a medical and socioeconomic triumph. In much of the world, increasing longevity has been matched by radically declining birth and infant mortality rates. Women choose the timing and frequency of childbirth with the confident expectation that their infants will thrive.

In Japan and Italy — now the two "oldest" countries, with a median age above 40 and climbing — the United Nations projects nearly one-quarter of the population is already older than 60 and that will pass 40% by 2050. But U.N. experts say these countries aren't the demographic anomalies they were once thought to be. Nations where the 60-plus population is expected to swell to about 40 % in half a century include Germany, Spain, Switzerland, Greece, Sweden, Bulgaria, Slovenia, the Czech Republic and Armenia. Most other developed countries aren't far behind. The exceptions are nations with many young immigrants — led by the United States, where the 16% of the population now older than 60 is expected to rise to 27% by 2050.

Worldwide, the number of people age 60 and up will more than triple, to 1.96 billion, in the next 50 years, according to U.N. forecasts, to one-fifth of the world's predicted population. Even in places where the median age is extraordinarily young — in most of Africa and the Middle East, just 5% of the population is older than 60 — U.N. demographers predict similarly stunning shifts in a generation or two.

Most striking of all is the expected rapid growth in the population of those 80 and up, nearly two-thirds of whom are women. Centenarians, once revered anomalies, now number about 210,000. By 2050, there will be 3.2 million people 100 or older, the United Nations estimates. This boom will produce economic strains as the group is supported either directly by families or indirectly through taxes.

As Population Boom Goes Bust, World Economy Faces Grim Future

If you're driving with a "Zero Population Growth" bumper sticker on your car, it may be time to get rid of it. According to the latest U.S. Census and U.N. data, worldwide birthrates have fallen 40% in the last half century and the decline is continuing. In fact we're heading into a global baby bust.

It's not just a European and American phenomenon. In more than 80 countries, including many large Third World nations, birthrates are so low that there are fewer births than deaths each year. That's true in the U.S., Canada, all of Western and Eastern Europe, Japan, China, Taiwan, South Korea, Thailand and Singapore. Birthrates are slightly higher in Brazil, Turkey and Iran, but are dropping quickly.

Nearly everywhere (except sub-Saharan Africa) the big challenge ahead isn't too many people. It's too few working-age people to support economic growth. This threatens Europe and Japan with economic stagnation and it could keep poor countries from making the leap to economic modernity.

Too Many Retirees?

Zero population advocates insist that reducing fertility rates spares the environment and improves quality of life, especially for women.

Discouraging fertility may yield unintended consequences for Third World countries. Curtailing birthrates at a time when people are living longer results in an increase in the ratio of elderly people to young people and retirees to workers. This means Third World countries will have a large dependent elderly population and not enough young workers to support a growing economy.

Three demographic experts, Wolfgang Lutz, Warren Sanderson and Sergei Scherbov, announced in a recent *Nature* magazine article that the world's population will peak between mid-century and 2100, and then decline. They based their forecasts on U.N. population projections. Forecasting population growth for the next 100 years is admittedly speculative, but more concrete short-term population data also contradicts the myth of overpopulation.

Nicholas Eberstadt of the American Enterprise Institute finds that the global annual population growth rate, which was 2% in the 1960s and is now down to 1.3%, will drop to 0.8% by 2015. His conclusion? Zero population is an ideological "preoccupation" unjustified by facts.

Zero Growth Or Bust

Eberstadt's article, "The Population Implosion," in the March/April 2001 issue of *Foreign Policy* magazine, caused a stir. Groups such as Zero Population Growth, Population Action International and Planned Parenthood Federation of America don't question his data, but say they're "alarmed" by his conclusions. In a letter co-signed by these three groups and several others, Eberstadt's opponents charge that "he ignores the community benefits of a smaller population — reduced pressure on the environment and public services — the benefits to women and children for more options for their own lives."

Eberstadt responds that the zero population advocates are in denial about the grim reality ahead. Virtually every industrialized nation is struggling with the impact of lower birthrates on its future labor force. In 1998, the Organization for Economic Cooperation and Development said these nations should consider raising their retirement ages to avert a serious drop in standard of living.

The U.S. population is looking more and more like an upside-down pear, with a huge elderly population tottering on a working-age group too small to support it. The Social Security Administration estimates that between now and 2020, the 65-plus population will grow 100% while the group who are 20 to 64 years old will grow only 15%. According to the Congressional Budget Office, that could lead to economic slowdown in future decades due to a severe shortage of workers.

Possible remedies? The two discussed most often are keeping people working beyond age 65 and expanding the work force through immigration. A third remedy, having more babies, is rarely broached.

The U.S. is sitting pretty compared with Europe and Japan, which have even older populations.

By 2025, Japan's median age will be 49 years, more than 10 years older than in the U.S. Japan also faces the severest crisis because immigration is such an unlikely solution. Japan hasn't been willing to take in ethnic newcomers at any time over the last 1,000 years. So it faces a tough choice — racial purity or economic well-being — brought about in part by its steady drop in birthrates.

Immigration also sparks controversy in Europe. Demand is high for agricultural laborers — Moroccans are picking tomatoes in Spain, Poles are harvesting vegetables in Germany — and for outsiders to work as household help. European political leaders are calling for more skilled labor, such as computer technicians, from countries such as India.

Figure 15-1: WHO'S GROWING, WHO'S SHRINKING

Countries or areas with the highest and lowest annual population change, 2000-2005 and 2045-2050.

Country or area	Annual growth rate	Country or area	Est. annual growth rate
Highest rates	**2000-2005**		**2045-2050**
1. United Arab Emirates	6.51%	1. Uganda	2.39%
2. Qatar	5.86	2. Niger	2.12
3. Dem. Rep. of Timor-Leste	5.42	3. Burundi	2.10
4. Afghanistan	4.59	4. Liberia	2.08
5. Eritrea	4.26	5. Congo	2.07
6. Sierra Leone	4.07	6. Guinea-Bissau	2.05
7. Kuwait	3.73	7. Chad	2.03
8. Chad	3.42	8. Mali	1.84
9. Uganda	3.40	9. Afghanistan	1.83
10. Niger	3.39	10. Burkina Faso	1.75
Lowest rates			
1. Ukraine	-1.10%	1. Guyana	-2.25%
2. Georgia	-1.07	2. Tonga	-1.96
3. Bulgaria	-0.69	3. Samoa	-1.54
4. Latvia	-0.57	4. Ukraine	-1.52
5. Belarus	-0.55	5. United States Virgin Islands	-1.34
6. Estonia	-0.55	6. Georgia	-1.31
7. Russian Federation	-0.46	7. Micronesia (Fed. States of)	-1.19
8. Armenia	-0.43	8. St. Vincent and the Grenadines	-1.19
9. Lithuania	-0.40	9. Bulgaria	-1.09
10. Romania	-0.37	10. Cuba	-0.93
WORLD	**1.21%**	**WORLD**	**0.38%**

Source: Population Division of the Department of Economic and Social Affairs of the United Nations Secretariat (2005). *World Population Prospects: The 2004 Revision. Highlights.* New York: United Nations.

How many workers should be let in, and from where? These are questions hotly debated in almost every Western European nation. Current immigration is minuscule compared with what will be needed in future years. Net immigration would have to quadruple over the next 25 years, according to Eberstadt, to avert a work force decline, literally changing the face of Europe.

More People, Richer Nation

The industrialized nations became rich before their populations aged. In the Third World, declining birthrates threaten to push many nations into the dilemma of having a large elderly population and too few young people to work. Historically, an adequate labor force — both educated and sufficient in number — has been vital for a poor nation to make the leap into a modern, diversified economy.

Nearly all of the largest underdeveloped countries today have birth rates too low to produce an adequate working age population in the coming decades. That's a stark contrast to the youthful population that helped make the Industrial Revolution possible. The question is whether these countries, deprived of an adequate labor force by falling birthrates, can make it.

It's amazing how a myth persists even when the facts are in. There will be no population problem for most nations of the world in the foreseeable future. Instead, they'll be struggling with the unintended negative consequences of declining birthrates.

But don't throw away that "Zero Population Growth" bumper sticker. Just cross out the word "Zero."[3]

Population Trend Worrisome

Projected Steep Decline Has Experts Asking Quality-of-Life Questions

Imagine Japan 50 years from now with a third fewer citizens. Or a child born today reaching age 100 in a country with only half its current inhabitants — the same number of people it had in 1928.

Would Japan be a gloomy place mired in a semi-permanent recession, where the voices of children were rarely heard? Where the pulsing streets of Tokyo's Shibuya district, now so jammed that it is difficult to open an umbrella, were filled not with outrageously dressed youth but with white-haired and relatively poor seniors?

Or would it be a paradise where robots did most of the menial jobs and well-paid, hyper-educated men and women as old as 85 spent short but stimulating work shifts jousting with competitors in a high-tech global economy? Where Tokyo residents, for the first time in a century, could enjoy unobstructed sunlight, reasonable land prices, clean air, no traffic jams and room to sit down on a rush-hour subway and spread open a newspaper (or its digital equivalent)?

This is not a theoretical exercise. It's a dead-earnest debate among intellectuals, environmentalists and government planners, prompted by the steep Japanese population decline projected to begin by 2007. The debate resonates worldwide.

About 39 countries are expected to experience population declines over the next 50 years, even as the global population swells to about 9.3 billion, according to the United Nations Population Division. The dimensions of Japan's population decline are still uncertain. But even if its women begin having more babies, Japan will lose 14% of its population by 2050. If fertility does not recover, the population will halve in a century.

"We've never seen it," said Joseph Chamie, director of the U.N. agency. "We do not have enough experience to say what happens when a population declines by 50 percent." Chamie says it would be a mistake to dismiss the projections as merely hypothetical.

In 1953, the United Nations projected that world population in 2000 would be 6.2 billion. It is now estimated at 6.1 billion. Demographic projections are far more accurate than weather or economic forecasts, Chamie said. The number of people worldwide over 80 will increase fivefold by 2050. China alone will have about 400 million people over 60. Japan will have nearly 1 million people over the age of 100. Aging will have far-reaching effects on the leading industrialized nations, including potential pension shortfalls, labor shortages, falling savings rates and asset values, and eroding military capabilities, according to a study by the Center for Strategic and International Studies in Washington.

But there are key differences by country. Europe tends toward high unemployment and early retirement and has already absorbed millions of immigrants and guest workers. Japan's economy is built around low unemployment, with hard-driving people who want to keep working for as long as they can — all the more so in the decade since the economy began to falter.

The only country that has a population older than Japan's is Italy. But while Italy has bolstered its graying population with young immigrants, xenophobic Japanese are already worried about an increase in illegal immigration, and there are widespread fears that labor shortages will necessitate guest workers who may never go home. To keep its population stable, Japan would need 17 million immigrants by 2050, according to a U.N. study. That would mean 18 percent of the population would be immigrants — compared with just 1 percent now.

And while countries such as Italy have reduced public debt, Japan's government debt is skyrocketing — just when medical and pension outlays for the elderly are also about to soar. Private analysts, including Moody's Investors Service, have been warning for some time that the coming demographic upheaval could have dire fiscal consequences. They caution that a smaller work force shouldering higher taxes to support retirees will further depress consumption and growth. Reneging on pension commitments would undermine public confidence, but running up the red ink makes Japan more vulnerable to rising interest rates.

Political Crisis in the Making

Some warn of political tension between the generations, or even potential default. "There is probably going to be a crisis of large proportions within a decade," said Paul Hewitt, former director of the Center for Strategic & International Studies (CSIS) Global Aging Initiative study. "You can see the outlines of it in a potential default. This will essentially wipe out their welfare state and young people are not going to be taking old people in, because there won't be enough young people." Hewitt believes that both Japan and Europe will find themselves in recession for much of the period between 2025 and 2050.

The Japanese government is deeply concerned about a population that is growing older and smaller. Evidence of its distress is a chart, published in the Ministry of Health and Welfare's 1998 White Paper, showing that if the current birth rate were to continue for the next 1,400 years, Japanese would die out by the year 3500. The fertility rate fell further in 1999, moving the projected extinction date forward 100 years. However implausible its assumptions, the chart has been widely circulated, adding to the general climate of pessimism.

One major question being debated now is what a sustainable population for Japan would be. Some scholars and environmentalists argue that a declining population is inevitable, perhaps even desirable. Paul Ehrlich, a Stanford University biologist and author of the seminal 1968 book "The Population Bomb," argues that Japan should let its population decrease quickly now, while it has the economic vigor to manage the transition.

Shinji Fukukawa, head of the Dentsu Institute for Human Studies think tank in Tokyo, says the issue is not the size of the population so much as the ratio of elderly to young. "There is now much discussion that 100 million (population) is too much, so maybe 50 million is better," Fukukawa said. "But the problem is in the transition process."

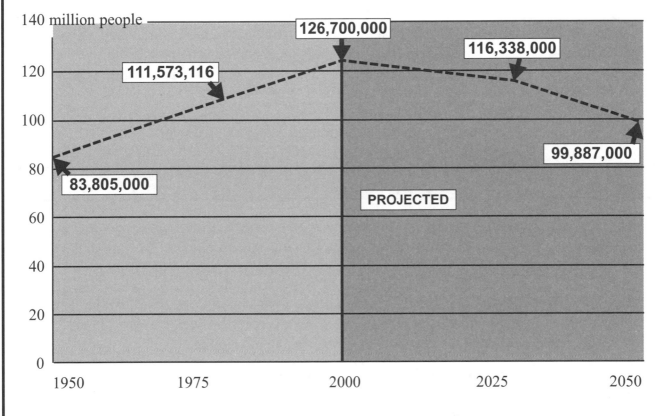

Figure 15-2: JAPAN'S SHRINKING POPULATION

The U.S. Bureau of the Census projects that Japan's 100-year population high will occur in 2007, when the projection is 127,492,699.

126,700,000

111,573,116

116,338,000

99,887,000

83,805,000

PROJECTED

140 million people

120

100

80

60

40

20

0

1950   1975   2000   2025   2050

Source: U.S. Census Bureau, International Data Base, April 26, 2005

Ehrlich argues that the optimum world population is one-quarter of its current level. He says Japan in particular, with its dearth of arable land, dependence on imported food and energy and great vulnerability to climate change from global warming, should adopt that goal. "It would be a great country to live in with 30 million people," Ehrlich said. Ehrlich's ideas are still outside the mainstream in Japan, where economic growth continues to have priority over environmental concerns.

But many Japanese liberals, environmentalists and feminists argue that their country's fixation on economic growth has been misguided. Overcrowding, high land prices, the rigid employment system, inflexible gender roles and quality-of-life issues should have equal attention, they say. "Why must we automatically have a recession when the population declines?" asks Keiko Higuchi, a specialist in gender studies and aging society at Tokyo Kasei University. "Whenever I go to places that are less densely populated, I think life there is so good. I believe our current population is too high."

Others argue that the common interpretation of many of the demographic statistics is too gloomy. For example, Japan's life expectancy — already the highest in the world at 81.5 years — is expected to increase to 88 by 2050. That is a pension planner's nightmare, but a public health triumph.

Nor must an aging work force be inherently inferior, some say. Japan has a history of stunning efficiency improvements, Fukukawa notes. He says the demographic crunch could spur innovation, productivity gains and better use of capital.[4]

16 Volunteer Support: A Link in Long-Term Care

According to an article published in the March 1, 1999, issue of *Newsweek* magazine, "In 30 years, there will be almost 70 million retirees in America – more grandparents than grandchildren. The Senior Boom is coming, and it will transform our homes, our schools, our politics, our families, our lives and our deaths. And not just for the older people. For everybody."[1] How will these aging Baby Boomers be cared for when chronic disease and frail older age intersect with a lack of support systems? Contra Costa County in the San Francisco Bay Area is on the cutting edge of this issue.

What is Caring Hands?

The Caring Hands Volunteer Caregivers Program was established to address just such issues for the county's already large senior population. Research by five Bay Area Agencies on Aging in the early 1990s indicated that, for the period 1990-2010, the county would experience a 237% increase in residents 85 and older (an increase of 17,000 individuals). These individuals are often very frail. Their spouses and peers have already died or are in poor health themselves and cannot provide support. The adult children, often living in other parts of the country, are overstressed, trying to juggle their own careers and the demands of raising their children while needing to care for their aging parents.

The research also indicated that during the same 20-year period the county would experience a 103.8% increase in those age 55 and over (an increase of 155,000 people). After months of discussion and planning, Caring Hands, a community-collaborative effort based on a national model, emerged to match volunteer caregivers to seniors in need. There are more than 1,200 volunteer programs similar to Caring Hands operating in counties across the nation.

Caring Hands seeks to expand and strengthen the network of care available to the chronically ill and frail by integrating the services of trained volunteers. The goal of the program is to enable seniors and other disabled individuals to maintain independence in their own homes as long as is safely possible, while seeking outpatient assistance for medical needs. The program is offered free to those who need its services, regardless of income.

How It Works

The statistics reported in the Bay Area study were certainly accurate. Even before starting services, Caring Hands already had a waiting list. Caring Hands is a collaborative of the John Muir/Mt. Diablo Health System, religious congregations of various faiths, the Interfaith Council of Contra Costa, and social service agencies. As a collaborative, the program has a sponsoring agency and fiduciary agent — the John Muir/Mt. Diablo Health System — which assumes in-kind and actual financial support, and whose board of directors is legally responsible for it. Others of the collaborative serve on the Advisory Committee and work closely with the Program Manager to direct the operations of the program through monthly meetings.

The work of Caring Hands is providing social support (not personal hands-on care) for those who contact the office or are referred to the program. Caring Hands enlists, trains and assigns volunteers, who provide assistance, support, respite and referral to those in need. In reality, the trained volunteers offer the type of support traditionally provided by family members. The intent of Caring Hands is to create long-term relationships through "matches" of volunteers and seniors, rather than one-time or short-term contact. Volunteer services are matched with seniors' needs, and include visiting, calling, transportation and escort, shopping and errands, light household chores, meal preparation, minor home repairs and yard work, letter writing, reading assistance, and respite care.

Referrals come to Caring Hands from the county's Senior Information and Referral Hotline; from the John Muir/Mt. Diablo Health System's Senior Services Program, Home Health Services and Discharge Planning/Case Management; from physicians; from other hospitals and home health services; and from social service programs such as the Lions Blind Center of Diablo Valley, Jewish Community Services, Senior Outreach Services, and Rossmoor Counseling Services (Rossmoor is an exclusive retirement community with a population of over 8,000). Calls also come directly from seniors who themselves realize their need for help, or from their family members, neighbors or friends who have heard about Caring Hands. An additional source of referrals is the religious congregations to which the seniors belong. These may be the first to become aware that an individual, once an active participant in the congregation, is now struggling with chronic health problems, is grieving the loss of a spouse, or is in the early stages of Alzheimer's disease or other dementia. Caring Hands works closely with religious congregations who sometimes recruit volunteers to participate in the program.

How Does A Caring Hands "Match" Occur?

First, a home assessment visit is conducted to assure the individual's needs can be met by a volunteer. The presence of a family member is encouraged during the home assessment whenever possible. Often the Caring Hands volunteer will assist a senior who is receiving care from other services as well, such as a home health aide who provides bathing assistance, or a home health nurse who may check on the healing of a wound. It is important to know in what other ways the senior is being assisted. Often, during the home assessment it is found that an individual has waited too long to call Caring Hands. He/she has become too frail and requires around-the-clock services, or referral to an assisted-living center or a nursing home.

If Caring Hands services are found to be appropriate during the home assessment visit, the care recipient signs a form that outlines the Caring Hands program and services the program will provide. The recipient retains a copy of the signed agreement.

If the individual or couple is considered appropriate for Caring Hands services during the home assessment, the Caring Hands Program manager and/or volunteer coordinator tries to "match" the senior with a volunteer from the program's Volunteer Bank who wants to provide the particular service needed by the senior.

How Are Volunteers Screened?

All volunteers have an interview with the program manager or volunteer coordinator. They must provide three references which are checked, have a professional background screening, and provide a copy of their driver's license and the declaration page from their automobile insurance (which are retained in their file). Each volunteer then undergoes tuberculosis testing. Upon being accepted, a photo identification badge is made for the volunteer.

Each volunteer is asked to make a six-month commitment to the program because of the bond the program wishes to create between the volunteer and the frail senior. During the interview, each volunteer determines which service or services he or she would like to perform, in which communities, and how many care recipients to assist in any six-month period. Each volunteer caregiver must participate in an all-day training seminar before he or she can be "matched."

The mandatory training for volunteers includes information on:

- The aging process and the county's Senior Information and Referral Program, presented by a manager or supervisor from the Contra Costa County Office on Aging;
- Confidentiality and the Health Insurance Portability and Accountability Act (HIPAA), presented by a nurse educator in the John Muir Medical Center Education Department;
- Signs of elder abuse, and setting limits, presented by a social worker who is the manager of John Muir's Senior Services program;
- "Active Listening" (stresses the importance of physical presence and the desire to listen without judging as healing tools when dealing with a person who is grieving over a loss);
- How to work with a person who is hard of hearing;
- Caring Hands policies and procedures, presented by the director of John Muir's Home Health Services;
- Sensitivity to cultural and religious diversity, presented by the director of Pastoral Care for the Medical Center;
- "Caring for the Caregiver," "Back Care for the Volunteer" and "Senior Use of Ambulatory Aids," presented by a physical therapy staff member of John Muir's Rehabilitation Services Department;
- The visually impaired, conducted by an instructor from the Lions Center for the Visually Impaired of the Diablo Valley; and
- Logistics of being a volunteer caregiver.

Caring Hands provides ongoing education for volunteers in five or six sessions each year. Some of the topics from the mandatory training are covered in more depth, while other subjects are new. Time in each session is set aside for socializing, for questions to the program manager and for group discussion and support. Continuing education sessions focus on such topics as "active listening," and grief and loss.

During the first four years of the program, Caring Hands touched the lives of more than 3,000 people, trained more than 350 volunteers ranging in age from 21 to 81, and served over 350 seniors with one-on-one service. More than 700 seniors received home assessment visits. A number of those were referred to other programs, while others were placed on the Caring Hands waiting list. Caring Hands provided information about, and referral to other senior services in the community, and in other parts of the country to more than 1,250 individuals. Volunteers provided over 35,300 hours of service in the first four years. The number one request by seniors in the service area is for transportation, and the number two request is for assistance with shopping and errands.

There have been some heartwarming matches. An 81-year-old volunteer is providing transportation for an 83-year-old. They are on their way to becoming good friends. An early member of the John Muir Auxiliary, who is now housebound, is having her grocery shopping done by a recent John Muir Auxiliary president.

Those involved in Caring Hands' development believe that what we see today is merely the "tip of the iceberg" of the contributions well-trained volunteers can make to people needing long-term care in the next few decades, as the 75 million or so Baby Boomers seek support during their later years.

CONTACT INFORMATION

Telephone: 925-952-2999 / Fax: 925-952-2998 / Website: *www.johnmuirhealth.com*
Mt. Diablo Medical Center, 1601 Ygnacio Valley Rd, Walnut Creek, California

138

17 The California Partnership for Long-Term Care

The California Partnership for Long-Term Care is a plan designed by the state of California, private insurers and consumers. It has the following goals:

- To educate consumers on the risks and costs of long-term care;

- To provide high-quality coverage; and

- To protect the assets of Californians when they need to pay for long-term care.

These policies are sold by private insurance companies. They are available to any citizen or legal resident of California, although they are primarily designed for individuals whose net worth is less than $600,000. Even a millionaire would receive the same promise of asset protection (a dollar for every dollar of coverage purchased), but would not be eligible for public assistance until all of his or her unprotected assets were exhausted.

You must live in California at the time you purchase the policy. To claim the asset protection, and to file for Medi-Cal, you must reside in California. If you leave California, your long-term care policy protection will still be in force to the limits of your policy, no matter where you choose to live.

Asset Protection

The "asset protection" feature of these policies helps people retain or protect more of their assets if they incur long-term care costs. Each dollar your Partnership policy pays in benefits will protect one dollar of your assets. For example, if you have $50,000 in assets and purchased a long-term care Partnership policy covering that amount, the policy would pay for your long-term care needs up to the policy limits of $50,000. If you still need long-term care after your benefits are exhausted, you may apply for Medi-Cal and keep the entire $50,000 you have in assets, instead of the $2,000 (for a single person) that would otherwise apply.

These policies have several other important features:

- Inflation protection (5% simple or compound for puchasers over 70). This will help your benefits keep up with some of the rise in cost of care;

- The premium is waived from the first day you receive care in a nursing home or assisted-living facility;

- Care in a residential care facility is covered;

- Premium increases are limited; and

- Each policy has standardized terms and a core set of benefits that make it easier to compare policies from different companies.

Insurance companies participating in the California Partnership Plan must have their policies approved by both the Department of Insurance and the California Department of Health Services.

Types of California Partnership Approved Policies

There are two kinds of California Partnership approved policies:

- Facility only: Covers care in a nursing home or residential care facility; and

- Comprehensive: Covers a full range of benefits for home and community services, such as home health care, personal care, homemaker services, adult day care, hospice and respite care. Care in a skilled nursing or residential facility is also provided.

Note: Both kinds of policies have built-in inflation protection, which means your asset protection increases at 5% compounded interest each year you keep the policy.

Inflation Protection

Both of these policies have inflation protection. The daily benefit and lifetime benefit maximums automatically increase by 5 percent simple or compound each year. The lifetime policy maximum is available to pay for any benefit covered by the policy. You may use your "pool of money" for any covered home and community care services that you choose, in the amounts that you select. You are not limited to any particular amount of care each day, as with some policies, but you may use the full month's benefit to construct the most effective care plan to meet your needs.

These policies pay for your care the same way other long-term care insurance policies do. If you still need care after you have spent all of your benefits ($50,000 in the example above), you must begin paying for your care yourself. However, you will qualify for Medi-Cal when you still have $50,000 in assets instead of $2,000 (Medi-Cal's current requirement for single people). Because the Partnership policy has the 5 percent inflation protection, the amount of assets you can keep and the benefits the policy will pay will increase by 5 percent simple or compound every year. When you purchase a policy you can select your daily benefit amount and the number of years you want the policy to cover.

A special plan is available to public employees of the state of California.

California Long-Term Care Insurance Plans for Public Employees and Their Families

The California Public Employees' Retirement System (CalPERS) offers a long-term care program. This program is available for nearly 5 million people, including all public employees and retirees, (all city, county and state employees; schoolteachers, legislators, judges and University of California employees). Employees may also enroll their spouses, parents and parents-in-law. Since the program was first offered in 1995, approximately 1.5 million employees and their families have enrolled. As of June 30, 2006, CalPERS provided benefits to 1,048,895 active and inactive members and 441,277 retirees.

The CalPERS program is a self-funded program and not an insurance company program. The funding for benefits comes from premiums members pay directly into the program. These premiums are invested at the direction of the CalPERS Board of Administration by an insurance administrator who manages the funds for CalPERS. Because CalPERS is self-funded and not-for-profit its plans tend to be less costly than comparable commercial policies.

Types of CalPERS Plans

CalPERS offers three types of plans:

- Nursing home/assisted-living facility *only*;

- Comprehensive: Covers both facility care and home care;

- California Partnership Plan: Covers both residential and home care and offers a "spend-down" protection feature.

A Partnership policy costs about the same or slightly less than other policies that offer similar coverage. But Partnership policies include lifetime asset protection and access to Medi-Cal services should you ever need them – an invaluable added benefit at no extra cost.

Because of the Partnership asset protection feature, you don't have to worry that you may run out of insurance benefits and end up spending the savings that you hoped to protect as you pay for ongoing care needs. The asset protection feature enables you to purchase policies with coverage equal to the amount of assets you want to protect from approximately $47,000 up to your total assets – with the assurance that these assets are protected for life, no matter how extended or expensive your long-term care needs may be. Without a Partnership policy, you could only achieve lifetime asset protection by purchasing lifetime insurance coverage . . . something most people cannot afford. This added protection and peace of mind comes only with the purchase of a Partnership policy. Each insurance company offering Partnership policies has its own premium rates. However, the younger you are when you purchase coverage, the less expensive your premium will be. That is a good reason to buy earlier. Any retirement planning needs to consider how you will pay for your long-term care.[1]

The Partnership Plan only protects assets, not income. When you receive Medi-Cal services you must still apply a portion of your income to the cost of your care if you have more income than the Medi-Cal limits allow. Please see *Figure 17-1* for a list of benefits with the CalPERS plans, including their Partnership policy, compared to their other offerings.

CalPERS

CalPERS Long-Term Care Program

Plan Features	Comprehensive Plan	Facilities Only Plan	Partnership Plan
Covered Services	• Nursing Home • Assisted Living Facility • Hospice Care • Respite Care • Home and Community Care	• Nursing Home • Assisted Living Facility • Hospice Care (Facility Based) • Respite Care (Facility Based) • *Does **not** cover Home and Community Care*	• Nursing Home • Assisted Living Facility • Hospice Care • Respite Care • Home and Community Care
Daily Benefit Amount (DBA)	$130, $150, $170, $200, or $250	$130, $150, $170, $200, or $250	$130, $150, $170, $200, or $250
Total Coverage Amount	Lifetime (Unlimited) **OR** Maximum Benefit (3 Years = 1,095 x DBA) or (6 Years = 2,190 x DBA)	Lifetime (Unlimited) **OR** Maximum Benefit (3 Years = 1,095 x DBA) or (6 Years = 2,190 x DBA)	Maximum Benefit: (1 Year = 365 x DBA) or (2 Years = 730 x DBA)
Inflation Protection (IP)	**Built-in IP*** increases your benefit amounts by 5% Compounded Annually. **OR** **Benefit Increase Option** lets you increase your benefit amounts periodically at an additional cost.	**Built-in IP*** increases your benefit amounts by 5% Compounded Annually. **OR** **Benefit Increase Option** lets you increase your benefit amounts periodically at an additional cost.	**Built-in IP*** increases your benefit amounts by 5% Compounded Annually. *Benefit Increase Option not available.*
Deductible Period	**90** calendar days once per lifetime.	**90** calendar days once per lifetime.	**30** calendar days once per lifetime.
Plan Benefit	• Nursing Home–100% of DBA per day. • Facilities Only–70% of DBA per day. • Home and Community Care–70% of DBA per day.	• Nursing Home–100% of DBA per day. • Facilities Only–70% of DBA per day. • *Does **not** cover Home & Community Care.*	• Nursing Home–100% of DBA per day. • Facilities Only–70% of DBA per day. • Home and Community Care–70% of DBA per day.
Benefit Eligibility	• Severe Cognitive Impairment or • 2 of 6 ADLs** for all benefits.	• Severe Cognitive Impairment or • 2 of 6 ADLs** for all benefits.	• Severe Cognitive Impairment or • 2 of 6 ADLs** for all benefits.
Care Advisor	**Available** to help develop Plan of Care and identify quality providers.	**Available** to help develop Plan of Care and identify quality providers.	**Required** to develop Plan of Care and identify quality providers.

Return of Premium Death Benefit	**Yes.** Returns some or all of your premiums less any benefits paid under this coverage to your spouse or your estate if you die before age 75 while this coverage is in force.	**Yes.** Returns some or all of your premiums less any benefits paid under this coverage to your spouse or your estate if you die before age 75 while this coverage is in force.	**No.** Not applicable.

* A Special Note About Premiums and Inflation Protection: Buying inflation protection can help ensure that your benefits will keep pace with the rising costs of long-term care. However, premiums may increase should the CalPERS Board determine it necessary to ensure adequate funding to pay future benefits. This increase would take place for all members of the same age with similar coverage. Should a rate increase occur, all members would receive a 60-day written notice and would have the option to adjust their coverage in order to maintain the premium amount they had been paying, if that is more affordable for them.

** ADL means Activity of Daily Living

Information available online at: calstate.edu/Benefits/carrier.materials/2005_LTCPlans.pdf .

Eligibility for Benefits

Partnership policies use the same "benefit trigger" criteria as Tax Qualified (TQ) policies. You may receive insurance benefits from your California Partnership policy if you are unable to perform two of the six activities of daily living (ADLs), which include: bathing, dressing, toileting, transferring, continence and eating; or if you have a severe cognitive impairment or a complex yet stable medical condition. An independent care management agency will assess your needs and develop a plan to coordinate the services required and monitor the quality of your care.

You can contact the CalPERS Customer Contact Center at 1-888-CalPERS (1-888-225-7377). They also have a TTY (telephone typewriter) number available for people with speech and hearing impairments at 916-795-3829 (Sacramento, California). There are also two Customer Service numbers available that may be helpful. The first is for the CalPERS 457 Deferred Compensation Program at 1-800-260-0659. The second is for the CalPERS Long-Term Care Program at 1-800-982-1775. Or visit their web site at *www.calpers.ca.gov.*

Three Examples Regarding Partnership Policies

Example #1

A single man in need of LTC purchases a **non**-Partnership LTC insurance policy with a maximum payout of $100,000. He owns a home worth $100,000 and has a bank account with $2,000. He enters LTC and, after exhausting the benefits of the LTC insurance policy, he applies for and is granted Medi-Cal benefits. Medi-Cal pays an additional $100,000 for his care.

Question: When he dies, what action would the Department of Estate Recovery (ER) take?

Answer: Since Medi-Cal paid a total of $100,000 for his care, ER would present a claim for $100,000 against his estate. While he was still able to qualify for Medi-Cal benefits, based on his exempt residence and $2,000 in the bank account, there is no asset protection provided by the policy because this was not a Partnership-approved policy. The ER, therefore, would pursue collection for $100,000.

Example #2

A widowed woman in need of LTC purchases a Partnership-approved LTC insurance policy with a maximum payout of $150,000. She owns the following assets:

- A home, in joint tenancy with her son, appraised at $100,000;

- A separately held savings account with $100,000; and,

- Separately held stocks and bonds worth $25,000.

After utilizing the Partnership-approved policy for the maximum amount in benefits, she applies for and is granted Medi-Cal benefits. Medi-Cal pays an additional $200,000 in benefits.

Question: When she dies, what action would ER take?

Answer: A claim in the amount of $200,000 would be presented against her estate. At the time of her death, she had the following interest in her assets:

$ 50,000 interest in real property;
$100,000 balance in savings account; and
$ 25.000 current valuc in stocks and bonds.
$175,000 total assets

While the home would be exempt for eligibility purposes and allow her to qualify for Medi-Cal benefits, it is no longer exempt for recovery purposes and would be included in the value of her estate assets. After applying the exemption provided by the Partnership-approved LTC insurance policy ($150,000), the Department's ultimate collection on the claim would be limited to $25,000. This exemption is only applicable, however, when the Partnership-approved LTC Insurance policy pays out benefits <u>and is</u> <u>limited</u> <u>to</u> <u>the</u> <u>payout</u> <u>amount</u>. Without the benefits of this policy, not only would she probably not have qualified for Medi-Cal benefits (until she spent down her assets) there would not be any protection for her assets against any future ER claim and she would owe the Department the full $175,000.

Example #3

A husband and wife apply for Medi-Cal for the husband who is in a long-term care facility. The couple has the following assets:

- A home, held in joint tenancy, appraised for $141,500;

- A joint savings account with $83,500;

- Other joint real property appraised for $100,000; and,

- Stock certificates, held jointly, worth $125,000;

- A total of $450,000 in joint assets.

The husband owned a Partnership-approved LTC insurance policy and ER was provided with a service summary, which verified that $225,000 in benefits has been paid under the policy. Medi-Cal paid an additional $300,000 in benefits. The wife did not utilize Medi-Cal.

Question: When the husband dies, what action does ER take?

Answer: ER would take no collection action during the lifetime of the wife. When the wife dies, however, ER will present a claim against her estate for the husband's Medi-Cal usage.

At the time of his death, the husband's interest in the joint assets totaled $225,000 (or one half of their value) and passed to his wife upon his death. There were no statutory exemptions to the claim. Since the provided service summary indicated $225,000 in benefits, the dollar-for-dollar exemption will bar ER from collecting on its claim.

Appendix A

Additional Information on Reverse Mortgages

How Senior Citizens Can Claim Lifetime Tax-Free Income

"You saved my mother's life."

That was the opening sentence of the best letter I ever received. I should have saved it and framed it. The writer was a schoolteacher and the daughter of a senior citizen homeowner. She was worried her mother would be forced to sell her beloved home because she couldn't afford its property taxes and mounting repair costs. Unfortunately, the schoolteacher was not in a financial position to help her mother.

But the daughter read one of my articles about the benefits of reverse mortgages for senior citizen homeowners. She shared it with her elderly widowed mother, who enjoyed her home, especially tending its garden, and wanted to stay there as many years as possible.

After several months of daughter-mother investigation of reverse mortgage choices, the happy result was obtaining a "lump sum" to pay the property taxes and necessary repairs, plus lifetime monthly income for as long as the mother lives in the home.

Even if the mother lives to 120 she will never have any personal repayment obligation. She can never be forced out of her home, because the reverse mortgage lender doesn't own the home.

The mother's home equity can be tapped by the reverse mortgage lender for repayment only when she (1) decides to sell, (2) moves out for more than 12 months, or (3) dies. The remaining home equity after repayment of reverse mortgage principal and interest then goes either to the homeowner or the heirs.

Sounds too good to be true — but it isn't.

What is a Reverse Mortgage?

Unlike a customary mortgage or a home equity credit line, which require monthly payments from the borrower to the lender, a reverse mortgage requires payments from the lender to the borrower.

But the reverse mortgage homeowner never needs to make any repayments to the lender until the loan "matures" and the homeowner sells, permanently moves out, or dies. There is no personal liability. The principal residence is the only reverse mortgage security.

To qualify for a reverse mortgage the homeowner must be at least 62. If husband and wife own the home, both must be at least 62 because the reverse mortgage payments are based on the life expectancy of the youngest homeowner. For example, a 70-year-old homeowner married to a 25-year-old has no chance of getting a reverse mortgage.

The Older You Are, The Better for Reverse Mortgages

Homeowner credit and income are irrelevant for obtaining a reverse mortgage (though you can't be in bankruptcy). However, the older you are, the more reverse mortgage money you can receive.

To illustrate, if you own a $250,000 home and are 65, you can receive $805 per month lifetime income from an FHA reverse mortgage. However, if you are a 75 year-old owner of the same house, you can receive $1,057 monthly for the balance of your life, even if you live to 120.

If your home has a modest existing mortgage balance, that's all right. But it must be paid off from the reverse mortgage proceeds because a reverse mortgage must be a first lien against the owner's primary residence.

Vacation or second homes are ineligible, as are farms, co-op apartments, houseboats and mobile homes. But manufactured homes on their own foundations on separate lots are eligible.

Who Makes Reverse Mortgage Loans?

There are three major nationwide reverse mortgage lenders, plus several state and local lenders. However, all reverse mortgages are originated by local representatives.

The "big three" nationwide reverse mortgage lenders are FHA (HECM, which means "home equity conversion mortgage)," Fannie Mae "Home Keeper," and the Financial Freedom Cash Account.

FHA reverse mortgages have a current $313,895 maximum (lower in low-cost counties), Fannie Mae has a nationwide $359,650 maximum, while the Financial Freedom Cash Account has no maximum. However, all reverse mortgages are based on: (a) the principal residence's current market value, (b) the age of its youngest homeowner, and (c) the current interest rates.

As a general rule, a 65 year-old homeowner can borrow up to 60 percent of the home's market value, a 75 year-old can borrow 69 percent of the home's value, and an 85 year-old homeowner can borrow up to 79 percent of the home's value. The reason these percentages seem low is because they consider the homeowner's life expectancy and the accrued interest over that time period.

Reverse Mortgage Interest Rates Are Now Ultra-low

Most reverse mortgage interest rates are adjustable, tied to the U.S. Treasury market interest rate. At the time of publication of this book, FHA reverse mortgage interest rates in 2006 were very low, at around 4.5 percent.

For this reason, reverse mortgages have recently gained great popularity as retirees watch their stock investments and dividends plummet. As of 2006, reverse mortgage volume had increased every year for the past five years in both the number of originations and dollar amounts.

Where to Find Local Reverse Mortgage Lenders

Although there are only three nationwide reverse mortgage lenders, you'll find many local reverse mortgage originators. However, not all banks and mortgage brokers offer reverse mortgages.

The largest reverse mortgage originators are Financial Freedom, Wells Fargo Mortgage, and Seattle Mortgage. The easiest way to locate local originators is on the Internet at *http://www.reversemortgage.org/LocateaLender/tabid/255/Default.aspx*. This website, sponsored by the non-profit National Reverse Mortgage Lenders Association, lists state-by-state lenders with phone numbers.[1]

Reverse Mortgages Gaining in Popularity

Older homeowners are increasingly choosing these loans as rising property values and low interest rates converge.

Baby boomers aren't the only ones jumping on record low mortgage rates and high home values to finance their dreams.

According to a national group of lenders that make reverse mortgages, older homeowners are also getting in on the action. The owners see it as a way to stay in a home and draw on its value for living expenses, health care, or home improvements.

Private, or proprietary, reverse mortgage loans are also available and in some cases can be much bigger, but the American Association of Retired Persons (AARP) cautions that they tend to cost more.

In a reverse mortgage, a borrower can take the loan all at once, monthly or as needed or in amounts that the borrower selects. The borrower or his or her estate must pay the money back plus interest and any other charges when he or she sells, permanently moves out, or dies.

Because a borrower makes no monthly payments the amount owed grows larger over time. That means the money left after selling a house and paying off the loan generally grows smaller. The borrower must also continue to pay property taxes, insurance and repairs. If not, the reverse loan becomes due and payable in full. But a borrower can never owe more than a home's value at the time the loan is repaid.

Bronwyn Belling, AARP's reverse-mortgage expert, cautions that potential borrowers must still do the fairly complicated math to determine whether a reverse mortgage is better than a home equity loan, buying a less-expensive house, renting an apartment, or moving to an assisted-living facility. A reverse mortgage would be expensive for those who sell a house quickly, in part because of high closing costs attached to the loan.

To order a free copy of the AARP brochure "Home Made Money: A Consumer's Guide to Reverse Mortgages," call 1-800-209-8085 or visit their website, *www.aarp.org/money/revmort/revmort_basics/a2003-04-07-homemademoney.html*. You can also download a PDF version of the brochure from the website.

The National Reverse Mortgage Lenders Association offers free brochures by phone at 202-939-1760 and their website is w*ww.reversemortgage.org*.[2]

Giving Seniors New Options

Lillian Hunter's life hadn't been the same since her husband Henry died last year. As a homemaker for 42 years, Lillian's career was raising their three children while Henry worked at one of the big oil companies in Houston. Unfortunately, he wasn't one of the privileged few executives, and during their retirement years they had come to rely upon Henry's pension checks to help them make ends meet.

It was only after he died and the pension checks went away that Lillian realized they hadn't developed a very effective retirement plan. To make matters worse, Lillian's HMO had shut down in her area the previous year and she suddenly was faced with high Medicare supplement premiums. She also was struggling with drug prescription costs and even began to skip a few doses to stretch her dollars. Every little penny counted now, so the cherished "girlfriends only" weekend tradition looked impossible to attend this year. In fact, Lillian began taking steps toward selling her house as a last-ditch effort to try to live the rest of her retirement years with grace and dignity. She would never ask the children for help because she knew they had financial concerns and responsibilities of their own.

Retired seniors with few assets and a poor retirement plan face serious issues, especially when they realize that they may have to downgrade their lifestyle just to fill prescriptions or pay for long-term care. No senior wants to swallow his or her pride, especially those with relatively good health and a comfortable life. A 1998 *New York Times* survey indicated that only 11 percent of the population who are 65 and older live in retirement communities, while 84 percent of all older Americans would prefer to stay in their own house and never move.

One morning, while having coffee, Lillian was reading the newspaper and glanced at an article about reverse mortgages. Because she had been considering selling the house, Lillian read how a widow — much like herself— watched her retirement income dwindle. To solve this income problem the woman took a lump sum reverse mortgage payment and used it to fund an immediate annuity. That solved her cash flow problem and the woman could continue living in her house.

Lillian made a few calls, and by the end of the day, a loan officer gave her 65,000 reasons why she shouldn't cancel her girlfriends' weekend. Without hesitation, she picked up the phone: "Darlene? Count me in for this weekend. I'll be there!"

A Brief History

Lillian Hunter isn't a real person, but her "house rich, cash poor" situation is. Records dating back to the 19th century show European investors purchasing homes from aging individuals and then permitting them to live in the home rent-free. During the 1920s in Great Britain, the business of home-equity reversion, a precursor to the current reverse mortgage, gained popularity although it took 50 years for the concept to catch on in the United States. Even then, these loans usually were sponsored by local government agencies and were available only for property taxes and home repairs.

In 1988, President Ronald Reagan signed legislation to launch the Federal Housing Administration's reverse mortgage program known as the Home Equity Conversion Mortgage (HECM). In 1995, the Federal National Mortgage Association (Fannie Mae) entered the scene with its HomeKeeper program. Currently, both programs are available in all 50 states and, according to the National Reverse Mortgage Lenders Association, about 90 percent of all reverse mortgage loans are processed through the Department of Housing and Urban Development. NRMLA also lists Financial Freedom Senior Funding Corp. as the nation's primary private lender of jumbo reverse loans, although the company operates in only 21 states.

Counseling Session

Whether a senior is looking to secure a Home Equity Conversion Mortgage or HomeKeeper loan, that applicant must first talk with an approved reverse mortgage counselor (see Figure App-1). The counselor is obliged to discuss the types of reverse mortgages available to an applicant and which would best suit his or her needs. They also must provide alternatives to a reverse mortgage, depending on the applicant's situation. These meetings usually are in person, but Fannie Mae allows phone counseling.

Reverse Mortgages and Long-Term Care

With the backing of HUD and the emergence of Fannie Mae, reverse mortgages have become a popular choice for seniors looking to uncover some much-needed retirement income.

Jeff Ludwick, CPA with Matthews, Ludwick, & Follender in Temple, Texas, agrees. "We believe that the reverse mortgage is one of the best kept secrets in estate and retirement planning. If used correctly, a reverse mortgage can assist many mature Americans and in doing so, often removes a financial burden from their children by providing immediate monthly income in what sometimes appears to be a hopeless situation."

In some cases, the initial mortgage insurance premium charged by FHA for a reverse mortgage can be waived if some of the proceeds of the loan are used to purchase a qualified long-term care insurance plan. For seniors who could not afford long-term care insurance previously, this becomes an attractive benefit.

Tax and Estate Implications

Once a senior homeowner with a reverse mortgage sells the house, moves out permanently, or dies, and the reverse mortgage is satisfied, amounts available under the homestead exemption are paid to the homeowner before involuntary lien creditors receive anything. The first and second liens required by the reverse mortgage plus the home exemption amount may exceed the fair market value of the home. The homeowner can then establish that there is nothing remaining for other judgment creditors to collect even if the house is sold. This exemption planning uses up the home equity with first and second mortgages and can make the residence judgment-proof against non-mortgage creditors.

Example: North Dakota provides an $80,000 homestead exemption. Assume a widow, age 72, has a $125,000 residence. Upon applying for an HECM reverse mortgage and obtaining a cash payout of $62,951, she has effectively judgment-proofed her home. Any involuntary lien creditor could not execute judgment against the residence because the home equity of $62,049 ($125,000 minus $62,951) is below the $80,000 exempt amount.

Tax Implications

Reverse mortgages are treated similarly to regular mortgages for tax purposes. Interest on reverse mortgages is classified as qualified residence interest, is deductible, and is subject to limitations from adjusted gross income. The interest is only deductible when it is paid. For a reverse mortgage the interest is usually paid when the loan is repaid at the time of death or when the borrower leaves the residence. Loan proceeds used to pay accrued interest or points on the same loan are not deductible until the loan is repaid.

A way to make loan points currently deductible is to pay the points with out-of-pocket cash at closing. The homeowner could then deduct the out-of-pocket points expense over the estimated life of the homeowner. This payment by the homeowner also increases the loan balance available for a tenure lifetime payout or increases the HECM line of credit that continues to grow tax-free.

The interest expenses accumulated during the life of the decedent are deductible as qualified residence interest. Qualified residence interest is interest paid on debts that are secured with a qualified residence of the taxpayer. A qualified residence is the taxpayer's main home or second home. Since reverse mortgages can only be taken out on the borrower's principal residence, the interest qualifies.

After the homeowner dies, an estate tax deduction for all interest and principal balances due on the reverse mortgage reduces the amount of federal estate taxes otherwise payable on the fair market value of the residence.

The loan interest that is deductible for income tax purposes is limited to the interest on the portion of the loan that does not exceed the borrower's qualified loan limit. For most reverse mortgages, the qualified loan limit is the same as the home equity debt limit, which is the smaller of $100,000 ($50,000 if married, filing separately), or the fair market value of the home. However, if part of the reverse mortgage is used to construct or substantially improve the residence, that part can be classified as acquisition indebtedness. For improvements the qualified loan limit is $1 million. Generally, interest on debt that exceeds the qualified loan limit is classified as personal interest and is not deductible for income tax purposes. However, the interest expense may be tax-deductible if the loan proceeds were used for investment or business purposes.

If the reverse mortgage ends in a foreclosure, the rules are the same as regular mortgage foreclosures. The foreclosure results in a realized gain to the borrower to the extent that the debt forgiven exceeds the adjusted basis in the property. If a loss results, the residence is a personal asset, and losses on personal assets are not allowed. For a qualified residence, realized gains up to $500,000 for married taxpayers ($250,000 for singles) are excluded for tax purposes. The home must have been the principal residence of the taxpayer for at least two out of the last five years before the foreclosure. This exclusion can apply to only one sale every two years.

Example: A homeowner has a $100,000 loan balance to pay on a reverse mortgage and the adjusted basis in the residence is $50,000 when the homeowner permanently moves to a home for the elderly. If the lender forecloses, the homeowner has $50,000 of realized gain. The $50,000 gain is excluded for income tax purposes if the homeowner lived in the residence for at least two of the last five years. The borrower must also not have used this exclusion in the last two years.

If the homeowner dies, the adjusted basis for the heirs is stepped up to the fair market value of the property. If the lender forecloses, the heirs have zero income because the terms of the mortgage limit the decedent's liability to the proceeds from the sale of the residence.

Example: A homeowner has a $100,000 loan balance to pay on a reverse mortgage and the adjusted basis in the residence is $50,000, and the homeowner continues to live at the residence until death. Assume the sale of the decedent's home provides net proceeds of $90,000. When the homeowner dies the heirs have at least a $90,000 stepped-up basis in the residence. The heirs are liable for only $90,000 of the $100,000 outstanding mortgage under the terms of the non-recourse debt and report zero net income.[3]

Conclusion

A retired homeowner should consider setting up a line of credit under the HECM plan, even before monthly payments are necessary, because there is a statutory limit on the aggregate number of reverse mortgages available. Currently the aggregate number of mortgages allowed to be insured under present statutory authority is 50,000.[4]

The U.S. Department of Housing and Urban Development's loan limits by area are available on the HUD Web site, *www.hud.gov*. Fannie Mae, a private company that invests in reverse mortgages, has a loan limit of $417,000 as of 2006.

REVERSE MORTGAGE SUMMARY

Basics	Reverse mortgages are home equity loans; The borrower doesn't make monthly loan repayments; The debt is repaid when the borrower(s) die(s) or permanently leave(s) their principal residence; The loan repayment is always limited to proceeds from the sale of the residence (non-recourse debt).
Who Qualifies?	Must be at least 62 years old; Home is your principal residence; Must own or nearly own your home.
Main Plans	Home Equity Conversion Mortgage (HECM by HUD [FHA]); Home Keeper (by Fannie Mae); Cash Account (by Financial Freedom Senior Funding Corp.).
Things to Be Aware of	Compare plan payout options and expenses charged at different lending institutions; Have lender give objective comparisons of average loan costs against HECM and Home Keeper plans.
Tax Effects	Interest is income tax-deductible when the loan is repaid; If borrowers permanently leave the residence, foreclosure gain is excluded up to $500,000 for married filing jointly ($250,000 for single taxpayers); If the heirs inherit the residence upon borrowers' death, basis is stepped up to the fair market value, resulting in no gain on foreclosure; Loan principal and interest are both deductible for federal estate tax purposes.
Payout Options	Lump sum; HECM line of credit (unused balance grows tax-free; most used plan); Home Keeper line of credit (larger initial dollar amount but unused balance never increases); Tenure option (constant monthly payout for as long as you live in your residence); Term payment (constant monthly payment for a fixed number of years); Combination (at any time any payout method can be changed or added if sufficient equity in the residence remains).

Source: Journal of Financial Service Professionals, *September 2002*

For More Information On Reverse Mortgages

Contact Fannie Mae at 800-732-6643
or the
American Association of Retired Persons (AARP)
at www.aarp.org or 202-434-2277.

Appendix B

For Financial Professionals

In conjunction with the Health Insurance Portability and Accountability Act of 1996 (HIPAA), the guidelines (or lack thereof) from the Treasury and the Congress and the insurance companies' interpretation of the new rules and regulations, we provide the following overview. We believe the information to be correct as of the date of this letter, but you must verify this information with your income tax sources before use with clients due to ongoing changes from the IRS.

The Act and subsequent regulations from the Treasury regarding tax-qualified policies are interpreted presently, as follows:

1. Long-term care (LTC) insurance premiums paid by a regular C corporation are fully deductible as a general business expense under Section 162 of the Internal Revenue Code (IRC) with no maximum limit. The deduction is for coverage provided for the employee, as well as the spouse and dependents of the employee.

2. The policy may be paid up in a limited number of years to ensure lifetime benefits.

3. Under HIPAA, LTC policies are treated as accident and health insurance.

4. Premiums paid by a C Corporation are not included in the employee's taxable income.

5. Benefits for services for nursing home, assisted living and home care-related services are not considered taxable income, unless payments exceed certain per diem rates. Benefits are taxable only to the extent they exceed actual expenses above the per diem rates. "Actual expense paid" policies have no limitation.

6. The LTC coverage is not subject to federal antidiscrimination rules, so carve-out groups within the corporation are acceptable.

7. If the employee pays a portion of a premium it is a deductible item on the employee's tax return.

8. LTC premiums may not be paid through a Section 125 "Cafeteria" plan, or a flexible spending account. Interestingly, LTC premiums paid through a Health Savings Account (HSA) are permitted.

It is also important for the agent and the client to clearly understand the tax effect on making changes in long-term care policies that were issued prior to the HIPAA Act of 1996, versus the new tax-qualified or non-tax-qualified policies being issued after that time (January 1, 1997).

(See the Table titled "Tax Liability on Premiums and Benefits" on our website, *www.longtermcarebooks.com*, for additional tax information. Be sure to review with your current tax advisor for actual regulations regarding your particular circumstances.)

Footnotes/References

Introduction

[1] Thomas, Trevor. "Long-Term Care: Average Annual Nursing Home Cost Hits $74,000, Survey Finds." *National Underwriter*. October 3, 2005. Page 10.

[2] U.S. Census.

[3] U.S. General Accounting Office.

[4] U.S. General Accounting Office.

[5] Leimberg, Steve. *Steve Leimberg's Elder Care Planning Newsletter #7* (February 23, 2006). Website: http://www.leimbergservices.com. Copyright 2006 Leimberg Information Services, Inc. (LISI).

[6] Leimberg, Steve. *Steve Leimberg's Elder Care Planning Newsletter #7* (February 23, 2006). Website: http://www.leimbergservices.com. Copyright 2006 Leimberg Information Services, Inc. (LISI).

Chapter 1

[1] "The MetLife Study of Employer Costs for Working Caregivers." (Based on data from *Family Caregiving in the U.S.: Findings from a National Survey*). Metropolitan Life Insurance Company, June 1997.

[2] "Caregiving Costs U.S. Business $29 Billion." Excerpted from: *AWNings*, The newsletter of the Academic Women's Network at Washington University. Vol. 6, No. 3. July 1997.

[3] G.E. Financial.

[4] *National Nursing Home Survey*, 1999. Website: http://www.cdc.gov/nchs/about/major/nnhsd/nnhsd.htm.

Chapter 2

[1] *Contra Costa Times*, September 12, 1999. (*Names are fictitious*).

[2] *GCM: Questions & Answers (When Looking for a Professional Geriatric Care Manager)*. A brochure printed by the National Association of Professional Geriatric Care Managers (GCM), 1604 N. Country Club Road, Tucson, AZ 85716-8008. Website: http://www.caremanager.org. © 2005.

Chapter 3

[1] Copyright © 2002 by Maryland Health Care Commission. All rights reserved. Website: http://hospitalguide.mhcc.state.md.us/Definitions/define_drgs.htm.

[2] "Medicaid." ElderLaw Answers. © 2006 ElderLawNet, Inc. Website: http://www.elderlawanswers.com/elder_info/elder_article.asp?id=2751.

3 Website: http://www.medicare.gov/Choices/Original.asp.

4 "Medicare Advantage (Part C)." National Education Association Member Benefits, Copyright ©2004. Website: http://www.neamb.com.

5 "Medicare Part D Overview." © California Health Advocates – The California HICAP Association, August 30, 2005. Website: http://www.calmedicare.org.

6 The Centers for Medicare and Medicaid Services. Website: http://www.cms.hhs.gov.

7 Goldfarb, David. *Medicare and Medigap Insurance Policies: Maximizing the Benefits.* New York State Bar Association Elder Law Section. Originally printed March 12, 1992. Updated January 2006. Copy of text available at: http://www.seniorlaw.com/medicare.htm.

8 *2005 – Choosing A Medigap Policy: A Guide to Health Insurance for People with Medicare.* Page 75. Available free for download at: http://www.medicare.gov/Publications/Pubs/pdf/02110.pdf.

9 "Medicare Part D Overview." © California Health Advocates – The California HICAP Association, August 30, 2005. Website: http://www.calmedicare.org.

Chapter 4

1 The Centers for Medicare and Medicaid Services. Website: http://www.cms.hhs.gov.

2 Website: http://www.elderlawanswers.com/content/attorney_search.asp.

Chapter 6

1 The Centers for Medicare and Medicaid Services. Website: http://www.cms.hhs.gov.

2 The Centers for Medicare and Medicaid Services. Website: http://www.cms.hhs.gov.

Chapter 7

1 U.S. General Accounting Office.

2 *Long-Term Care: Medicaid's Role and Challenges.* Publication 2172, The Henry J. Kaiser Foundation, November 1999.

3 California Partnership for Long-Term Care.

4 *Health Savings Accounts.* Free brochure available on The Department of the Treasury website at http://www.treas.gov/offices/public-affairs/hsa. Last updated April, 2005.

5 *HSA Frequently Asked Questions.* Free brochure available on The Department of the Treasury website at http://www.treas.gov/offices/public-affairs/hsa. Last updated June 7, 2006.

6 U.S. Department of Labor, Employee Benefits Security Administration, Frances Perkins Building, 200 Constitution Avenue, NW, Washington, DC 20210. http://www.dol.gov/ebsa/faqs/faq_consumer_cobra.html. November, 2006.

7 Saleem, Haneefa T. "Health Spending Accounts." U.S. Department of Labor, Bureau of Labor Statistics website at http://www.bls.gov. Revised December 19, 2003.

[8] Gaunya, Mark S. *Consumer-Driven Health Plans – The Next Evolution in Health Insurance.* Presentation at the 2005 Top of the Table Annual Meeting. © 2005 Million Dollar Table. September 29, 2005.

Chapter 8

[1] Moorhead, Mary B. "Pioneers Set to Change Nursing Homes." *Contra Costa Times*, November 16, 2002.

Chapter 9

[1] "Tax Resource Center: Are You Self-Employed?" © 2006 Jackson Hewitt Inc. All rights reserved. Website: http://www.jacksonhewitt.com/resources_library_topics_self.asp.

[2] Trader Status.com. "My Medical Plan Options including the new HSA." Copyright ©2004 Colin M. Cody, CPA and TraderStatus.com, LLC, All Rights Reserved. http://www.traderstatus.com/medicalplan.htm.

Chapter 10

[1] All information for Chapter 10 was adapted from the following source: Slott, Ed. *Ed Slott's IRA Advisor: Tax & Estate Planning for Your Retirement Savings.* © 2005 Ed Slott, CPA. October 2005. Pages 5-7.

Chapter 11

[1] Slott, Ed. *Ed Slott's Elite IRA Advisor Group, Workshop 3, January 13-15, 2006.* Rockville Centre, NY. Copyright © 2006 Ed Slott, CPA. Page 79.

[2] Slott, Ed. *Ed Slott's Elite IRA Advisor Group, Workshop 3, January 13-15, 2006.* Rockville Centre, NY. Copyright © 2006 Ed Slott, CPA. Page 4 of 13.

[3] Slott, Ed. *Ed Slott's Elite IRA Advisor Group, Workshop 3, January 13-15, 2006.* Rockville Centre, NY. Copyright © 2006 Ed Slott, CPA. Pages 2 and 3 of 13.

[4] Greene, Kelly. "Encore: How Retirees Are Blowing Their Nest Eggs." *The Wall Street Journal.* © June 27, 2005 Dow Jones & Company, Inc. Page R1.

[5] "Create A Legacy That Passes the Test of Time." American Legacy℠. © 2005 Lincoln Financial Distributors, Inc.

[6] Haberman, Zach. "Pension Pickle: The Mistake of Failing to Update Pension." *New York Post.* New York, NY. © January 31, 2005. Page 16.

[7] Moody, Errold F., Jr. "Estate Planning Basics." © Copyright 1998-2005, San Leandro, CA. Website: http://www.efmoody.com/estate/estatebasics.html.

[8] Greene, Kelly. "Encore: How Retirees Are Blowing Their Nest Eggs." *The Wall Street Journal.* © June 27, 2005 Dow Jones & Company, Inc. Page R1.

[9] Greene, Kelly. "Encore: IRA Inheritance, Part 2." *The Wall Street Journal*. © January 2, 2005 Dow Jones & Company, Inc.

[10] Slott, Ed. *Ed Slott's Elite IRA Advisor Group, Workshop 3, January 13-15, 2006*. Rockville Centre, NY. Copyright © 2006 Ed Slott, CPA. Pages 64-66.

[11] Slott, Ed. *Ed Slott's Elite IRA Advisor Group, Workshop 3, January 13-15, 2006*. Rockville Centre, NY. Copyright © 2006 Ed Slott, CPA. Page 6 of 9.

[12] Greene, Kelly. "Encore: How Retirees Are Blowing Their Nest Eggs." *The Wall Street Journal*. © June 27, 2005 Dow Jones & Company, Inc. Page R1.

[13] Greene, Kelly. "Encore: IRA Inheritance, Part 2." *The Wall Street Journal*. © January 2, 2005 Dow Jones & Company, Inc.

[14] Slott, Ed. *Ed Slott's Elite IRA Advisor Group, Workshop 3, January 13-15, 2006*. Rockville Centre, NY. Copyright © 2006 Ed Slott, CPA. Page 5 of 7.

[15] Greene, Kelly. "Encore: How Retirees Are Blowing Their Nest Eggs." *The Wall Street Journal*. © June 27, 2005 Dow Jones & Company, Inc. Page R1.

[16] *Individual Retirement Arrangements (IRAs): For use in preparing 2005 Returns*. Department of the Treasury, Internal Revenue Service. Publication 590, Cat. No. 15160x. Chapter 1: Traditional IRAs. Page 25. Website: http://www.irs.gov/pub/irs-pdf/p590.pdf.

[17] Greene, Kelly. "Encore: How Retirees Are Blowing Their Nest Eggs." *The Wall Street Journal*. © June 27, 2005 Dow Jones & Company, Inc. Page R1.

[18] Gagne, Gregory B., ChFC. "Financial Planning: Net Unrealized Appreciation." *Advisor Today*. Falls Church, VA. © June 2005 National Association of Insurance and Financial Advisors. Page 20.

[19] Slott, Ed. "The Client: Pop Quiz." *Financial Planning*. © July 2003 Financial-Planning and SourceMedia, Inc. Pages 77-79.

[20] Greene, Kelly. "Encore: Help on IRA Withdrawals." *The Wall Street Journal*. © December 11, 2005 Dow Jones & Company, Inc. Page 104.

[21] "The Roth IRA Alternative." *Cenco Street Journal*. © January/February 2004. Sacramento, CA. Vol. 4, Issue 1.

Chapter 12

[1] Stein, Arthur, CFP. "Long-Term Care Insurance As An Estate Planning Tool," *Estate Planning Newsletter*, Society of Financial Services Professionals, Spring 2001, Vol. 3, No. 2. Additional information is available on his website at http://www.ltcguide.com. You may contact him directly at 240-235-1325 or via e-mail at astein@ltcguide.com.

[2] Public Probate Records.

[3] ©1998-2006 SaveWealth.com. Website: http://www.savewealth.com/planning/estate/taxes.

4 SmartMoney.com © 2007 SmartMoney. SmartMoney is a joint publishing venture of Dow Jones & Company, Inc. and Hearst SM Partnership. Website: http://www.smartmoney.com/estate/index.cfm?story=grandparent-tax.

5 ©1998-2006 SaveWealth.com. Website: http://www.savewealth.com/planning/estate/taxes.

Chapter 13

1 *Life & Health Advisor*, April 1997.

2 "Workplace Injuries and Illnesses in 2005." U.S. Bureau of Labor Statistics, Washington, D.C. 20212. October 19, 2006. Website: http://www.bls.gov/iif/home.htm.

3 Disability and Employment – #11. Disability Statistics Abstract, 1997.

4 U.S. Bureau of the Census, No. 594.

Chapter 14

1 "Genworth Financial 2006 Cost of Care Survey: March 2006 Nursing Homes, Assisted-Living Facilities and Home Care Providers." ©2006 Genworth Financial, Inc. and National Eldercare Referral Systems, Inc. (CareScout).

2 "Key Long-Term Care Costs Increase More Than 5% From 2004." *General News: 2005 and 2004 Press Releases.* 2005 MedLife Mature Market Institute Survey Reports. Website: www.metlife.com.

Chapter 15

1 Orme, William. "World Graying Quickly, Population Study Finds." *Los Angeles Times* (edition unknown).

2 *World Population Prospects: The 2004 Revision,* vol. III, Sex and Age Distribution of the World Population (United Nations publication, Sales No. E.05.XIII.6). © 2004 United Nations Department of Economic and Social Affairs/Population Division.

3 McCaughey, Betsy. "As Population Boom Goes Bust, World Economy Faces Grim Future." *Investor's Business Daily*, Tuesday, August 28, 2001.

4 Efron, Sonni. "Population Trend Worrisome." *Los Angeles Times* as published in the *Contra Costa Times*, July 8, 2001.

Chapter 16

1 Peyser, Marc with Esther Pan and Elizabeth Roberts. "Home of the Gray." *Newsweek*, © March 01, 1999 Newsweek, Inc. Volume 133, Issue 9. Pages 50-53.

Chapter 17

[1] Partnership Policy information on the State of California website. Information available at: http://www.dhs.ca.gov/cpltc/HTML/Consumer_Pages/Partnership_Policies.htm. © 2004 State of California.

Appendix A

[1] Bruss, Robert. "How Senior Citizens Can Claim Lifetime Tax-Free Income." *Contra Costa Times*, November 3, 2002.

[2] Fleishman, Sandra. "Reverse Mortgages Gaining in Popularity." *Washington Post,* September 7, 2002.

[3] "Reverse Mortgages: Tax-Free Money You Don't Pay Back While Living in Your Home." *Journal of Financial Service Professionals,* September 2002.

[4] "Federal Housing Administration: Managing Risks from a New Zero Down Payment Product." GAO report number GAO-05-857T. June 30, 2005. U.S. Government Accountability Office (GAO). Website: http://www.gao.gov/htext/d05857t.html.

Notes

Notes

Notes

Notes

Notes